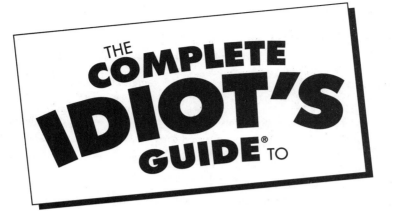

The Kama Sutra

Second Edition

*by Johanina Wikoff, Ph.D., and
Deborah S. Romaine*

ALPHA

A member of Penguin Group (USA) Inc.

THE COMPLETE IDIOT'S GUIDE TO and Design are registered trademarks of Penguin Group (USA) Inc.

International Standard Book Number: 1-59257-184-0
Library of Congress Catalog Card Number: 2003112980

05   04   8   7   6   5   4   3   2

Interpretation of the printing code: The rightmost number of the first series of numbers is the year of the book's printing; the rightmost number of the second series of numbers is the number of the book's printing. For example, a printing code of 03-1 shows that the first printing occurred in 2003.

Printed in the United States of America

Note: This publication contains the opinions and ideas of its authors. It is intended to provide helpful and informative material on the subject matter covered. It is sold with the understanding that the authors, publisher, and book producer are not engaged in rendering professional services in the book. If the reader requires personal assistance or advice, a competent professional should be consulted.

The authors, publisher, and book producer specifically disclaim any responsibility for any liability, loss, or risk, personal or otherwise, which is incurred as a consequence, directly or indirectly, of the use and application of any of the contents of this book.

Most Alpha books are available at special quantity discounts for bulk purchases for sales promotions, premiums, fund-raising, or educational use. Special books, or book excerpts, can also be created to fit specific needs.

For details, write: Special Markets, Alpha Books, 375 Hudson Street, New York, NY 10014.

Publisher: *Marie Butler-Knight*
Product Manager: *Phil Kitchel*
Senior Managing Editor: *Jennifer Chisholm*
Acquisitions Editor: *Gary Goldstein*
Book Producer: *Lee Ann Chearney/Amaranth Illuminare*
Production Editor: *Megan Douglass*
Illustrators: *Hrana Janto and Wendy Frost*
Cartoonist: *Jody Schaeffer*
Cover/Book Designer: *Trina Wurst*
Indexer: *Angie Bess*
Layout/Proofreading: *Becky Harmon, Donna Martin*

Contents at a Glance

Appendixes

Contents

Foreword

"Nothing is either good or bad, but thinking (or society) makes it so."
—St. Paul

That I would be asked to write the foreword to a book on the Kama Sutra was, at first, surprising to me, since I am not an expert on sexuality and its literature, nor published in the field. When I thought further, however, I was not so surprised, as I am a *relationship* expert, with a special interest in marriage, and published in that field. After all, sex usually happens in a relationship, and sometimes sex is relational! And it is not uncommon for it to happen in a marriage, although great sex in a marriage seems to be uncommon.

I, like most of you, am a product of the social construction of sex in Western culture. Sex did not have much press in our culture until the nineteenth century when Freud made the problems of the repression of sexuality the centerpiece of his psychoanalytic theory. Since then, many studies of sexuality have been undertaken—ostensibly to bring sex out of the closet and integrate it into life—thus documenting the West's negative attitude toward sex. A negation so severe that the appearance of the Kama Sutra in mainstream bookstores a few decades ago was a little-heralded but radical event.

Until the substantive challenge posed by the modern sexual revolution, and studies such as by Masters and Johnson, sex had been viewed as dangerous and bad in the West. But, according to those who study such matters, that revolution has been more talk than action. Sexual education in schools is still very controversial. Guilt about sexual curiosity is alive and well. Pornography is a political hot potato and a legal crime. The sex life of most couples is vastly overrated; experimental sex with one's partner is illegal in some states. The desire level of both sexes seems at an all-time low. And the idea that sex has anything to do with spirituality is a cutting-edge idea for an enlightened minority who subscribe to New Age values (whatever they are!).

Over time, it has become clear to me that the problem with sex in the West is essentially a problem with pleasure; not just sexual pleasure, but any kind of pleasure. Although the West is the world's largest pleasure industry, pleasure is bad. Why? Because it is dangerous, or so it has been thought for a long time. Sex has been preserved for procreation—in marriage—and love, if it comes at all, was to come after marriage. St. Paul cautioned even married people not to enjoy sex too much and advised singles to marry so "as not to burn." Given these authoritative negative constructions of a universal human activity, it is no wonder that the Western world has been ashamed to have a body, much less to enjoy it.

All this began to change in the middle part of the twentieth century with the arrival of the spiritual traditions of the East, which paradoxically led to our recovery of the body. Along with the Vedas, which gave us Transcendental Meditation; Zen Buddhism, which extols the power of compassion and balanced living; Confucianism, with its emphasis on ethical living; and Taoism, which taught "the way"; has come the Kama Sutra, from the second century B.C.E., with its bold assertion that sex is a natural part of a balanced life.

It was not too many years ago that the Kama Sutra was available only in some public libraries and in adult bookstores. Now, it graces, in abbreviated form, the checkout counters of airport bookstores, replete with illustrations of a variety of sexual positions. While Western studies of human sexuality, a la Havelock Ellis, Magnus Hirschfield, and the team of Masters and Johnson, tended to describe what couples do without recommendations, the Kama Sutra prescribed what couples *can* do, with restrained enthusiasm. Whether, with all this information, sex is being enjoyed more by its Western consumers, it is clearly the case that sexual information—including data about a variety of sexual positions and the enhancement of sexual pleasure, hitherto forbidden by law—has become mainstream.

I, for one, welcome *this* introduction of the Kama Sutra, *The Complete Idiot's Guide to the Kama Sutra, Second Edition*, especially its clear location of sex in a balanced life and its exposition of sex as a spiritual experience. My first introduction to the spiritual dimension of sex was Andrew Greeley's book, *Love and Sexuality*, where a priest of the Roman Catholic Church chides men who are not attentive to a woman's orgasmic pleasure as depriving her of the experience of God. After reading him, I understood that the exclamation "Oh, God!" in the sexual climax was a statement of contact with the "holy." Since then, in my work with couples and in the development of Imago Relationship Therapy, I have taught that orgasm and the belly laugh is an expression of the core self, our true essence, which is the experience of full aliveness and relaxed joyfulness.

The Complete Idiot's Guide to the Kama Sutra, Second Edition, shows how the playful and disciplined exploration of the physical pleasure of sexual love is one of the ways to open the door to the joy of union with the Divine, which is the birthright of us all. Read, experience, enjoy.

—Harville Hendrix, Ph.D.

Harville Hendrix, Ph.D., is the author of the *New York Times* bestseller *Getting the Love You Want: A Guide for Couples*, with over one million copies in print, and *Keeping the Love You Find: A Personal Guide*.

Introduction

Though global generalizations are often exaggerations, it's probably safe to say that all of us want to experience the kind of intimate, erotic sexual loving that fulfills us physically, emotionally, and spiritually. And it's no doubt equally safe to say most of us don't really know how to create such experiences with our partners.

It might seem a little odd to look to a book for guidance and advice on such a sensitive matter. To our counterparts 2,000 years ago, however, it would have been odd *not* to do so. The Kama Sutra ushered countless couples into sexual harmony through clear explanations and explicit directions. The sages of the time recognized that sexual loving was an integral and essential component of a committed relationship.

Now we look back in time to this comprehensive love text for guidance with and insights into our modern relationships. *The Complete Idiot's Guide to the Kama Sutra, Second Edition*, interprets the Kama Sutra to accommodate the needs and desires of contemporary couples.

How to Use This Book

There are six parts to this book:

Part 1, "The Book of Love," presents the context of the Kama Sutra. These four chapters discuss the origins of the Kama Sutra, the culture of ancient India, the foundations of Eastern philosophy, and the mind/body connection.

Part 2, "What Does Love Have to Do With It?" discusses the elements of sex, love, and relationships. These four chapters explore what we seek, how we find love and partners, what we expect from ourselves and from others, and what happens when relationships sour.

Part 3, "Friends and Lovers," takes a look at the foundations of a relationship. These three chapters investigate matters of trust, intimacy, and communication.

Part 4, "Bodies Beautiful," tells you everything you want to know about his body, her body, and your bodies united. These four chapters cover the structure and functions of the male and female bodies and how to enjoy them safely and pleasurably through sexual loving.

Part 5, "The Art of Loving," presents the Kama Sutra's famed 64 arts of lovemaking. These six chapters take you through the sacred cycle of sexual loving, from arousing beginnings to erotic love play and exotic unions, to intimate closures.

Part 6, "Beyond the Kama Sutra," explores what can come after the Kama Sutra. These five chapters look at special applications of the Kama Sutra, introduce other love texts, and look at how sexual loving might shape relationships of the future.

Sutra Shorts

Each chapter contains boxes that provide interesting and helpful information.

Out of Touch

These boxes provide cautions and warnings.

Sutra Sayings

These boxes recreate and paraphrase sayings from the Kama Sutra to bring the flavor of this ancient text into a modern context.

Sutrology

These boxes define and explain Sanskrit words and technical terminology.

Kama Knowledge

These boxes present tidbits and facts about the Kama Sutra and related information.

Dr. Josie Suggests

These boxes feature tips and suggestions from Johanina Wikoff, Ph.D., who is known as Dr. Josie in the column she writes for www.Tantra.com that answers the questions people ask about love, sex, and relationships.

Acknowledgments

The efforts of many go into bringing a book to life, and to all of them we offer our appreciation and respect for work well done. We thank the hard-working team at Alpha Books, especially publisher Marie Butler-Knight and production editor Megan Douglass. Thanks also to two fabulous and soulfully sensual artists, Hrana Janto and Wendy Frost for their artful interpretations of the Kama Sutra.

Debbie especially thanks the following people: Mike, her soul mate and husband of 27 years, for his loving and enthusiastic support; Lee Ann Chearney, for following the wisdom of her intuition in pulling together the team for this book, and for sustaining the beauty and sensitivity this subject deserves; and co-author and collaborator Johanina, for the knowledge, insight, and spirituality that gives this book its soul.

Johanina especially thanks the following people: Rhoda Wikoff, her mother, who was the first person to teach her about sex and who throughout her life embodied the vitality, energy, and openness of healthy sexuality. She is grateful to all her teachers and mentors, particularly Abby Cohen Smith, Sylvia Goodman, and Al Bauman in the work of Wilhelm Reich; Bob Rosenbush, Hameed Ali, Karen Johnson, her teachers in the Ridhwan School, and Suzie Heumann, for her vision of Tantra and for providing a forum at Tantra.com for her to develop her view of transformative sexuality. Johanina thanks Debbie Romaine and Lee Ann Chearney for bringing a real spirit of collaboration to the process of making this book.

Special Thanks from the Publisher to the Technical Editor

The Complete Idiot's Guide to the Kama Sutra, Second Edition, was reviewed by an expert who not only checked the accuracy of what you'll learn in this book, but also provided invaluable insight to help ensure that this book tells you everything you need to know about the Kama Sutra. In its pages, you'll learn how to unlock the Kama Sutra's ancient secrets to enhance your experience of sexual loving and increase intimacy in your relationship with your life partner. Our special thanks are extended to Suzie Heumann.

Suzie Heumann has studied, taught, written, spoken, and produced instructional videos on the subjects of the Kama Sutra, Tantra, and other sexual disciplines since 1987. Suzie is CEO of Tantra.com and is a well-known radio personality and syndicated writer. Suzie has co-produced three instructional videos: *Ancient Secrets of Sexual Ecstasy, Multi-Orgasmic Response Training for Women,* and *Multi-Orgasmic Response Training for Men,* which involved collaboration with many of the world's best-known teachers of Western Tantra. Suzie lives in Northern California with her husband and Tantric partner of 22 years and their three daughters. Schooled in the biological sciences, she has a keen interest in physiology, the Sanskrit language, and its relationship to modern language, and women's studies, including ancient cultures that held the feminine principle as sacred. She has been a colleague of Dr. Johanina Wikoff's for 13 years.

Trademarks

All terms mentioned in this book that are known to be or are suspected of being trademarks or service marks have been appropriately capitalized. Alpha Books and Penguin Group (USA) Inc. cannot attest to the accuracy of this information. Use of a term in this book should not be regarded as affecting the validity of any trademark or service mark.

Part 1

The Book of Love

Eastern concepts and perspectives may seem confusing and unfamiliar to Westerners. We tend to look for separation, while Easterners tend to see integration. The Kama Sutra is both Eastern and ancient. Though its message and guidance remains amazingly relevant 2,000 years after its writing, to understand its content you must first understand its context.

The chapters in this section introduce both ancient Eastern culture and Eastern concepts. This gives you the foundation you need to appreciate and explore the Kama Sutra's version of sexual loving.

Who Wrote the Book of Love?

In This Chapter

◆ How we learn about sexual loving

◆ The origins of the Kama Sutra

◆ Sex through the ages

◆ Why the Kama Sutra remains so popular today

Most of us are intrigued by the Kama Sutra because we've heard it details exotic sexual positions and alluring new ways to make love. You've heard right. But the Kama Sutra is not just a sex manual. It is not about dazzling sexual performances, or one-night stand extravaganzas. Yes, the Kama Sutra does provide detailed and explicit directions for an astounding assortment of sexual positions and activities. But indulging in them is as much about pleasing your partner as it is about enjoying yourself. (Surely you've heard that the greatest pleasure is in the giving!) The result can be a truly *mind-blowing* experience—and what happens to your body is pretty amazing, too. The whole point of the Kama Sutra is to meld the physical, emotional, and spiritual aspects of love in a way that strengthens and expands your relationship.

The Kama Sutra is about sex, yes. Unquestionably—and intentionally—the Kama Sutra puts sex at the center of adult relationships. But this is sex for grown-ups who want to make their partner's pleasure at least as important as their own, and frequently even more important. This is sex as the ultimate communication between two people who are committed to connecting with each other emotionally and spiritually as well as physically. This is sexual love as you've never known it before and, perhaps, secretly wished it could be.

Beyond the Birds and the Bees

What do you know about sex and love, and how did you learn what you know? Most of us bump along the road of such learning blindfolded by misinformation and misunderstanding in a climate that subtly and not so subtly suppresses any interest in learning about sex. What we learn in high school health classes, from locker room bragging, and in back seat explorations blends to present a bewildering and limited view of human coupling. In our ignorant bumblings, love has little, if anything, to do with it. Few of us learn what it takes to love another person well—sexually, emotionally, and spiritually. To the contrary, our life experiences are more likely to teach us how not to communicate, especially about sex.

The very concept of sex education is often a contradiction of terms. Instead of learning the important arts of wooing, touching, communicating, and respecting one another, young people hear about hormones and acne and pregnancy and sexually transmitted diseases. These are all very important topics, to be sure. But there is more to sexuality than movies featuring swarms of sperm swimming in desperate search of their destiny and dry lectures offering dire warnings about what misfortunes await when they succeed. Distilled to passionless physiology, such lessons give sex all the appeal of a trip to the dentist.

No one says, or even hints, that sexual love can be one of the most pleasurable, emotionally connecting, and spiritual experiences humans can have. No one mentions that pleasure is our natural birthright, and as such is an inherently good and desirable experience. No one discusses the complexities, subtleties, and nuances of achieving sexual fulfillment. Instead, most often these topics are at best given only rudimentary and passing attention; often they are sidestepped, and at worst are treated as taboo. Sadly, Western cultures pretty much leave the education part of sex up to the individual.

> **CAUTION**
>
> **Out of Touch**
>
> Despite the Kama Sutra's staying power, few other documents are so misunderstood and misrepresented. There are numerous translations and interpretations of the Kama Sutra, each offering a different perspective and social context. While in Western cultures the Kama Sutra has become somewhat of a synonym for amazing, often convoluted sexual positions, not many who talk of it have actually read a translation.

This hasn't always been the case. Once, education in the ways of sexual loving was just as important as learning the rules of commerce and the laws of the land. Whether through wisdom or intuition, many ancient civilizations recognized relationships as the core of human culture. They also recognized sexuality and sexual loving as integral, essential aspects of human relationships. These civilizations revered and honored the mysteries of love and sex, and taught the skills of loving. One of the most formal structures for such teaching was in ancient India, where a centuries-old document called the *Kama Sutra* instructed young men and women in the ways of love, sex, and relationships.

Sutrology

Loosely translated, **Kama Sutra** means "Love Aphorisms." An aphorism is a succinct statement of truth or principle. "Kama" is a Sanskrit word that means pleasure or desire. In Sanskrit, "Sutra" means rules. The document we know today as the Kama Sutra originated in India during the fourth century C.E., though scholars believe it existed in oral form for centuries before that.

The Kama Sutra: 2,000 Years and Still Going Strong

The Kama Sutra is one of the world's oldest written documents. Elements of it have been traced to the early part of the first century C.E., a time when written language was just beginning to record the information that passed from one generation to the next in the form of stories and verse. When people were born, lived, and died within the same small community, oral storytelling was a fine way to convey history and lessons on life. But as societies evolved and became more sophisticated, their codes of behavior became more complex. It became difficult for the average person to remember all the rules and procedures.

The Kama Sutra is one of the first known attempts to record such instructions. The original document was written in the ancient language of Sanskrit. Scholars believe the original intent of this document was to provide a summary, sort of an ancient "cheat sheet" to jog the memory. The brevity of the Kama Sutra's messages made it easy to memorize them. Community elders and religious leaders then taught the full meanings and interpretations. While best known for its detailed instructions in the art of making love, the Kama Sutra was first and foremost a guidebook for moral behavior.

Dr. Josie Suggests

When you're finished with this book, you might want to read an actual translation of the Kama Sutra. Appendix B lists several translations that scholars consider true to the Kama Sutra's original content and intent.

Time and Place: The Kama Sutra's Historical Context

While many aspects of the Kama Sutra remain relevant for modern times and Western society, this document is very much an element of its time and place in Eastern history. In the fourth century C.E., when the Kama Sutra came into existence as a written document, Hindu culture was male-dominated. Women, though revered for their sensuality and childbearing capabilities, had few rights of their own. Nonetheless, the Kama Sutra urges men to seek marriages based on love (or, at the very least, mutual agreement) rather than convenience. It featured a great deal of instruction in the fine art of wooing a woman through gifts and kindnesses, ranging from sumptuous foods and drinks to attentive conversation. In a manner surprising for its time, the Kama Sutra presents the differences between men and women as endless opportunities for mutual pleasure awaiting proper exploitation.

Ancient Hindu Culture: Passionate Loving

Ancient Hindu culture featured a complete and comfortable integration of religion and sex. Physical love was a natural element of spirituality. A core belief of ancient Hinduism was that passionate loving in this life would lead to eternal bliss in the next. Much of the art that survives from this period of time reflects this belief, showing couples in various forms of ecstatic coupling.

Ancient Hindu sculptures embrace the Kama Sutra as an expression of spiritual sexuality.

Statues and paintings considered erotic by modern Western standards adorned ancient Hindu temples and other public buildings. The Kama Sutra reflects this integration, too. What Western readers viewed as risqué and even pornographic by the time translations made their way to Europe was, in the context of the Kama Sutra's place and time in history, perfectly ordinary.

Kama Knowledge

Sanskrit was one of the earliest forms of standardized written language. A classical language originated by Hindu scholars around 1500 B.C.E., Sanskrit means "cultivated" or "refined." As a language, Sanskrit was very precise and complex, as was its European counterpart, Latin. Sanskrit remains a language of scholars in modern India, primarily in written form. Though thousands of documents exist in Sanskrit, only a few hundred have been translated into Western languages. Until the nineteenth century C.E., few Westerners were permitted in Eastern countries such as India, making this body of writing largely unknown until fairly recent times.

Castes and Social Status: Everyone in the Proper Place

Early society in India was rigidly structured, or stratified, into social classes called *castes*. The caste of your birth was the caste of your life; in this inequitable culture, there was no caste hopping. This is very different from most Western cultures, where individuals can alter social status through achievements such as education or business success. In the time of the Kama Sutra, people could interact with one another across caste lines, though they could not marry. Only the higher castes had the ability to read and the resources to accumulate property, such as books and art.

Sutrology

In ancient Hindu culture, a **caste** was a social level into which a person was born. Castes determined everything about how a person lived, from his or her occupation to whom he or she could marry.

Polygamy, Concubines, and Courtesans

While the Kama Sutra encourages men to marry just one carefully chosen wife, *polygamy* was common in early Hindu society. It was quite common for ancient Hindu men to have multiple wives, though a woman usually had just one husband. This had more to do with the need to make babies than to make love; infant mortality was very high in

Sutrology

Polygamy is the practice of having more than one mate. A **concubine** was a man's mistress, a woman with whom he had a sexual relationship. A **courtesan** was a woman with significant social status whose social and sexual favors were available for a price to men of equal or superior status.

this time, and heritage was everything. The Kama Sutra stresses the importance of a husband providing equal attention to all of his wives, without showing favoritism (and offers detailed instructions about how to do so).

Concubines and *courtesans* were also an accepted part of ancient Hindu life. While the Kama Sutra promises that a man, who learns well the lessons of love, could enjoy with one wife the pleasures other men must seek from many women, it also gives instructions for managing additional relationships.

Other Partnerships

Ancient Hindu society was quite accepting of same-sex and multiple partnerships. The Kama Sutra provides specific instruction for woman-to-woman and man-to-man interactions. While the Kama Sutra encourages men, for the sake of equitable treatment, to enjoy sexual love with one wife at a time, it also offers an array of techniques for the talented man to please several women at once.

Sexual Love in Other Cultures

The ancient Hindus were not alone in their efforts to establish moral guidelines for behavior. Ancient Western cultures also recognized the importance and role of sexual love. Erotic art, such as drawings, statues, and carvings, exists in all cultures from the Aztecs to the Vikings. In large part, Greek and Roman mythology is based on the amorous (and sometimes vengeful) romantic indulgences of the gods who cannot resist involving themselves with mere mortals. The Greek god Eros and his Roman counterpart Cupid were well known for their adventures. On the female side were the goddesses of love, Aphrodite (Greek) and Venus (Roman).

By the Middle Ages, however, Rome was no longer the center of the Western world. Europe was coming into its own, bringing new ideas and practices regarding sex. Sexual desire and activities became synonymous with decadence. Celibacy replaced indulgence as the idealized (though not very practical) standard. Dialogue about sex was veiled in metaphor and suggestion. Sexual love took place behind closed doors, hidden from acknowledgement that it was happening. Centuries later, it is this legacy that lingers to create challenges for contemporary couples.

Other Eastern cultures had their versions of the Kama Sutra, too, that were equally explicit and popular. *The Secrets of the Jade Bed Chamber*, which was popular around the same time as the Kama Sutra, was one of several books that kept many adventurous Chinese couples awake nights, detailing more than 30 sexual positions with exotic, evocative names such as fluttering phoenix and cranes with joined necks. Ancient herbalists concocted elaborate *aphrodisiacs* to aid couples in intensifying and enjoying their conjugal activities. Sexually explicit art was very common in ancient Japan, providing graphic illustration for those who wanted to explore new experiences.

Sutrology

An **aphrodisiac** is a substance that increases or enhances sexual arousal. The word comes from the Greek "aphrodisiakos," which means sexual pleasure. Aphrodite was the Greek goddess of love, whose allure was irresistible to men and gods alike.

The Greek sculpture, Aphrodite of Melos, a lost treasure of antiquity, was discovered in 1820 and has become a popular symbol of love and beauty.

Enlightening the Eastern World: Vatsyayana

The Kama Sutra that exists today is the work of many writers, perhaps a dozen or more. Because the doctrines it records predate written language, no one knows for sure when the Kama Sutra came to represent collective, not just individual, wisdom and guidance. It has been common practice throughout history to credit famous individuals with writing famous documents, whether or not they actually had a role in authoring them. Like most documents that have survived through thousands of years and many cultural and societal changes, the Kama Sutra is a compilation of the stories and writings of numerous authors, some who will never be known.

The person credited with doing the most to compile the writings and lessons that became the Kama Sutra was an ancient religious scholar and educator named Mallinaga Vatsyayana. Though the precise dates of his life are difficult to determine, it appears that Vatsyayana lived sometime between 400 and 500 C.E. Not much is known about him beyond his work to collect the writings of the Kama Sutra. While freely acknowledging he was not the author of the materials, Vatsyayana often interjects his observations and comments into the document. Many of these comments refer to his personal experiences with the practices of sexual love he is describing. Others encourage male readers to share the writings with their female partners, so they, too, might understand and appreciate the finer points of lovemaking.

> **Sutra Sayings**
>
> Some people believe there is no need for a book on the subject of Kama. They say the force of procreation drives the required acts. Those who believe this way are misguided. Men and women must learn the proper means of sexual loving, so the required acts become pleasurable and desirable. Only then will the drive to procreation be successful.

The Laws of Life: Artha, Kama, and Dharma

Though best known for its sexual instructions, the Kama Sutra's main purpose was to establish a code of conduct based on the laws and practices that governed life in ancient India. The culture of the time viewed life as consisting of three aspects—survival, reproduction, and social order. Artha, or material possessions such as food and shelter, secured survival. Kama, or sexual love, assured reproduction. And dharma, or ethics, guided the behaviors that protected social order. Every person, no matter what caste, had responsibilities and obligations. The Kama Sutra documents and explains these roles.

The Rules of Love

Fundamental to all aspects of life, of course, was love (or at least sex). The best-known part of the Kama Sutra is the section introducing the rules of love. It is within this context that the Kama Sutra provides the explicit details of both sex and love, striving to keep the two connected. Guidance begins with counseling about how to find the right woman, then entice her into a relationship and ultimately into marriage. Courtship and compatibility were very important.

With the goal of establishing a lifelong desire for sexual love, the Kama Sutra instructs that newlyweds wait 10 nights after the wedding before consummating their marriage. During each of those 10 nights, the couple is to engage in a progression of erotic activities, starting with conversation and rather chaste kissing, and gradually escalating to caresses, embraces, and finally the Big Moment. In ancient India, it was the man's responsibility to be sure his bride found the entire experience pleasurable (talk about performance anxiety!).

Kama Knowledge

At the same time Vatsyayana was compiling the writings of the Kama Sutra, the writings that would become known as the gospels of the Christian Bible were being recorded. St. Augustine was writing his famous treatise "The City of God." St. Jerome, who was known as Eusebius Hieronymus during his lifetime, was translating the Bible from Hebrew into Latin. Meanwhile, Attila, ruler of the Huns, was laying siege to much of Western Europe. Those who escaped the bloody battles fled to a cluster of islands off the coast of northern Italy, where they established the city we now know as Venice.

Enlightening the Western World: Sir Richard Burton

A hundred years or so before the Richard Burton of stage and film fame, there was Sir Richard Burton (1821–1890), a world traveler extraordinaire. Burton is best known for introducing Westerners to the mysteries of Eastern culture through his comprehensive translation of *Arabian Nights*. He also wrote numerous travelogues and was an accomplished linguist, fluent in more than 40 languages. Despite his gift for languages, Burton managed to get expelled from the prestigious Oxford University (England) for disciplinary reasons. He joined the British army and served in India as an intelligence officer. While there, his expertise in language earned him the dubious assignment of infiltrating, in disguise, the local culture to report on, among other activities, the homosexual brothels popular among the soldiers. His most famous undercover operation was his infiltration of the Muslim holy city of Mecca in Arabia.

After leaving military duty, Burton wrote several books about India. But he soon tired of the leisurely life and set out to study and document the erotic practices of different cultures. He began traveling again, to Africa and other exotic locations to study and record sexual behavior. In 1883 Burton completed his translation of the Kama Sutra, which he published through the secretive and private organization he co-founded for just this purpose, the Kama Shastra Society (a name that means "art of love").

Kama Knowledge

Though first published in the English language in 1883, the Kama Sutra remained underground for nearly 80 years due to Western restrictions on sexually explicit materials. It wasn't until the 1960s and the "sexual revolution" that copies of the Kama Sutra became openly available in the United States and other Western countries. Since then, the Kama Sutra has appeared in dozens of translations and versions. It remains one of the most enduring titles in book sales worldwide.

Though *erotica* enjoyed great popularity at the time, its fans did not flaunt their interests. In fact, they went to great lengths to conceal them. Burton's Victorian contemporaries were not nearly so open-minded as was the adventurer who had experienced cultures well beyond Western imagination. Many scorned the "obscenity" of the manuscript (though they may well have secretly purchased it through the Kama Shastra Society, which did a good amount of business). Because the translation was published without Burton's name on it, only his closest collaborators in the Kama Shastra Society knew of his participation in bringing the art of love, Eastern style, to the West.

Sutrology

Erotica is material, usually illustrations or writings, that is sexually arousing. The term comes from the Greek word "eros," which means sexual love.

Following the success of the Kama Sutra translation, Burton translated two other documents, the Ananga Ranga and the Perfumed Garden. The Ananga Ranga is a Hindu document, written in the fifteenth century C.E., that incorporates elements of the Kama Sutra with aspects of other writings on love and sex. The Perfumed Garden is an Arabian document written in the sixteenth century.

Unfortunately Burton's wife didn't share her husband's enthusiasm for Eastern culture, particularly its erotic elements. When Burton died of a heart attack in 1890, his Victorian-principled spouse burned all of his diaries, journals, and writings—four decades of accumulated observations. Many details about Eastern life and love during the mid 1880s are lost forever.

Transcending Time and Place

It is no mistake of translation that the Kama Sutra emphasizes the "art" of sexual love. The many unknown authors of this incredible document consistently linked sexual loving with other arts such as music and drawing, and encouraged readers to study all with equal dedication. There are no cold, clinical descriptions of the body and its functions. There are no calculated connivings to get a prospective partner into bed.

Instead, there is poetic imagery, erotic metaphor, and a respectful mystery about the opposite gender. There is gentleness and excitement, anticipation, and the promise of satisfaction. The language of the Kama Sutra is itself a form of art. The courtship activities it describes are playful, emphasizing mutual respect and pleasure. It is the journey, not the destination, that matters.

The structure of modern Western society differs considerably from the ancient Hindu culture in which the Kama Sutra evolved. Birth status is far less significant than individual achievement. Our relationships are based on sharing, not belonging. Yet our needs and desires are very much the same as those of the ancient couples who read the instructions of the Kama Sutra by candlelight, curled together in the warm glow of each other's love.

> **Sutra Sayings**
>
> A person should study the 64 arts and sciences, as well as the 64 aspects of sexual union. The practices of Kama, or love, are learned from the Kama Sutra and from other knowledgeable people.

No one denies that part of the Kama Sutra's appeal lies in its detailed sexual instruction. Most adults enjoy sex, and want to learn more about how to keep their sex lives fun and fulfilling. But there are hundreds of sex manuals out there—testimony, perhaps, to their inability to provide what we truly seek. The Kama Sutra emphasizes relationship in its wholeness, not just its physical aspects. The Kama Sutra appeals to our desire for connection and deep intimacy as well as sexual satisfaction. It addresses our desire to be seen, appreciated, accepted, revered, and adored. And it addresses our spiritual hunger.

We are becoming aware that as we race through our fast-paced lives we are speeding past some of life's most precious moments. Food, family, and sex are not deeply nourishing or satisfying when we do not take time to enjoy and savor them.

We turn off the bedroom television after a long busy day and turn to our partner for a little skin contact. But we haven't got much to give and we don't want to spend too long. It is not surprising that one of the main complaints that committed couples have is lack of sexual desire. Sometimes it seems like nothing squelches sexual desire like a relationship!

Even with today's more open-minded attitudes toward sex and love, there is no teaching in the West that addresses the art of loving with as great an attention to detail, subtlety, nuance, and refinement as the Kama Sutra. As a manual for navigating the often unfamiliar aspects of the other sex in love, the Kama Sutra both recognizes and honors the differences between man and woman. It teaches the art of loving in ways that bridge the mysteries of gender.

Join us in a journey of discovery that will enhance your knowledge both of yourself and your partner as you explore together the Kama Sutra: the art of sexual love. Enjoy!

The Least You Need to Know

- The Kama Sutra has endured through the centuries because of its emphasis on sexual loving as a means to support and strengthen relationships.

- The Kama Sutra recognizes and validates the importance of sexual love. Though the Kama Sutra contains explicit sexual instructions, it is not a document of pornography.

- The Kama Sutra will help you enjoy yourself while you learn how to increase your partner's pleasure and deepen your sexual union.

- Despite its ancient roots, the Kama Sutra appeals to contemporary couples who are searching for increased fulfillment in their intimate relationships.

Chapter 2

Morality Rules

In This Chapter

- ◆ Establishing a balance between manners and morals
- ◆ The Kama Sutra's comprehensive guidelines for daily life
- ◆ How you define sexual morality: a self-exploration
- ◆ How attitudes and values shape ideals and expectations

Nothing focuses the magnifying glass on sexual morality like a good scandal. Americans revisited this lesson *ad nauseum* in 1998, when the country's highest elected official, President Bill Clinton, got caught with his pants down. His transgressions thrust the issue of sexual morality into the national spotlight. Though the vast majority of people quickly tired of the endless discussions, the situation had a startling, unexpected effect. Suddenly everyone was talking—openly and in public—about sex.

In Vatsyayana's India, such public discourse would not have been so surprising or unusual. Sex was not hidden or ignored, but instead was openly accepted, welcomed, and included as an essential and enjoyable aspect of daily life. The Kama Sutra combines the poetic with the pragmatic in defining just how that integration should take place. It offers extensive, explicit instructions for lovers, to be sure. But equally important were the spiritual and practical dimensions of relationships, and this comes before any discussion of sex.

First Things First: Education and Etiquette

The first part of the Kama Sutra counsels the reader in the ways of achieving artha (wealth), dharma (virtue), and kama (love). It then describes the formal learning process for both men and women to follow, which not surprisingly includes studying the Kama Sutra. Women were expected to learn the same things as men, even though their roles in society were quite different. The introductory material concludes with a precise discussion of daily habits, detailed to the level of describing the placement of furniture and the steps of personal hygiene. The Kama Sutra was, for its time, a manual for living, not just a guide to having good sex.

Though the Kama Sutra describes sexual practices that seem to permit just about any behavior a person desires to indulge in, there were actions that were out of bounds. Vatsyayana cautions against secret relations with another man's wife, warning that this would likely lead to violent vengeance. Straying from the culture's moral standard would not have been viewed any more positively than it is in contemporary cultures. Rather than issuing condemnations or proscriptions, however, documents such as the Kama Sutra clearly and succinctly describe the actions an individual needed to follow for a return to acceptable behavior.

> ### Kama Knowledge
>
> The Kama Sutra spoke to ancient India's middle and upper levels of society. Those merchants or proprietors, who operated businesses selling or trading goods, enjoyed both wealth and status. Those middle- and upper-class citizens had plenty of time for leisure and recreation. They spent their days eating mangos and other fruits, picking flowers, and playing in the water (after all the dangerous animals were relocated, of course). Evenings were meant for heavier dining, drinking, and partying. And nights were meant for sexual adventures.

We don't live in Vatsyayana's India, of course. Western moral standards have always differed vastly from their Eastern counterparts. Even contemporary India differs greatly from the India of Vatsyayana's time, in both moral standards and everyday life. *Sexual morality* is fluid and dynamic, changing with cultures and times. But one constant remains. Men and women continue to desire and form intimate relationships. And they still need guidance and instruction to help make those relationships successful. Amazingly, despite its antiquity, the Kama Sutra has the ability to transcend time and culture to meet this need.

Sutrology

Sexual morality is the set of values and attitudes individuals and cultures hold and follow regarding sexual behavior.

A Prescription for Living

The Kama Sutra outlines a comprehensive prescription for pleasurable living for the merchant, or middle-class, citizens of ancient India. Vatsyayana and the sages who came before him understood that sexual pleasure was the cornerstone of a happy life, and its pursuit was an aspect of nearly all activities. Consistent with this view, the Kama Sutra perceives pleasure and morality as inseparable as it defines the rules and protocols of relationships. By so intimately describing myriad ways to improve and enjoy sexual love, the Kama Sutra makes it more desirable to follow, rather than break, the rules.

At the same time, the Kama Sutra clearly recognizes and accepts that people, in their humanness, sometimes follow their desires instead of the rules. This often leads to situations that are outside the accepted moral and cultural standards. Rather than condemning those who stray, the Kama Sutra instead provides prescriptions for how to deal with such situations. Rather than spewing fire and brimstone, the Kama Sutra offers understanding and guidelines for returning to accepted behavior. This is not to say that anything goes and all is forgiven. Hindu culture lives by the law of Karma, which believes that there are consequences for all actions. At times Vatsyayana quite sternly lectures his readers to remember and follow the rules, even though others may not.

Preserving the Social Order

Particularly in ancient India, social status was important. It was also fixed. There were no opportunities to invent a better whetstone and leap to the top of the caste ladder. Where you were born was pretty much where you would die, socially speaking. This structure was deeply imbued in the religious beliefs and practices of the day. By detailing every aspect of relationships from courting to courtesans, the Kama Sutra supported and reinforced the caste system of its time.

There was a practical side to this, one befitting the culture's rigid caste system. The most reliable form of birth control, abstinence, wasn't any more popular then than it is now. The second-most reliable form of contraception, the Pill, was still 2,000 years away from its debut. Pregnancy was a very real and very common consequence of sexual love. Children born as the result of a union between two people of different castes were themselves outcasts, belonging to neither the mother's nor the father's caste. They could not inherit property, which doomed them to lives of poverty.

Dr. Josie Suggests

Morals are guidelines that give us a sense of what has worked for people in a culture. They give us the room to make inevitable mistakes and the opportunity to use the lessons learned by others to self-correct.

The Kama Sutra merely observes this consequence, however. Vatsyayana doesn't threaten or lecture about it. Instead, the emphasis of the Kama Sutra is to make appropriate sexual relationships so appealing that men and women have no reason to seek excitement with others. This is perhaps one of the earliest and no doubt most successful examples of positive reinforcement as a tool for shaping behavior!

Of Marriage and Morality

A man of high social status married a woman who was a virgin. Their marriage could not be consummated for 10 days after the wedding. This was to allow them to first become comfortable in the presence of each other, so they could experience the pleasures of each other without fear. The Kama Sutra gave explicit instructions for the level of acceptable sexual activity to take place on each of the 10 nights leading to sexual union. This, Vatsyayana believed, was essential for the couple (and especially the virginal woman) to enjoy a long and pleasurable relationship with each other. In this way they would build a strong and sustaining marriage, uninterested in sexual liaisons with others.

It was also acceptable for a man to pursue a woman through an elaborate courtship that culminated in sexual union. The two then lived together as man and wife, ultimately participating in a marriage ceremony to formalize their matrimony. Not all of ancient Indian society observed the tenets of the Kama Sutra, however.

Paradoxically, polygamy—having multiple wives—was also an accepted and common practice in ancient India. Though the Kama Sutra provided extensive instruction for both men and women about how to behave in such a situation, Vatsyayana nonetheless encouraged monogamy. He astutely observed that a man could find himself exhausted rather than exhilarated in his efforts to satisfy many wives with equal attention—with fairness being of paramount importance to prevent jealousy and disagreement among the wives.

Forbidden Love

As a scholar, Vatsyayana was committed to transcribing and recording the original sutras of his predecessors, even when he felt the practices they described were reprehensible or immoral by his standards. In his wisdom, the ancient scribe inserts his own comments to remind readers that the inclusion of such lessons did not mean they had to attempt them.

Among the relationships forbidden, or at least strongly discouraged, by the Kama Sutra were those with prostitutes, those between close relatives, and those with close (especially childhood) friends. Nonetheless, Vatsyayana acknowledges that such relationships were likely to occur, and he offers instructions for making the most of them. Vatsyayana strongly discourages certain kinds of sexual behavior that existed in some regions of India, though he includes them in the Kama Sutra with the observation that some people had different tastes in pleasure. For these men and women, Vatsyayana notes, such behaviors—which ranged from ways of kissing to violent sex—were both normal and acceptable.

Acknowledging and Honoring the Feminine

Sexuality has been kept in the dark for ages in the West. Just a few generations ago our Victorian grandmothers believed sex was something you did for a man, as a duty of marriage. After all, he had certain needs, however unpleasant his wife found the task of meeting them. It was worse for her if she found herself enjoying her duties, though, because even if she recognized that she also had needs and desires, it wasn't acceptable for her to desire pleasure or sexual fulfillment for herself. A generation or two later, our mothers started waking up to the idea that there might be something in sex for them as well—though they weren't always sure what to do about it. By the 1960s, most women (and many men) finally reached the recognition so well known 2,000 years earlier, that a woman is entitled to experience sexual pleasure and orgasm. How she was to achieve this was up for more discussion, however, because the Kama Sutra and other Eastern love texts were still relegated to reading by a privileged few.

Despite the reality that ancient India was a male-dominated culture (as were many ancient cultures), the Kama Sutra emphasizes a man's responsibility for assuring a pleasurable sexual experience for the woman. He is to teach her in the ways of love, so that her joys might become his joys. And in a display of enlightenment that would not resurface for many centuries, the Kama Sutra instructs women in how to extend the sexual experience by "acting the part of a man," empowering her to fulfill her own pleasures. In the Kama Sutra we find a culture and a sexual morality that honors the feminine at the most fundamental level by revering her as a full equal in sexual union.

Sutra Sayings

A woman should also learn the Kama Sutra. For guidance in acquiring this learning, she can turn to a trusted and experienced woman friend, a sister, or an aunt who can teach her. She should also study the arts and sciences. Though some men may object, they are wrong. A knowledgeable woman is respected, praised, and favored.

During the nineteenth century, Victorian morality kept sexuality under the covers and behind closed doors in Western society. The woman must protest as the man "steals" a kiss.

Kama Knowledge

The Victorian period encompassed the years from 1837 to 1901, during the reign of England's Queen Victoria (1819–1901). Victoria brought a great formality to her tenure on the throne, and correspondingly to her country. Under Queen Victoria's rule, everything had a time, place, and procedure—even love and sex. Ultimately, the term "Victorian" came to be synonymous with repression and restriction. In 1876 Victoria extended her formal, structured methods to the East when she became Empress of India (which was under British rule at the time).

Ancient Ways in Modern Times

The Kama Sutra recognizes and addresses the mystery of the feminine and masculine in relationships. This ancient document features elegantly explicit attention to the subtleties and nuances of the feminine response. If the people of ancient India in fact lived as the Kama Sutra prescribed, it's hard to imagine being unhappy in a relationship. Even those short on experience could learn the lessons of love and relationships in detailed, step-by-step directions (not unlike *The Complete Idiot's Guide to the Kama Sutra, Second Edition* offers for today's lovers!).

The Kama Sutra, in its depth of understanding of the differences between women and men, psychologically and spiritually, adds to our understanding of sexual loving even now, 2,000 years after a wise man named Vatsyayana decided to record his culture's love lessons. Westerners have not always had the good fortune of such learning. Many of our books are more like technical manuals, telling what parts to press for which results. Pleasure becomes predictable, which makes it, well, less fun—and less fulfilling. What this approach lacks—and the Kama Sutra hinged on—is the awareness of the soulful meeting. We don't want formulas, recipes, and techniques. We want to awaken sexually, to feel the flow of our masculine and feminine energies through the dance of sexual union. We want to find completion, connection, and spiritual union through sexual love.

Sutra Sayings

Kama exists when the five senses, together with the intellect and the spirit, consciously and intentionally explore the full and complete pleasure of bodily contact.

The Kama Sutra encouraged the soulful—and equal— meeting of both partners.

(Hrana Janto)

What Does Sexual Morality Mean to You?

Sexual morality is deeply personal. Sure, there are guidelines, rules, and even laws that border and shape a society's standards for acceptable sexual practices. But these are only a starting point for most people. Belief systems and life experiences contour societal standards to fit individual attitudes. You and your partner may share all, some, or few of the same views and values about sex. As well, your feelings and beliefs may change over time.

Out of Touch

If you do choose to share and discuss your responses to the sexual morality self-exploration, do so without commenting on each other's responses. It is important to respect your partner's differences and to honor each other's privacy.

Dr. Josie Suggests

Many people adopt attitudes and values about sex without thinking about whether they truly believe and accept them. This can cause confusion and feelings of guilt when what you enjoy conflicts with what you define as your sexual morality. Exploring the sources of your attitudes about sex helps you clarify your values.

Your Sexual Morality: A Self-Exploration

How do you feel about sex? What do you believe is right, wrong, or dependent on circumstances? The following self-exploration can give you some insights. This is not a quiz; there are no definitive answers or scores. The only purpose of this exploration is to increase your understanding of your individual attitudes and values about sex. Even if you feel you know yourself well, see how you feel about these statements. Your responses could surprise you.

It's often enlightening for a couple to complete the self-exploration individually, then share and discuss their responses with each other. (Make a copy of the questions, or write your responses on a separate sheet of paper so you don't influence each other.) For the most meaningful insights, your responses must be honest—even if you just keep them to yourself.

For each of the following statements, circle (or write on another piece of paper) the number that best describes how you feel about what the statement says. Remember, there are no right or wrong responses.

1. Having sex with someone I'm attracted to requires no commitment beyond the physical experience.

1	2	3	4	5
Strongly agree	Moderately agree	Neither agree nor disagree	Moderately disagree	Strongly disagree

2. Sex should happen only within marriage.

1	2	3	4	5
Strongly agree	Moderately agree	Neither agree nor disagree	Moderately disagree	Strongly disagree

3. Sex should happen only in relationships where the partners are committed to each other.

1	2	3	4	5
Strongly agree	Moderately agree	Neither agree nor disagree	Moderately disagree	Strongly disagree

4. It's okay for committed or married partners to have sex with other people.

1	2	3	4	5
Strongly agree	Moderately agree	Neither agree nor disagree	Moderately disagree	Strongly disagree

5. It's okay for committed or married partners to have sex with other people as long as both partners agree.

1	2	3	4	5
Strongly agree	Moderately agree	Neither agree nor disagree	Moderately disagree	Strongly disagree

6. Gay and lesbian relationships should be viewed and treated no differently than heterosexual relationships.

1	2	3	4	5
Strongly agree	Moderately agree	Neither agree nor disagree	Moderately disagree	Strongly disagree

7. Learning about sex through experience strengthens a couple's relationship.

1	2	3	4	5
Strongly agree	Moderately agree	Neither agree nor disagree	Moderately disagree	Strongly disagree

8. Sex education classes should teach about the joys and techniques of sex, not just the biology.

1	2	3	4	5
Strongly agree	Moderately agree	Neither agree nor disagree	Moderately disagree	Strongly disagree

9. Communities and cultures should be able to pass laws that regulate sexual behavior among consenting adults.

1	2	3	4	5
Strongly agree	Moderately agree	Neither agree nor disagree	Moderately disagree	Strongly disagree

10. Anything goes when it comes to sexual practices, as long as the partners are willing.

1	2	3	4	5
Strongly agree	Moderately agree	Neither agree nor disagree	Moderately disagree	Strongly disagree

11. Sex is an essential aspect of a committed relationship or marriage.

1	2	3	4	5
Strongly agree	Moderately agree	Neither agree nor disagree	Moderately disagree	Strongly disagree

12. New sexual experiences within the relationship help committed or married partners keep their relationships exciting.

1	2	3	4	5
Strongly agree	Moderately agree	Neither agree nor disagree	Moderately disagree	Strongly disagree

13. When it comes to sex, "If it's not broken, don't fix it."

1	2	3	4	5
Strongly agree	Moderately agree	Neither agree nor disagree	Moderately disagree	Strongly disagree

14. It's okay to have sex with someone outside a committed relationship or marriage, as long as you keep it secret so you don't hurt your partner's feelings.

1	2	3	4	5
Strongly agree	Moderately agree	Neither agree nor disagree	Moderately disagree	Strongly disagree

15. I could be happy without sex in a relationship.

1	2	3	4	5
Strongly agree	Moderately agree	Neither agree nor disagree	Moderately disagree	Strongly disagree

16. Sex is a duty in my relationship that I tolerate because my partner expects it.

1	2	3	4	5
Strongly agree	Moderately agree	Neither agree nor disagree	Moderately disagree	Strongly disagree

17. Couples should be required to have marital and sex counseling before getting married.

1	2	3	4	5
Strongly agree	Moderately agree	Neither agree nor disagree	Moderately disagree	Strongly disagree

18. I have had, or would consider having, a sexual friendship without the intention of creating a committed relationship.

1	2	3	4	5
Strongly agree	Moderately agree	Neither agree nor disagree	Moderately disagree	Strongly disagree

19. I have had, or would consider having, a sexual relationship with someone of the same gender.

1	2	3	4	5
Strongly agree	Moderately agree	Neither agree nor disagree	Moderately disagree	Strongly disagree

20. Gay and lesbian couples should be allowed the rights and privileges of legal marriage.

1	2	3	4	5
Strongly agree	Moderately agree	Neither agree nor disagree	Moderately disagree	Strongly disagree

Assessing Your Attitudes and Values

Did any of your responses surprise you? You may be unaware of your views about certain sex practices until something forces you to think about your views in a different way. This can happen when you meet someone whose sexual interests excite you in a new way, or make you feel uncomfortable. Your attitudes about sex define what you perceive to be an ideal sexual experience, and these perceptions in turn shape your expectations. This makes the bed, so to speak, for success or failure in your sexual relationships.

The Least You Need to Know

- Attitudes and values about sex and love vary widely, even within the same culture or society.

- The attitudes and values others—parents, educators, religious leaders—have about sex and love strongly influence your views and perspectives.

- A strong morality frames the Kama Sutra's sexual teachings.

- The Kama Sutra honors the woman in sexual union by empowering her as a full equal.

Eastern Philosophy, Western Style

In This Chapter

◆ The different perspectives of East and West

◆ Breathing as life and as energy

◆ The seven chakras

◆ Joining sexuality, intimacy, and spirituality

The India that adventurer Sir Richard Burton infiltrated had been largely closed to Westerners for centuries. His travels took him across both geographical and cultural boundaries, finding wonders beyond imagination—among them, of course, the Kama Sutra and other erotic texts. These writings treated sexuality as an integral dimension of healthy, enjoyable living. This was a clear contrast to Burton's homeland, where sex and health were considered mutually exclusive. Rigid protocols regulated both attitudes and behaviors in Victorian England.

By contrast, India appeared exotic and free. Because he hid his Western appearance behind clothing and actions that made him seem less like an outsider, Burton had tremendous access to everyday life and activities on his lengthy forays into this foreign and exciting culture. As a result, he was able to view Indian society and practices with rare depth and perspective. In deciding to publish his translations of the Kama Sutra and other erotic texts, Burton hoped to create a bridge between the two worlds in which he felt equally comfortable.

Blending Dualities

Western philosophies, such as those of Burton's lifetime as well as those of contemporary times, tend to be mutually exclusive. They are based on a system of *duality* or "either/or" thinking. An action or a thought is either good or bad. Lines of acceptable behavior are clearly drawn, and there are often consequences for crossing them.

Eastern philosophies, such as those of Vatsyayana's India, allow for the mutually harmonious existence of multiple viewpoints. Such philosophies are based on a system of *nonduality*. A thought or behavior contains a blend of what a Western viewpoint would consider good and bad. Consequences exist more as options—a particular action has taken place, so here are the choices for what to do next.

Sutrology

Duality, also called dualism or dichotomy, holds the view that mutually exclusive opposites, such as good and evil, govern existence. **Nonduality** holds the view that opposite or conflicting perspectives exist simultaneously and can be harmonious.

Burton's translation of the Kama Sutra, even in the limited quantity he published and secretive manner in which he distributed the books, proved a great awakening for Westerners. Here was a text, authored by spiritual leaders, that offered more explicit information about sex than had ever been accessible to any Westerner. More astonishingly, it did so without embarrassment or secrecy. This forthright document not only encouraged what Westerners typically thought of in the Victorian period as "sins of the flesh," it actually condoned sexual union that attended to women's pleasure as vitally important, and elevated the sexual embrace to a place where it was required learning for the average citizen.

Kama Knowledge

Psychiatrist Wilhelm Reich (1897–1957) was one of Freud's most gifted psychoanalysts. Noted for his discovery of "orgone" (a form of energy Reich believed to have healing properties), Reich's understanding of the breath as a conduit of energy was the Western equivalent of the Tantric energetic current known as Kundalini. By the time of his death, Reich had contributed to our understanding of the importance of full orgasmic functioning in health. He also stirred up a great deal of political, analytical, and socio-sexual controversy, and by the end of his life was seen as a dangerous person.

The Kama Sutra introduced Western lovers to a startling recognition—there is a connection between spirituality and sexuality. Not surprisingly, it was, and remains, a welcome correlation for many Westerners (of Burton's time and beyond) who wondered if there might be more to sex than procreation. It didn't make sense that bodies containing such vast stores of untapped pleasure should be limited to the routine of reproduction. The Kama Sutra offered proof that people had been enjoying and discovering intimacy in "the pleasures of the flesh" since the beginning of time.

May the Life Force Be with You: Prana

Breathing is the essence of life. No one questions this, East or West. But East and West define "essence" in different ways. In the Western view, breathing is the basis of biological function. Without it, the heart stops beating and life ends. Breathing is an unconscious act the body engages in without control or direction from the mind.

In the Eastern view, the breath, called *prana*, is recognized as an important conduit between flesh and spirit. As the breath flows, so flows life. If we breathe in a shallow limited way, our organs receive a limited amount of oxygen and this can ultimately result in oxygen-starved cells, tissues, and organs that become diseased. Breathing, Eastern style, is both biological and spiritual.

The Eastern schools of *esoteric sexuality* use practices that focus on the breath. Learning to charge the body with energy through the breath, channeling the breath through breathing practices, and directing the breath through visualization practices are important life force-enhancing practices that bring spirit and flesh into harmony, and balance the masculine and feminine energies.

The Tantric exercises that harmonize the masculine and feminine energies within an individual are practiced alone and with a partner. Through a conscious knowledge of the breath, along with meditation, visualization, and breathing, partners come into the harmonic union that Eastern sexual practices honor and seek.

Sutrology

Prana means life energy or life force. **Esoteric sexuality** refers to the Tantric philosophy, which recognizes love and sex as powerful aspects of life that can be vehicles to our self-realization.

Out of Touch

When you practice harmonized breathing, or any other breathing technique, be sure to breathe slowly and deeply, in and out. Breathe from your belly, not just from high up in your chest. If your breaths are too shallow and too fast, you could hyperventilate, which causes you to feel woozy and lightheaded. If this happens, return to a normal breathing pattern until the lightheadedness passes.

> ### Kama Knowledge
>
> Tantra is a mystical and spiritual philosophy, art, science, and psychological system that translated from the Sanskrit means "weave," "continuum," "web," "context." Tantra seeks to create a balanced union between opposites as a way to liberate mind and body from unconsciousness. To facilitate this, it focuses on the union of opposites, holding that paradoxical states arising on physical, mental, spiritual, and astral levels exist as one. Women and men are viewed as embodying and mirroring the creative energies represented by the goddess Shakti and the god Shiva. Tantric knowledge is concerned with the transmutation of energy, freeing the mind, and realizing one's potential. We'll discuss Tantra in more detail in Chapter 25.

Breathing in Harmony: Two Exercises

Harmonizing your breathing helps synchronize your body and your feelings with your partner's. This can turn satisfactory sex into amazing lovemaking. Try the following two exercises, and see what differences you experience.

Paired Harmonized Breathing

1. Sit with your back touching your partner's back and begin breathing in unison to harmonize your breaths.

2. Pay equal attention to both your own and your partner's breathing until you are breathing together.

3. Once you are breathing together, turn to face each other. Sit as close to each other as you can. Look into each other's eyes and continue to breathe in unison. Do this for at least five minutes.

4. Notice what feelings come up. You may find this is difficult to do at first, because we're not accustomed to either extended eye contact or consciously breathing with another. You may notice a feeling of peacefulness, well-being, a sense of harmony with your partner.

Dr. Josie Suggests

When making love, often we hold our breath as we approach orgasm. We tighten up and focus on the elusive "Big O" as though we can will it to happen. But we can't. Orgasm is surrendering, losing control, letting pleasure have its way with you. The fuller and deeper you breathe while you are riding the waves of pleasure, the looser and more relaxed you are, and the more intense your orgasm.

Harmonized Breathing While Making Love

While making love, notice your breathing. Many people stop breathing when they become aroused. Ask your partner to breathe with you, so the two of you inhale and exhale in unison.

1. Open your eyes and look into your partner's eyes. Now, extend the length of the breath. Inhale for the duration of four or more heartbeats.

2. Retain the breath for two or more heartbeats. Focus on heartbeats instead of seconds so you listen to your body rhythms rather than count.

3. Visualize your entire nervous system being charged with life force, or prana, as you hold in the breath.

4. Exhale evenly for the duration of four or more heartbeats.

The Wheels of Energy Keep on Rolling: Chakras

In the ancient Tantric texts, the term *chakra* describes the seven major and minor centers of psychic energy that are located along the spine. Westerners tend to think of the chakras in physiological terms, viewing them as corresponding to physical centers or vital organs at the base of the spine, the sexual organs, the diaphragm, the heart, the throat, and the point between the eyes in the center of the forehead and the top of the skull. Channels called *nadis* connect the chakras. Chakras are typically represented as circles of energy surrounded by lotus petals. Each circle is associated with a color, sound, and deity.

Sutrology

A **chakra** is a center, or wheel, of psychic energy within the human body. **Nadis** are the invisible pathways or channels this energy follows as it moves through the body.

The chakras are energy vortexes that vibrate with energy corresponding to the center where they are located. While early Tantric systems identified just four chakras, later Tantric schools worked with a seven-chakras system, which is the system we in the West currently use. On a physical level, the organs of the endocrine system match up to the chakra system.

Chakra	Location	Related Endocrine Gland	Energy	Color	Sanskrit Name
First	Base of the spine	Ovaries/testes	Survival	Red	Muladhara chakra
Second	Sexual organs	Pancreas	Sexual and emotional	Orange	Svadhish-tana chakra
Third	Solar plexus	Adrenals	Personal power and how we use it	Yellow	Manipura chakra
Fourth	Heart	Thymus	How we give and receive love and affection	Green	Anahata chakra
Fifth	Base of the neck (throat)	Thyroid/parathyroid	Creativity and expression	Turquoise	Vishuddha chakra
Sixth	"Third eye" region of the forehead	Pituitary	Clear vision, perception, and understanding	Blue	Ajna chakra
Seventh	Crown of the head	Pineal	Our connection to spiritual truth, the god of our heart, the great spirit, existence, and how we see our cosmic connection	Violet	Sahasrara chakra

Our bodies tend to give us straightforward information about what we are feeling. Chakras symbolize energetic centers and the location where we hold emotions. When we pay attention to the location where our emotions are centered, we can access valuable insights into our selves and how we are handling our emotions. For example, anger or fear frequently causes a response of tightening or contraction in the chest/heart chakra or the belly/power center. Sexual desire is experienced as a pleasant fullness and excitement in the sex center/second chakra. Self-consciousness or difficulty with communication makes us feel choked up or we lose our voice, a throat chakra/fifth chakra issue.

The chakras are seven centers of psychic energy located along the spine.

(Hrana Janto)

Opposites Attract

The attraction of opposites is certainly one of life's most compelling mysteries. As human beings, we now are in the unique position of no longer being dependent upon one another for survival. This frees us to explore the nature of our attraction and longing to unite with another in a pairing that establishes us as equals.

Still, we long for the fulfillment that comes with being loved deeply and well. No matter how much we lament the differences between ourselves and our opposites, one thing is certain: Whether straight or gay, our fascination with the dance between self and other is powerful and pulls at our attention on physical, emotional, and spiritual levels.

The Kama Sutra acknowledges and honors the differences between men and women. In its view, the male and the female bodies are opposites that fit together in such a way that when united, they form completeness. The Kama Sutra recognizes, too, that not all male bodies are the same, nor are all female bodies the same. It offers numerous suggestions for accommodating these additional differences to create the most enjoyable sexual union possible.

Yin: The Feminine Mystique

In the Eastern view, *yin* represents the feminine principle, or femaleness. Yin is that aspect of existence that is passive, cold, dark, and wet. Yin is the force of the earth, and must be awakened and aroused to prepare it for union with the *yang*. The Kama Sutra instructs men in the methods of creating such arousal, and recognizes one of the most important distinctions between men and women: The feminine, as a rule, takes longer to arouse. The Kama Sutra goes to great lengths instructing lovers in the ways to arouse the feminine. Vatsyayana compares this process to preparing dough for baking.

To Western thinking, yin and yang might sound sexist. But remember, no one is purely female or male. We all have qualities that could be interpreted as belonging to the other gender. A woman might be a terrific athlete, hate to cook, and be the primary breadwinner. A man might love to cook and stay home to raise his kids while his partner pursues her career. A man also has yin, just as a woman also has yang. When partners can stimulate both yin and yang energies in each other as they make love, the experience becomes more powerful and enjoyable. The Kama Sutra also instructs women in "acting the part of a man," describing techniques for taking the yang role during lovemaking, and for awakening the yin energy in the man.

> **Sutrology**
>
> Yin and yang are Eastern terms for opposites that together form a whole. In the context of sexuality, yin designates the feminine and yang designates the masculine.

The Eastern symbol for the balance in energetic harmony of yin and yang.

Yang: The Energy of

Virility

Yang represents the masculine, or the male principle. It is active, warm, light, and dry. Yang is the force of the heavens. Yang is the initiating energy, and as such (according to the Kama Sutra) is responsible for assuring that the sexual experience is enjoyable for both partners. The Kama Sutra also advises the man to get in touch with his feminine side by exhibiting gentleness and tenderness. Male tenderness is not such a contemporary concept after all!

Sex, Kama Sutra style, strives to balance the yin and the yang or masculine and feminine energies, not just between the partners but also within each partner. Without balance and the meeting that takes place when two sovereign people claim their full potential, partners cannot reach the ecstasy available to them in sexual loving. The goal of both the man and the woman, Vatsyayana writes, is to strive toward this balance in every act of sexual union.

Kama Knowledge

In Vatsyayana's time, it was common for men in the higher social castes to demonstrate their cooking expertise during courtship. Cooking was among the 64 arts and sciences the cultured ancient Indian citizen studied. Men and women alike also studied using flowers to beautify the home, stringing necklaces, making and wearing jewelry, applying perfumes and cosmetics, and arranging beds, carpets, and couches for comfortable reclining. These elements of the arts balanced learning in the sciences and in kama, or loving. Fluency in all three areas established both men and women as desirable citizens and spouses.

In Union with the Universe

In the Eastern view, sex is seen not only as pleasure and procreation, but also as a vehicle for balancing disparate energies within one person as well as within the couple. Sexual union is a way to exchange these energies as well as balance them within one person. A man who makes love to a woman to her full release and opens himself to receive her *yin* essence takes that energy into himself. A woman who rides wave after wave of bliss opening and releasing into full orgasmic pleasure and takes in the *yang* essence of her partner (whether the partner is male or female) becomes more energetically balanced.

The ideas of cultivating a balanced feminine and masculine energy and visualizing each other as an embodiment of the divine is a common practice in the sacred schools of erotic spirituality that evolved in India, Tibet, the Middle East, and China. These practices draw attention and awareness to the attributes of each gender. This allows partners to be witnessed by each other in the full potential of their gifts as woman and man. Revering our partner as our beloved adds a note of sacredness to the relationship and cultivates loving as a path to an enlightened way of living together.

Sutra Sayings

The man and the woman who can feel the same kind of pleasure, and arouse this pleasure in each other, should marry. They will love each other forever.

Learning to Be Spiritually Intimate

Most people want intimacy and closeness in their relationships. Couples whose relationships are coming apart often complain that they wish their partners would be more intimate. When couples come to the counseling office and the therapist asks what intimacy means to them, responses range from "I want him to talk to me" to "I want her to watch me surf."

Perhaps, sadly, people fail to realize that it isn't the shared space that makes you feel intimate. It isn't what you do that creates an intimacy. It is the quality of your presence. It is how much of yourself you share with your partner when you are together. Do you offer your feelings and thoughts, share insights and tenderness through affectionate touching? Do you notice changes and compliment your partner?

Sutra Sayings

A man should show the woman he loves the truth of his emotions. He should confide his feelings to her, and have long conversations with her, so she can come to know the true state of his mind. He should look for the same ways from her, so he can know the true state of her mind.

Intimacy and closeness are not the same. A couple may tell the therapist that they have lots of closeness yet still don't feel intimate. When the therapist asks them to describe how they spend their time together, they rattle off a list of activities that puts most social calendars to shame. They share time going to movies, having dinner with friends, watching television, attending the kids' soccer games. Their favorite pastime, they may say, is to sit side-by-side on the sofa and read. Clearly this couple, like so many others, has plenty of closeness. They spend a lot of time in close proximity, sharing activities and spending quality time together. What they are missing, however, is intimacy.

"Into Me, You See"

Intimacy evolves in a relationship when we reveal ourselves to one another. Look at the word intimacy—"into me, you see." To be intimate with another person, we must reveal ourselves to one another. When a relationship is young, we share little bits of intimacy and take little risks. Saying "I love chocolate, too" establishes a common connection, but it isn't much of a risk. If one person says, "Your loving me makes me aware of how I sometimes don't feel like I deserve your love and don't always let you in," that is putting your heart out there in a vulnerable way that establishes an intimate connection.

To grow and feel more connected in an intimate relationship, partners need to reveal themselves in a vulnerable, undefended manner. When you expose your fears to one another, your hearts soften and you can continue to grow and evolve in an open, tender, and dynamic relationship. If couples harden, withdraw, and stop revealing themselves to each other, relationships stagnate. Couples that adopt a "let's not rock the boat" attitude and play it safe miss out on the growing intimacy that happens by revealing yourself to another.

Those couples who find themselves dining in silence are often not at a loss for words, but rather they are unwilling to say the difficult things that would bring them back into an intimate connection. Rather than jeopardizing closeness, telling each other the truth and saying what might be the hard things usually bring couples closer because speaking of such things clears the air between them. There are no unspoken conversations.

This fear of saying something that would shake things up keeps couples locked out of real intimacy. Sure, this offers shelter from disturbance and vulnerability. But it also closes out passion and desire. In this "no risk" zone, it's tempting to turn to an erotic text like the Kama Sutra in search of ways to revive faltering intimacy with exotic techniques of pleasure. This will almost certainly reinvigorate interest in sex. But each partner also must again be willing to take the risks true intimacy requires.

> **Dr. Josie Suggests**
>
> When you are making love and nearing orgasm, deepen your breath and extend the exhale. Let sound out on the exhale as you climax. This extends the orgasm.

Reuniting Sexuality and Spirituality

It is easy to see how the Kama Sutra includes emotional intimacy as an important element of sexual loving. In Vatsyayana's view, sexuality and spirituality are also intertwined. Western perspectives are moving closer to this unity of body and soul. During the past 40 years we have begun to view sexual loving as a pleasurable way to cultivate intimacy. More recently, we have started to see that sexual loving is also a way to honor our longing for a deeper and more profound spiritual connection to life. Eastern writings such as the Kama Sutra, in which the divine extends to the human experience through sexual union, have encouraged Westerners to permit spirituality in the bedroom, too.

Still, we remain self-conscious in our treatment of spiritual intimacy and sexuality. We tend to think in terms of having better sex rather than viewing a loving relationship as a way to grow in self-knowing, acceptance, and compassion. It is these qualities that we can develop in loving another well that will allow us to bridge the differences that exist between us. We can be sexual without being intimate. We can have orgasmic, good-enough sex (which is all some of us feel we dare ask). But do we feel intimately, spiritually, connected in our lovemaking? Do we open our eyes and see who it is that we are sharing our bodies and our love with?

The intimacy that we long for can be found when we are fully, unconditionally present in our love play with our beloved. When we make love without a goal of "getting off or getting our beloved off" and focus on being present in our breath, in our touch, in our open-eyed meeting of the other, when we can share fear or joy during the height of pleasure, when we participate with all of our being, and when we risk being honest, then real intimacy is present in our lovemaking.

The Least You Need to Know

- Breathing gives your body life and your spirit energy.

- Each person, male or female, has both masculine and feminine (yin and yang) dimensions.

- Intimacy can exist only when partners are willing to risk sharing themselves, their joys, and their fears.

- While Eastern cultures have always viewed sexuality and spirituality as inseparable, Western cultures are just beginning to recognize that it is okay to feel spiritual about sex.

Chapter 4

Pleasing the Body, Nurturing the Spirit

In This Chapter

- ◆ The connections between body, mind, and spirit

- ◆ The joy of using all of your senses when making love

- ◆ Exercises to help you enjoy taste, touch, smell, hearing, and sight during lovemaking

- ◆ The importance of "being present" when making love

"I love you, body and soul." Eastern cultures might express this sentiment simply as "I love you," because in the Eastern view, body and soul are inseparable elements of human existence. In the Western view, however, the body and the soul exist independently. Though the soul resides in the body, this is less than suitable housing. The Western view sees the body as flawed, devious, and inherently destined to lead us astray. We certainly can't trust it, and would do best to try to tame it, deny it, or ignore it.

In the Western view, the soul, then, is everything the body is not—pure, sincere, inherently good. Often, religious beliefs and practices foster this division. What's good for the body can't possibly be good for the soul, and the soul's desires don't satisfy the body's cravings. Life, then, becomes a battle between body and soul.

Everyone knows the troubles that result. Otherwise, sensible, caring, intelligent adults behave like adolescent children rebelling against overly strict parents. Throwing caution aside, we push past inhibitions and limits to discover what it feels like to live beyond them. For many people, the experience is exhilarating. For the first time, they feel alive, awake, free.

Still, there's something missing. Without guidelines and traditions, there remain the feelings of being hungry and lost. The quest for fulfillment continues as people seek relationships that offer spiritual sustenance as well as physical satisfaction. And in the process, most people discover that, indeed, body and soul belong together.

What's Good for the Body Is Good for the Soul

Culturally, Westerners seem to have a built-in fear of abandoning themselves to pleasure. This is especially true of women, who are taught from early childhood to be "good" girls. A good girl doesn't throw her legs wide and revel in pleasure. She hides her desires, joys, and expertise as a lover. She appears discreet and virginal, no matter how old or experienced she may be. Ultimately, all that holding in and holding back creates a backlog of tension and stress that's not good for the body (or the soul, but more on that in the next section). It's difficult, if not impossible, to be a good girl and enjoy sex by Western standards.

There's also this body-image obsession that grips Western cultures (and particularly the trend-setting United States). We see our bodies as too old, too fat, too short, too hairy. Our image of what is attractive—for men as well as for women—is distorted and fleeting. What looks good today is ugly tomorrow. It's seldom possible to feel comfortable about yourself when the standard is a moving target. (Body image is such an important topic that there's much more about it in Chapter 7.

Dr. Josie Suggests

Our youth-oriented culture causes us to reject and fight the natural process of aging. Ironically, our aging bodies are better equipped to enjoy sex. As hormone levels change, the urgency that men felt in their twenties slows. Many women come into their sexual prime after menopause, when they can finally focus on pleasure without fearing pregnancy.

This obsession with image interferes with our ability—and need—to slow down and enjoy all of the senses, not only when making love, but in all aspects of our lives. It deprives us of the full experience, whether that is sexual union or a walk in the woods, leaving both the body and the mind wanting something more.

Get in touch with your body! Pay attention to how your body feels and reacts to its environment, whether the touch of a cool breeze or a lover's warm breath. Notice the multitude of sensations your body experiences. For most people, heightened awareness intensifies sensation.

If something feels good to the body, it becomes a pleasant emotional experience as well. It "feels good all over"—not just on the outside, but inside as well. Eastern sages like Vatsyayana stress the need to please both body and soul. Doing so nurtures each, resulting in a harmonious existence. We connect with our souls through our bodies, through "being present" to the sensations our bodies experience.

Activate Your Senses

When we first fall in love, we feel as though all of our senses are heightened. We notice and enjoy smells, touches, sights, sounds, and tastes as though they are entirely new experiences. We feel an intensified awareness. We feel alive and "on top of the world." We're more willing to say how we feel, to abandon ourselves to the pleasures of our senses, to trust in the attraction that draws us together.

As human beings, we learn at an early age to shut our senses down. Parents work very hard to thwart a baby's natural inclination to put everything in the mouth. Adults spew a litany of don'ts at children—don't put that in your mouth, don't touch, don't play with your food, don't stare, don't listen to that. We learn that it's okay to say a meal smells good, but wrong to say a person stinks. While all of this conditioning makes us more polite citizens, we lose spontaneous sensuality in the process.

Using our senses becomes, like so many other aspects of our conditioned dualistic thinking, a matter of "good" and "bad." By the time we are grown, an entire structure of socially acceptable responses governs the ways we taste, touch, see, hear, and smell. Little wonder that we find it confusing to taste when we kiss or see when we touch! Yet for sexual partners to fully enjoy each other, they must come to all their senses.

Kama Knowledge
Numerous studies show that infants who are raised in environments where their biological needs are met but they are seldom held or touched fail to thrive. As they grow older, they weigh less than their cuddled counterparts, and have trouble relating to other children. Touch is as essential to survival as are nourishment and shelter, yet it is often overlooked.

"Come to your senses," we say. Wake up and smell the coffee. Listen to that annoyingly chipper early bird sing a greeting to the dawning day. Feel the wind beneath your wings (okay, that's a little much). But do come alive, be in your body, and feel the exhilaration of living a sensual life.

The Kama Sutra emphasizes using all the senses during sexual loving. It stresses that touching, seeing, smelling, tasting, and talking are all essential elements of foreplay and arousal. Sight, sound, and smell are especially effective in setting the mood early on—soft lighting, gentle music, and fragrances such as incense or scented candles help to establish an amorous atmosphere. As lovemaking progresses, touching becomes the most dominant force. Vatsyayana continually reminds his readers to remember to invoke their other senses, even as contact envelops them, to make the experience even more pleasurable.

When you walk outside today, feel the air on your skin. *Really* notice it. Is it cool or warm, moving or still? Do you have goose bumps, or are you sweaty? Stop thinking about that overdue report your boss has been nagging about or what to fix for dinner tonight. Instead, feel your feet as they make contact with the ground. Hear the sounds of your shoes. Are you walking on gravel or pavement? Is the pressure of each step even across the sole of your foot? What happens when you lighten your step, lessen the force with which it falls? How do the sounds and feelings of walking change?

Make it a part of every action to consciously identify the participation of your five senses. Try to involve all your senses in as many of your daily experiences as possible, and seek experiences that fully engage your senses. Taste, smell, and touch your food. Savor experiences. Indulge in pleasures of the flesh. Get (or give) a massage. Take a scented bath. Turn down the lights and light candles. Play music in all the rooms of your house. Become sensually engaged in life.

Touch Me, Feel Me

The body's organ of touch is the skin. A typical adult has about two and one half square yards of skin containing between 600,000 and 700,000 *receptor cells* that detect sensation. The numbers and kinds of receptor cells vary depending on location. Your fingertips, for example, are loaded with pressure cells capable of detecting the footsteps of a fly but are rather light on pain receptors. Your corneas, on the other hand, are about 300 times more sensitive to pain than are the soles of your feet.

> **Sutrology**
>
> **Receptor cells** are specialized nerve cells in the skin that detect sensations such as pressure, temperature, and pain.

You've no doubt noticed that some parts of your body are far more sensitive to touch than others. Your lips, genitals, and the palms of your hands have the highest concentration of receptor cells. Hair follicles are also well-supplied with nerves. The areas of the brain that receive and interpret signals sent from these parts are correspondingly larger than the areas that handle neural transmissions from receptor cells on other skin surfaces.

The lips get the largest share of cerebral attention, nearly twice the size of that reserved for the genitals. The tongue, face, hands, and inner arms also command a good deal of brain space, too. It does take longer for a light, pleasurable touch to travel the neural highway to its terminal in the brain, however, than it does for pain to make the same trip. A tickle or caress cruises to your cerebrum at a rate of about three to six feet a second. Poke yourself with a tack, however, and the message races to your brain at a rate of more than 100 feet per second—about one tenth the speed of sound.

> **Out of Touch** _____
>
> Pleasure and pain exist at different ends of the sensory spectrum. What we might ordinarily experience as pain can become pleasurable when the senses are intensely aroused, such as occurs during lovemaking. The Kama Sutra suggests that lovers use a variety of touch, including gentle scratching, biting, and pinching. But it's important to communicate what is feeling good and what isn't and to stop when your partner asks you to.

Humans are sensual beings from birth. The skin is the first sensory organ to develop, so it should come as no surprise that babies love to be cuddled and stroked. Babies seem to bring out the touch in adults, too—few grownups can resist holding and touching a baby. Indeed, such contact is essential for survival—a human baby is completely dependent on the adults in its life to meet every need.

As babies grow up, however, and develop the ability to meet an increasing number of their own needs, contact from adults backs off. Way off. By the time their kids reach adolescence, few parents touch their kids at all. By the time we're adults, we've lost touch with the natural sensuality that is our birthright and replaced it with a false picture of what it means to be erotic. We don't lose our need to touch and be touched, however—we just don't know quite how to meet it.

In many cultures, it is common to see friends of the same gender kiss or hold hands without any sexual implications. Many Westerners are so restrictive about touching that nearly all physical contact immediately acquires sexual connotations. Ironically, this shuts down the sensuality of touch during lovemaking. We become as reserved about contact in bed as we are in public.

The Kama Sutra focuses much attention on touching. Touching is key to sexual arousal. Kissing, caressing, stroking, embracing, and even mutually agreeable biting, scratching, and pinching (taking great care not to hurt your partner) are all ways of sexual touching. Most people find that not all kinds of touching are erotic at all times, though sometimes anticipating how your lover will touch you next can heighten your arousal.

The following exercise focuses your awareness on how it feels to touch yourself or your partner, which we often overlook, as well as how it feels to be touched.

Exercise: Sensual Touch

1. Sit where you can be comfortable and free from distractions.

2. Focus your attention on and in your fingertips. Tune out other thoughts.

3. Place your fingertips on the soft inner skin of your arm or thigh and stroke very lightly. Focus your awareness on the skin you are touching. Notice how good it feels to be touched.

4. Now shift the focus of your awareness to your fingertips as they are doing the touching. Notice how good it feels to touch.

5. When you are aware and focused, it feels as good to touch as to be touched.

You can do this exercise with your partner, too. Be sure to concentrate first on what your fingertips feel as they stroke your partner's skin, noticing every detail about the contact. Then shift your attention to how it feels when your partner strokes your skin.

Eyes Wide Open

The eyes, as the saying goes, are the windows to the soul. But the path of vision starts with your eyes. About 60 to 80 percent of what we experience from the outside world comes to us through the function of sight. Patterns of light and color enter the eye through the *lens*, which projects them onto the *retina* at the back of the eye. This process is similar to projecting a movie onto a screen.

The eye uses two kinds of nerve cells to detect color and light, *cones* and *rods*. Rods respond to varying levels of light, and can become as much as 100,000 times more sensitive in the dark. Rods do not, however, respond to color. That's the job of the approximately five million or so cone cells each eye contains. Cone cells are further specialized to detect particular wavelengths of color. Your eye's ability to detect color diminishes in dim light and nearly disappears in darkness, reducing visual perception to shades of gray. Rods and cones send millions of signals to your brain, which interprets them and presents you with a perceived image.

Often your conscious mind intercepts an image on its way from your eyes to your brain. Taking interpretation beyond dutifully detecting color, shape, and size, your mind adds a few enhancements. Sights become pleasing … or not. What your mind's eye sees when you look at your partner is often arousing—and what you *can't* see can be even more so. Looking at each other, and especially into each other's eyes, while you make love can create an intimate and potent experience.

Sutrology

The **retina** is the light-sensitive membrane at the back of the eye. The **lens** sits at the front of the eyeball and focuses the light waves. **Rods** are the cells on the retina that detect light and dark, and **cones** are the cells on the retina that detect color.

So why do so many people close their eyes when making love? Some people find it uncomfortable to watch each other during lovemaking. They may find it somehow seems voyeuristic or naughty, like peeking into someone else's bedroom window. Of course, such a concept would sound silly in Eastern cultures of the Kama Sutra period where sex is a natural and good thing. For people who are used to just having sex, especially if they think it's good sex, it might feel like rocking the boat to try to make it better. Taking the relationship to the next level of intimacy—"into me, you see"—can be scary.

Looking someone in the eye is the traditional finger-in-the-wind test of truthfulness. Most (though not all) people have trouble lying when they're eye-to-eye with someone. The truth is, not all people can face being truthful during sex. Such truthfulness is a dimension of intimacy, and intimacy is risky. And sometimes people don't want to see beyond the surface, preferring to keep sex as nothing more than a physical act.

Many people close their eyes during lovemaking believing that doing so intensifies the experience. Sometimes this is true, as long as they can focus their attention on what the rest of their senses are telling them. Some sex therapists suggest that couples make love with their eyes closed so they can focus on specific sensations. This expands and intensifies the sensation receiving the attention. Couples who have difficulty touching and being touched often benefit from this approach because it reduces the sense of risk they feel about enjoying physical contact.

Sutra Sayings

An important prelude to sexual union is for the man to show his erect organ to his partner, so she may become aroused and desire for it to enter her.

Closing your eyes as part of a sexual fantasy has its place in love play, too. But ultimately, closing your eyes when you make love restricts your body's ability to fully respond. You're limiting the senses that can be involved. Keeping your eyes open and seeing your partner's pleasure adds another dimension to lovemaking, making the experience more complete and more intimate. Most lovers enjoy looking at each other's bodies. Whether by genetic programming or cultural indoctrination, this is a great turn on.

Watching your partner while you make love adds an exciting dimension to your sensual perception of each other's pleasure. For couples who are accustomed to making love in the dark, seeing each other's passion and joy is often a tender and revealing experience. The following exercise lets you practice using your sense of sight during lovemaking.

Exercise: Making Love with Your Eyes Open

1. Set the lighting so you can see each other. Keep your eyes open while you make love, and watch your partner.

2. "Drink" in the sights of your partner's increasing arousal.

3. Look into each other's eyes.

4. Make and keep eye contact during orgasm.

5. Pay attention to the feelings that arise while you look into your partner's eyes.

6. Later you can tenderly share your experience with each other.

Kama Knowledge

The French philosopher René Descartes (1596–1650), best known for "I think, therefore I am," was the first to view the eyes as windows to the soul. He believed the pineal gland, located deep within the brain, was the seat of the soul and the center of interaction between the soul and the body. A deeply religious man, Descartes theorized that visual information flowed into the body through the eyes and along the optic nerves, which he envisioned as hollow tubes, to the pineal. There, "passion" (the soul) joined matter (the physical world). Later studies in the structure of the brain disproved this theory, though the concept of a link between the eyes and the soul remains popular.

Love Sounds

What do you hear when you make love? Many people have music playing in the background, which helps create a pleasant, perhaps romantic, ambience. Different styles of music can stimulate different ways of lovemaking. But your bodies make erotic music of their own. All you have to do is tune in.

Listen, for example, to how your partner's breathing changes as your arousal increases. Hear whether it becomes shallow or deepens, and how it changes tempo. Listen to your own body, too. Can you hear your heart beating, the rushing of your pulse, the quickening of your breathing as you become aroused? Your body also makes other sounds and noises during lovemaking. When you become aware of them, you begin to connect them with sexual excitement. This awareness, this listening, creates anticipation as well as tells you how your partner is responding to your actions.

The organ of listening is the ear. The outer ear, the part you see and may adorn with earrings and other jewelry, collects and focuses sounds. It funnels them down the ear canal to the eardrum, which vibrates in response. Behind the eardrum are your body's three tiniest bones, which are called ossicles. They translate the eardrum's vibrations into signals the auditory nerves then carry to your brain.

Many people think of listening as the passive side of talking (which is why "you don't listen to me!" is such a common communication challenge among couples). But listening is an activity. It requires concentration and focus. It provides a dimension of information that you cannot obtain through your other senses, and also combines with other sensory perceptions to magnify your arousal. Listen to what your partner says while in the throes of passion, too. For some people, talking during lovemaking can be especially erotic.

Partners are sometimes uncomfortable talking with each other about their lovemaking, fearful of hurting each other's feelings or just unsure of what to say. Yet conversation is our primary means of communication. It greatly enhances the pleasures of sexual loving when you can tell each other what feels good and what you want. The following exercise helps you practice talking with each other about your sexual loving.

Dr. Josie Suggests

Your outer ear is very sensitive to touch. Many people enjoy having their partners kiss and gently tug their earlobes. Whispering into your lover's ear during lovemaking can be especially arousing. The tiny hairs inside the ear canal are surrounded by nerves that respond to the slightest stimulation. It is also an intimate way to talk erotically.

Exercise: Sex Talk

1. Have a conversation with each other about talking during sex. Take five minutes each to speak. While your partner is talking, just listen without responding.

2. When it's your turn to talk, be honest and direct. What do you want to say to your partner during lovemaking that you hold back because you're unsure of his or her response? Are you comfortable asking for what pleasures you? Do you wish your partner would let you know how good something feels? Tell your partner.

3. Practice talking during lovemaking. When making love, express your pleasure with sounds and words of delight. Tell your partner what feels good, and what would feel even better. Even just ooohs and aaahs will let your partner know you are enjoying the lovemaking.

Taste and Texture

It seems the first lesson parents strive to teach children is "get that out of your mouth." We grow up believing that unless it comes to us on a plate, it's yucky. Then we hit the age of sexual exploration, and an eager date thrusts a tongue during a kiss. Momma never said "yucky" would be so much fun! Using your tongue in lovemaking invokes the sense of taste as well as the sense of touch (and often the sense of smell, too, since your nose so closely follows wherever your tongue goes).

The tongue is muscular, flexible, and sensitive. Anchored at the back of your mouth right at the top of your throat, your tongue is necessary for swallowing and speaking. The surface of your tongue contains about 10,000 taste buds, which surround the hundreds of tiny bumps (called papillae) that give your tongue its rough texture. While these specialized cells can detect only four basic tastes—sweet, sour, bitter, and salty—they create thousands of combinations we perceive as flavors.

Taste buds tend to be grouped by their sensitivities. Those on the very tip of the tongue detect sweetness, flanked by those that detect sourness. The taste buds along the sides of your tongue sense saltiness, and the ones along the very back of your tongue send you into a shudder when they encounter bitterness. Interestingly, when we begin to like something, we "develop a taste" for it.

Your tongue also contains receptor cells that detect touch, which is one reason tongue thrusting during kissing is so arousing. It is such tongue-to-tongue contact during a kiss, according to the Kama Sutra, that establishes the kiss as erotic rather than merely affectionate. Such kissing, Vatsyayana counsels, is a necessary and enjoyable introduction to lovemaking. Using your tongue to explore other parts of your partner's body is also very erotic. The Kama Sutra encourages creativity in oral pleasuring.

Try the following exercise with your partner to experience the pleasures of kissing and being kissed. Each partner takes a turn of about 10 minutes.

Exercise: How You Like to Be Kissed

1. Begin kissing your partner the way you want to be kissed. Nibble, suck, bite, use your tongue. Start at the mouth and include the whole face, neck, ears, and any other parts of the body you wish.

2. Switch and become the receiver of your partner's kisses.

3. Share with each other, without judgment or criticism, how the kissing exercise was for you. Simply listen without responding. Thank each other.

4. This exercise may or may not lead to lovemaking. It is best to not have an expectation that sex will follow.

5. Take time to hold each other and be close after the exercise.

The Aromas of Love

The sense of smell is very closely linked to the sense of taste. Millions of nerve fibers line the inside of your organ of scent, the nose. Rather than being receptors that relay information to other nerves, however, these fibers are actually fringe-like extensions of the *olfactory nerve*, which gives them a direct path to your brain. Your sense of smell is far more sensitive than your sense of taste (which is actually why you can't taste very well when you have a stuffy nose).

Each one of us emits distinctive, unique odors. Perhaps the most familiar demonstration of this is in the use of tracking dogs such as bloodhounds to trail lost children and fleeing criminals. Dogs, with their highly sophisticated sense of smell, are able to distinguish an individual's scent from the odors of other people as well as the endless smells present in the surrounding environment. As well, a person gives off different odors when frightened or excited than when calm. Dogs are particularly adept at detecting these chemical changes, which is how police dogs can pick an otherwise unnoticed crime suspect from a crowd of people.

Unlike dogs and other animals, human beings are not so accustomed to using the sense of smell. Sure, we notice when body odors get especially strong, such as after intense exercise. We also respond to smells that we use intentionally. The associations between smells and emotions are very strong. A whiff of the perfume your grandmother wore when you were a child can instantly transport your mind back to childhood. Merchants such as bakers and florists use scents and fragrances to lure customers into their shops. The rush of fragrance in the wake of a passing stranger can send a flood of arousal coursing through you when the perfume or cologne is the same scent a lover wears.

Vatsyayana observes in the Kama Sutra that the smells men and women exude during sexual loving are both distinctive and changing. These scents foster sexual excitement, contributing to increasing arousal. Modern scientists call the chemicals responsible for such scents *pheromones*. It is believed that pheromones are effective whether or not we consciously detect them.

Sutrology

Olfactory comes from the Latin word "olfacere," which means to smell. The inside of the nose is filled with nerve endings directly attached to the olfactory nerve which conveys the nerve impulses carrying information about smells to the brain. **Pheromones** are chemical substances people and animals produce that stimulate responses in others. Though pheromones appear to activate the sense of smell, they are odorless.

Fragrances are an enjoyable, easy, and effective way to set the mood for romance. Incense and scented candles can fill the air with pleasant smells. Scented body oils, perfumes and colognes, and other substances also can be stimulating. Conversely, unpleasant body odors such as perspiration and bad breath can be real turnoffs. Many couples find the most erotic scent is that of their partner's clean, but otherwise unfragranced, body.

It is pleasurable and erotic to bathe together either in a tub of scented water or in a shower with wonderful smelling soaps. Here is an exercise to raise your awareness of how different scents can play a role in lovemaking.

Exercise: Sensual Bathing

1. Light candles and put several drops of aroma therapy oils in a tub filled with warm water. Put on some soothing music to play softly in the background.

2. Invite your beloved into the tub and soak and wash each other. If you are in a shower, take turns lathering each other slowly, sensuously, and playfully as if you were making love.

3. Dry each other off and, if you wish, you can put a towel down on the bed and take turns massaging a moisturizing lotion all over each other. Be sure to include the breasts and genitals.

Cultivate Mindfulness

The concept of mindfulness is important in many Eastern cultures. Someone who is mindful is fully aware of all that goes on around and within him or her. We often refer to this as being "present."

To experience the glory of sexual union as the Kama Sutra teaches, be present when you make love. When you touch, feel your fingers touching your partner's skin, and feel your partner's skin—its warmth or coolness, its smoothness or hairiness, its texture, its moistness or dryness. Be mindful of the breath, both your partner's and yours—feel it and hear it as it sets the rhythm of your bodies. Feel and listen to your bodies move against each other. Taste each other as though enjoying a gourmet meal. Call on all your senses to help you experience lovemaking to the fullest.

Out of Touch

Cigarette smoking interferes with both taste and smell. The smoke leaves residue on the delicate nerve endings, coating them and deadening their ability to detect tastes and odors.

Most importantly, make lovemaking an act of love. Focus on what feels good—to give and to receive—and give that your undivided attention. What you focus your attention on expands and intensifies. Just imagine the possibilities when your focus encompasses all of your senses!

The Least You Need to Know

- People are often not used to using all of their senses, either in everyday activities or in lovemaking.

- Human beings are sensual creatures. The need to touch and be touched is as fundamental as the need to eat and drink.

- Awakening all of your senses helps you to be "present" when making love. This intensifies the experience and your pleasure.

- Practice, practice. practice. It takes time to learn how to use all of your senses during lovemaking and you may feel awkward at first, but it will get easier and you can have fun along the way.

Part 2

What Does Love Have to Do With It?

Of all our human interactions, none are so important and so misunderstood as those we have with our partners. What attracts us to each other, what keeps us committed, and what drives us apart—these issues have confused and confounded us since the beginning of civilization. You'll learn what the Kama Sutra has to say about love, commitment, and sexual loving—and how you can use the Kama Sutra's teachings in your relationship with your partner.

These chapters go behind the scenes to show you the hows and whys of human relationships. You'll explore images and expectations—your own, and those of others (such as your partner). You'll learn how sex can—and can't—help a relationship. And you'll begin to understand why the intimate connections we seek through sexual loving so often evade us.

Chapter 5

Everybody Needs Somebody

In This Chapter

◆ Love and marriage

◆ Maslow's hierarchy of needs

◆ Love maps and how they influence your choice of partner

◆ The search for a soul mate

◆ The power of myth and ritual in relationships

In many traditional societies (often, but not always, Eastern), love and relationship or marriage have little connection, at least initially. Parents may arrange marriages when their sons and daughters are infants, or even before they are born. The marriage joins families for economic stability, social status, lineage (keeping a particular blood line going), or any number of other purposes. The boy and girl to become husband and wife when they grow up often know each other as children, and may even be close childhood friends.

Arranged marriages were fairly common in Vatsyayana's India, particularly among the wealthy and among royalty. Even when this was the case, the Kama Sutra encouraged a process of courtship. In this way, the couple could get to know each other and become attracted to one another. Parents were not above cultivating a close friendship between a young boy and a young girl, when an arranged marriage was not a feasible option (such as when the families were less wealthy). The two who were inseparable as children would naturally wish to continue their closeness as adults, according to the prevailing belief, leading them to marry.

This wasn't always the case, of course. Sometimes the two didn't get along as children, and had no attraction to each other as adults. In such situations, the Kama Sutra advised the two to consider finding other mates. Contemporary researchers who study social customs such as arranged marriages believe this is a classic example of "familiarity breeds contempt." A significant part of the attraction between two people is the exotic mystery of the unknown.

Arranged and encouraged marriages reflect an Eastern perspective on love that differs from the Western view. In the West, the order of things is marriage follows love. The reverse is typically the Eastern order—love follows marriage as the couple intimately bonds through the union of matrimony. This is natural and expected for couples raised in this cultural perspective, and they look forward to it in the same way that Western couples dream of falling in love.

We in the West have come to think that romantic love was an invention of the troubadours—the poets, musicians, and knights who romanticized courtly love in the eleventh to thirteenth centuries. But the Kama Sutra, drawing on teachings from perhaps as long ago as 1000 B.C.E., gave love and the art of loving a great deal of attention and study more than 900 years earlier.

Sex and Love: Basic Human Needs

The Western psychologist Abraham Maslow, known as the father of *humanistic psychology*, was the first to formally identify love and sex as basic human needs. In a groundbreaking departure from the probing psychoanalysis approach popularized by Sigmund Freud, Maslow identified a human *hierarchy of needs*.

Maslow's original model, developed in the late 1950s, contained five basic levels:

1. **Physiological**. Basic needs of life such as water, food, and oxygen, as well as sleep, sex, and shelter.

2. **Safety.** The need for protection (from disease, the elements, fear), structure, and order.

3. **Love and belonging.** The need for friends, lovers, children, family relationships, and a sense of community.

> **Sutrology**
>
> **Humanistic psychology** is an approach to understanding the human condition by looking within the individual, rather than to external factors, for answers and explanations. Maslow's **hierarchy of needs** is a theory in psychology that says human needs exist at different levels. A person must meet his or her needs at one level to move on to the next level.

4. **Esteem.** On what Maslow called the lower level of esteem needs is the need for self-esteem as it arises from status, recognition, attention, and appreciation. On the higher level is the need for self-respect as it arises from competence, achievement, independence, and confidence.

5. **Self-actualization.** This highest level in the hierarchy differs from the others in that it consists of values such as truth, goodness, realized potential. This level also includes what Maslow called "peak experiences of being."

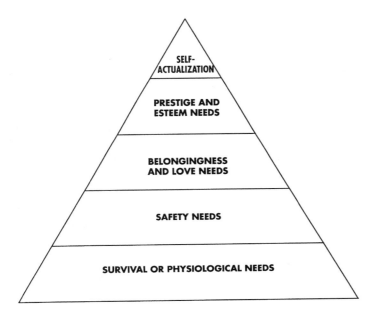

Maslow's hierarchy of needs.

According to Maslow, each time a person satisfies the needs at one level, he or she moves up to the next level. Because needs change and repeat, everyone moves back and forth among the levels. It is also possible to be meeting needs on different levels at the same time. Maslow's hierarchy has become widely accepted in contemporary psychotherapy.

The Drive to Have Sex

Is your desire for sex simply a hormonal response? Or is there more than the physical at play? Maslow identified sex as one of humankind's most basic needs, in line as a priority not far behind thirst, hunger, and shelter. He, like many psychologists who followed in his footsteps, believed that sex is a combination of physical and emotional functions.

Certainly sex can, and often does, exist as solely a function of biology, raging hormones, and plain old "horniness." Sex is, after all, the means by which we further our species. The urge to reproduce can exist somewhere between instinct and action—an insistent yearning we feel deep in our loins without always understanding why.

Kama Knowledge

Arranged marriages remain common in more than half of the world today, including modern India. Many families work through marriage brokers, who locate potential mates to meet the family's desires. In some situations, the bride and groom don't meet each other until their wedding day. In other cases, the prospective spouses spend some time together before the wedding, and may have the opportunity to choose from among several marriage candidates. Arranged marriages have a higher success rate than do marriages of choice worldwide, with many couples happy in their arranged pairings.

Just as there is an urge for the physical act of sex, most people experience a desire to merge body and soul with another. In Maslow's hierarchy, the act of sexual intimacy fosters love and belonging, esteem, and self-actualization. When it is an act of love or intimacy, sex draws people closer together. Sex that is emotionally and spiritually intimate helps create a bond of commitment, fostering both self-esteem and self-respect. Sex that lacks such intimacy can have the opposite effect, leaving partners feeling an emotional and spiritual void.

The need for sex, or to mate, is so strong that individuals sometimes forsake other needs. A small fish called a stickleback presents a particularly vivid example of this. Ordinarily, the male stickleback's coloring allows the fish, a favorite meal among sea birds, to blend into the shadows of the water. During mating season, however, the male stickleback's coloring becomes almost flamboyant. Though this makes the male more attractive to female sticklebacks, he loses his protective camouflage. His need to mate totally overrides his need to hide from predators.

Some people lose touch with their own hard-won truths about their boundaries when they fall in love (or lust) and put themselves at risk in order to have sex and love in their lives. Countless couples part ways because one partner strays to another attraction or infatuation. Some people are willing to risk their homes (shelter and safety), families (love and belonging), careers (security and belonging), respect within the community (belonging), and even their lives through unsafe sex practices (survival) just to have sex.

Even the Kama Sutra acknowledges that sometimes people have sex just for the sake of satisfying sexual urges, though it counsels that there is potential danger in such liaisons. Vatsyayana warns that while another man's wife may be irresistibly appealing, consummating a sexual union with her can incite her husband to a murderous rage. Such situations, Vatsyayana observes, seldom turn out good for anyone involved.

The Quest for Love

What does love have to do with it? Quite a lot, it seems, when it comes to sex, relationships, and partnerships. In the West we've come to the same conclusion the Kama Sutra presents—men and women need and want intimate relationships. And just as the Kama Sutra recognizes, these needs can differ vastly among individuals. The challenge is to find someone whose needs and wants match your own.

Western psychologist and sexologist John Money evolved the theory that even as young children we begin to develop a strong sense of what is attractive to us, what arouses us sexually, and what compels us to fall in love with one person rather than another. We store this information in our memories, constructing a subconscious guidance system Money termed "love maps."

> **Sutra Sayings**
>
> The man and woman who share in common the three aims of life (dharma, artha, and kama) are a good match. When a couple likes the same pleasures and has the same tastes, theirs will be a union of good fortune.

According to Money, between the ages of five and eight we form our earliest ideals of what we find attractive in others. These ideals incorporate the unique features of our caregivers and people we know who are compellingly appealing to us. We add to, refine, and alter our love maps throughout our lives, from the sexually intense times of adolescence to the more leisurely love relationships of maturity. We carry this love map with us like a well-worn picture of a fantasy lover. Mentally viewing the picture conjures images of all the erotic activities, settings, and conversations that we find arousing.

Every individual's love map is different and unique. When you meet someone who closely matches your dream lover, you feel an immediate attraction. At first, this person takes on the characteristics of your dream lover, and to your sense of perception, is your dream lover. You feel as though this person stepped from your love map into your life. This projection is not authentic, of course.

The real person that you meet, however closely he or she resembles the ideal you've been carrying with you for all these years, is a distinct individual with a love map of his or her own that you appear to match. Early in your relationship, it is the ideal representations you project onto each other that create an attraction. The longer you are together, the more clearly both of you will establish your independent identities.

If these identities truly match your respective love maps, your relationship will likely deepen and intensify. If it turns out that your dream lover isn't quite the dream (or lover) you expected, you will probably part ways.

We call this dance of discovery "falling in love." While some people land on their feet and find themselves in happy, enduring relationships, others crash into disastrous liaisons. Those who leap impetuously into their roles as dream lovers cut short the dance and suspend discovery. They may launch into "till death do us part" without really knowing the true other (and often not the true self, either). They don't see each other for who they truly are, as individuals with unique and specific needs and desires, until it's too late to end the relationship without significant hurt.

When Souls Connect

Love is an emotion that exists on many levels—and often simultaneously on several. There is physical love, the union of bodies drawn together by irresistible forces to satisfy physical and biological needs. There is emotional love, what we view as love of the heart (figuratively speaking). And there is soulful love, which is what we view as the joining of the very essence of our being, our souls.

Kama Knowledge

American psychologist John Gottman has developed a system based on more than 25 years of research that can predict, with 90 percent accuracy, whether a marriage will thrive or fail. From this research, Gottman has concluded that friendship is the foundation of a successful marriage. From friendship grows love, and from love grows romance and passion. Gottman designed a series of questionnaires and observed behaviors that evaluate how a couple communicates within their relationship. Key measures include how the partners treat each other when they argue. Those who can disagree and even become angry, yet remain respectful of each other, are more likely to stay together than those who become disdainful and derogatory toward each other.

There are more than a dozen dictionary definitions for love. The word comes from the Latin *libere*, which simply means "to please." Yet few other words, or concepts, are so complex and difficult to understand. We all seek love, usually in different forms at different times, yet we don't really know what love is until we find it. What love means to us also changes with time, maturity, and experience, further clouding our understanding.

Theologian and therapist Thomas Moore examines the needs and workings of the soul in his books *Care of the Soul* and *Soul Mates: Honoring the Mysteries of Love and Relationship* (see Appendix B). A former monk turned psychologist, Moore asserts that much of the unrest and discomfort people feel about their relationships arises from ignoring their spiritual, or soul, needs.

It's important to recognize and remember that religion and spirituality are not necessarily the same. Religion is a doctrine of belief or principles that often incorporates a structure of worship. The word comes from the Latin *religare*, which means "to constrain or hold back." Spirituality, on the other hand, appreciates and values the existence of a *sentient* self. *Spirit* comes from the Latin *spirare*, which means "to breathe." Breathing, as we discussed in Chapter 3, is the essence of life. In the Eastern view, the breath sustains both the body and the soul, uniting the two.

Human beings continually struggle to understand spirit and accept the soul as a dimension of existence. We see this in the richness of myth (the stories we tell to explain life's mysteries) and ritual (the ceremonies we engage in to give life meaning) that marks the human experience.

> **Sutrology**
>
> **Sentient** defines a state of presence based on feelings and awareness rather than on thoughts and intellect. It comes from the Latin *sentire*, which means "to feel."

The Myth of Love

Before we go any further, let us make it clear that calling love a myth is not denying the reality of its existence. To the contrary, to look at the myth of love is to explore our sense and understanding of how the soul functions. A myth is not an untruth, but simply a symbolic representation of an intangible concept.

Love and death are the two most extensive topics in myth. They are the two most powerful, yet most mysterious, experiences of human existence. Much of every culture's literature and art attempts to explain these mysteries. In the book *The Power of Myth* (see Appendix B), which Joseph Campbell co-authored with journalist Bill Moyers, Campbell identifies marriage (long-term relationship) as a "mythological plane of existence." Marriage, Campbell says, is a spiritual experience of the reunion myth. In the beginning of time, all souls existed as one. In birth they become separate. And in marriage, two souls are reunited.

Each of us looks forward to living the myths that define our perceptions and belief systems. The Kama Sutra is very rich in myth, and incorporates it into nearly every aspect of its lessons. Man and woman come together in sexual loving because that is the intent of their existence. Myth tells this story, and life fulfills it.

> ### Kama Knowledge
>
> In the mythology of India, Kama is the god of erotic love. His Roman and Greek counterparts are Cupid and Eros, respectively. In most depictions, Kama appears as a handsome young man surrounded by beautiful young women. He carries a sugar cane bow from which he shoots arrows of flowers. The arrows cause those who are struck by them to feel an intense and irresistible attraction to one another. Egged on by the other gods, Kama fired a love arrow at the god of gods, Shiva. The shot disturbed Shiva's meditation, outraging him. Shiva returned fire with a stream of flame from his third eye, incinerating Kama's body. Because he was a god, however, Kama lived on in spirit and continues his matchmaker ways.

The Power of Ritual

Much of life is ritual. Ritual gives a sense of consistency, of security, of assurance that this has happened before and it will happen again. Ritual also formalizes transformations, whether fleeting or lasting. Putting on a uniform, for example, whether to play baseball or go to war, allows us to transform from one perception of ourselves to another. We can then act in the manner expected of us.

Many rituals are relatively ordinary, serving to get us through our daily lives. Brushing your teeth, taking a shower, and eating breakfast, for example, may comprise the ritual of greeting the new day and getting ready for work or school. Some people always take the same route, stop at the same coffee shop, or park in the same space.

Other rituals have greater significance and may involve elaborate ceremony. A bar mitzvah ushers a boy into manhood in the tradition of his Jewish faith. New graduates don caps and gowns to receive formal and public recognition of their educational accomplishments. And, throughout history to the present time, couples pledge their commitment to each other, binding them together in the eyes of family, the community, and the legal system.

However simple or complex, ritual defines life. Without it, our existence would be chaotic and meaningless. Ritual joins and supports individuals with each other, with their families, with their communities, and with their cultural or religious belief systems. Ritual also helps us define our places in the various dimensions of our lives.

Ritual was quite formalized and ceremonial in the time of Vatsyayana. The ways in which a man and a woman acted toward each other in public were ritualized, with certain behaviors establishing them as potential spouses and others defining them as in defiance of custom. Ritual and ceremony guided much of the advice the Kama Sutra offered, especially for the elements of sexual loving. From setting the mood in the love chamber to luxuriating in the afterglow of sexual union, Vatsyayana presents prescriptions to assure a pleasurable experience for both partners. Ritual also helps to focus awareness, establishing a setting that supports a deep intimacy.

Finding Your Soul Mate

In the past 20 years or so, relationships have taken on a larger context in Western cultures, becoming a place to practice the spiritual values of acceptance, compassion, understanding, and generosity. By the 1980s, there was a name for the personification of this elusive dimension—*soul mate*. Rather than seeking just partners or lovers, men and women alike wanted to find someone they recognized from a deep place inside themselves as a kindred spirit. Someone who touched them in a deeply familiar way, someone they felt they knew deep down as though they had been together before or knew something that the other knew as well; they understood each other's hopes and dreams.

In his book *Soul Mates: Honoring the Mysteries of Love and Relationship*, Moore defines a soul mate as "someone to whom we feel profoundly connected, as though the communicating and communing that take place between us were not the product of intentional efforts, but rather a divine grace." Further, Moore writes, "this kind of relationship is so important to the soul that many have said there is nothing more precious in life."

Sutrology

A **soul mate** is another person to whom you feel deeply connected at a spiritual level. You feel as though you belong together and were meant to be with each other.

Sutra Sayings

The man and the woman should laugh together, and enjoy the same pleasures. They should be of like mind, and be well-matched to join their bodies in sexual union.

The Search for a Soul Mate

Vatsyayana counsels readers to follow their hearts whenever this is practical, but to make wise decisions that take into account other factors important to marriage and other relationships. While in ancient India these factors often had more to do with whether one had a full and healthy set of teeth or came from a wealthy family, the concept remains valid even today.

Vatsyayana, like contemporary counselors, advises men and women to seek partnership with those who share common interests. The man who enjoys singing will attract a woman who loves the beauty of song. The woman who writes in verse will attract the man who reads poetry. Those who try to act against their nature, Vatsyayana warns, are destined to find partnerships that soon disintegrate. Liaisons born of purely physical attraction are likewise doomed.

Letting the soul do the choosing doesn't always produce the desired result, either. Thomas Moore believed that, left to itself, the soul does not necessarily make wise choices when searching for a mate. It seeks to meet its need for connectedness and intimacy, and on its own can find these qualities in various souls without caring, if you will, whether the match also meets the needs of the mind or the body. It is the mind (or what some might view as the intellect), Moore says, that structures and balances the search.

The Kama Sutra spends a great deal of time addressing the roles of spirit and intellect in choosing partners. In fact, the Kama Sutra recognizes and supports a triad of existence—body, mind, and soul. First, writes Vatsyayana, bodies must attract each other, and match in their union. Second, lovers must give thought and attention to how well they match socially and within their communities. Third, they should be of like spirit and temperament—similar in emotion and belief. When these three dimensions exist, the body, mind, and soul are equally satisfied.

Dr. Josie Suggests

Someone once said to me, "I don't believe in soul mates. I think soul mates are souls that choose to mate." How your soul does this involves a blend of attraction and practicality. Sometimes the exuberance of falling in love overshadows more grounded considerations, such as whether you both want to have a child. Try to discover early in your relationship whether you and your soul mate are aligned about what you both want in a committed relationship.

The Mystery of Love

There is a great mystery at work when it comes to how souls find each other. Out of all the possibilities, you and an attractive stranger end up sitting next to each other at a concert or reaching for the same item at the bookstore. There's a spark, a flash of familiarity, a feeling of comfort or even a little exciting discomfort. Your body tingles with aliveness, and your attention is riveted. You feel *this* could be the one. When such magic is in the air, lovers feel the synchronicity of their meeting is fate.

When we fall in love we jump into the unknown with a familiar stranger who has touched the depths of our souls and awakened a sense of recognition. This feeling of fated connection we call falling in love makes us want to stay with this person forever. We feel and proclaim to each other, our friends, families, and communities that our two souls have found in each other a mate and a home. This is what we long to have in our lives.

When You Are Alone

Not everyone is part of a couple, of course. Some couples are parted by circumstances beyond their control, such as death. Others go their separate ways by choice, deciding to end their relationships. And some are somewhere in the middle, with one person wanting to stay and the other wanting to leave.

Many people come to enjoy being alone, though most people need a period of adjustment after a relationship ends. For some, the solitude presents a welcome opportunity for introspection and soul-searching. The "down time" lets them recharge and get to know themselves. Other people have a terrible time being alone. They fill their time with busy-ness to avoid pain and loneliness. When alone, they find themselves to be bad company. Their minds fill with self-destructive thoughts and negative images that play like continuous-loop cassette tapes.

Get Comfortable with Yourself

Each of us needs to learn to be alone. Whether happily married with wonderful children and a great career, or single working with a network of freelancers from a much-loved home base, we need to become good company for ourselves. One of the best ways to get acquainted with your inner self is to meditate—or engage in a meditational activity such as playing a musical instrument, writing, painting, practicing yoga, or taking part in other activities in which self-observation is central to the practice. Meditation lets you become aware of the repetitive stories and emotions that play continuously just beneath the surface of your consciousness. To explore the concept of meditation and to learn how to start your own meditation practice, consult *The Complete Idiot's Guide to Meditation* (Alpha Books, 1999).

Often, these voices chide that you are unworthy, unlovable, lazy, fearful—all of what you lack. If you pay attention, you'll be shocked to notice how much time your mind spends constructing such a negative self-image. You'll also be surprised to notice that your mind does something else. It spends a lot of time compensating for all that negativity. Your mind counters the negative talk with thoughts about how much better you are than other people and how absolutely great it's going to be when you get everything you want.

Though this sounds like a good balance, it really leaves you empty, alone, and without a sense of your own intrinsic goodness. The Buddhists call this cycle of building ourselves up in order to avoid the critical inner banter the Wheel of Samsara or the Wheel of Illusion. Until we can cultivate a relationship with our essential self—the part of us that exists outside of the building up and tearing down of our ego identity—as long as we keep running, controlling, filling ourselves with junk that doesn't satisfy, we will be bad company for ourselves. And when you're not good company for yourself, it's hard to be good company for someone else.

Here's an exercise in meditation that will help you develop a sense of comfort and acceptance with yourself. Choose a time and place where you can be alone without interruptions or distractions. Then, meditate for 20 minutes each day.

> **CAUTION**
>
> **Out of Touch**
>
> People who are new to meditation sometimes wonder, "What's the point? Nothing's happening." That *is* the point. Simply sitting, relaxing the body, paying attention to the breath, and noticing how thoughts just keep coming. Perhaps every so often there is a moment of stillness, of peace, of simple sweetness and space. This is the point.

Exercise: Get to Know Yourself Through Meditation

1. Sit up straight with your back straight, either on a cushion on the floor or in a chair with your feet flat on the floor.

2. Relax your body. With your eyes open focus on a spot six feet in front of you. Focus also on your breath, noticing and relaxing as you exhale.

3. If thoughts, feelings, and uncomfortable sensations arise, simply notice them without judgment and bring your attention to the breath again. In this way you can begin to observe your self and the stories that your mind tells again and again.

4. You may also experience a moment of sweet spaciousness where there are no thoughts or anything else to distract you from the pure experience of being that is you in relationship to your aloneness.

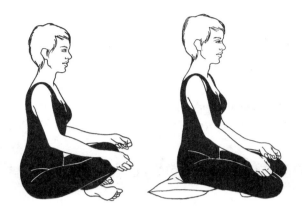

A pillow or a rolled towel placed at the base of your spine can help give you support when seated for meditation.

When Love Eludes You

The same mystery that makes the moment of meeting someone who is about to become very special in your life so magical and monumental plays a different hand when the intimate relationship you hunger for continues to elude you. At the times when you're anxiously seeking love, it often seems that no matter how hard you try, the magic passes you by.

Just as you can't will yourself to have an orgasm, you can't will yourself to fall in love. (Sorry!) The path most likely to lead you to your soul mate really requires only one thing of you—be yourself. Learn to like who you are and who you are becoming. Do the things you like to do, go to the places you like to be. Do the things that you've been putting off doing until you meet that special someone. Go ahead and have that adventure now. When you're having a good time in life, you become irresistible to yourself and to others.

Learning to Love Yourself

It's important to acknowledge your feelings about a relationship that ends. There is almost always a sense of sadness, no matter how bad things had become before the end, and often a feeling of betrayal. Healing from the loss of a beloved takes time and there are stages that you go through. The anger, grief, and denial eventually give way and your heart begins to soften and even open to receive love again.

Try this exercise: Look in the mirror and have a little chat with yourself. Say all the things to yourself you'd like to hear from someone who loved you (use your own words), such as the following:

- "Hi there, precious. I love you."

- "You look particularly beautiful/handsome tonight."

- "You sure are a dear and wonderful person."

You may have heard that there's something a little nutty about talking to yourself. Actually, self-talk is a good way to soothe and nurture yourself.

Touching the Dream Lover in You (or Your Partner)

Each of us has an image of what our dream lover would be like. This image comes from a variety of sources such as childhood memories, media influences, and dating experiences (your love map). But most people end up in relationships that aren't quite their dreams come true.

In reality, of course, few people measure up to an ideal. Human beings are imperfect, and human nature sometimes runs counter to the best decisions. Sometimes the reality is at best a distant match with the ideal. When this happens, couples often struggle to balance their expectations with their circumstances.

Some couples work through their struggles to believe they've come as close to the ideal as is humanly possible. Other partners may feel they've found their soul mates despite deviations from the ideal. The key is to understand your ideals, both for your lover and for yourself, and determine how they mesh with your reality. Sometimes the two are much closer than you realize.

Touching your dream lover is a very powerful experience. It unites the perceptions of your mind with the desires of your soul. When your bodies unite in sexual loving, they fuse a bond unlike anything you've experienced before. This is the quest of the Kama Sutra, and has been the quest of couples from the beginning of time.

The Least You Need to Know

- Myth and ritual are important aspects of everyone's lives.

- Finding your soul mate is a mysterious process that you cannot force or control.

- To truly love someone else, you must first accept and love yourself.

- We all have a deep and driving need to feel connected to a special someone with whom we can share all dimensions of our lives.

Chapter 6

The "C" Word (Commitment)

In This Chapter

- ◆ The importance of commitment in our relationships
- ◆ How committed are you? A self-exploration
- ◆ How to keep your sense of you strong in a committed relationship
- ◆ One or many? Monogamy and polygamy

Most people yearn for their lives to include close, loving relationships. Everywhere we look, we see that people who are single want to be part of a couple and those who have coupled want better relationships. But as much as we long for committed relationships, we fear them. We want what a committed relationship promises: closeness, good sex, companionship, family, a helpmate, someone who will be a partner along life's winding path.

But we get the other side of relationships as well. There is nothing like a committed relationship that evokes fears that we could be abandoned, rejected, humiliated, or engulfed. Learning to work with our ambivalence in relationships makes us grow up and become more tender and human. Committed partnership also holds the possibility of our healing and maturing into loving adult partners. A caring, loving partner can offer us the chance to use relationship issues as a steppingstone to become more aware of who we are.

Why Commitment Matters

Commitment is important in relationships because it creates the container within which couples can safely open themselves to one another. It is natural to want not to be ridiculed, criticized, or rejected for the important things we reveal to our partner. Committed relationships offer partners security and continuity. They also provide us with a witness, someone who sees us when we are at our best and worst. Knowing we are seen contributes to feeling vulnerable.

Intimacy, as we discussed in an earlier chapter, depends on this vulnerability, on our being seen and revealing ourselves to another. In order to do this we need to know it is safe. This safety creates the container for sharing yourself. The word *commitment* originates from Latin words that mean "to bring together" and "to send forth." In their book *The Conscious Heart* (see Appendix B), psychologists Gay and Kathlyn Hendricks define commitment as the idea of "pledging and binding yourself to a chosen course of action."

Commitment as Process

When you make a commitment to your partner, the very act of committing begins a process. The commitment acts as a bond between both you and yourself and you and your partner. As you move forward, the commitment will challenge you by flushing to the surface any ways that you are not aligned with your commitment. This can be disconcerting. However, if you are honest with yourself and your partner, you can stay on course with one another. Perhaps you will find that your commitments need to be adjusted. Remember, things change and so do relationship commitments. This way of making commitments is called process-oriented commitment and is different than the "till death do us part" approach.

Many people perceive commitment as static. It's black and white, either/or, carved in stone. Such an approach dooms commitment to certain failure in the context of a relationship. *Life* is dynamic, filled with ambiguity and change. Committed relationships can be no different. Often in the desire to create certainty and solidity, we impose expectations and structure on our relationships. When you think of commitment, like life, as fluid and dynamic, a relationship not only accommodates but desires change. Think of it as the difference between a string and a rubber band—both can hold two ends together, but one (the rubber band) anticipates and allows movement, while the other (the string) prevents movement.

> **Sutra Sayings**
>
> A husband and a wife are bound to each other. They should share the same thoughts and behaviors. They should not exaggerate their disagreements, but rather speak of concerns when they are alone.

In a relationship, you make a genuine commitment when you bring yourself to a chosen course of action with your body and soul united. The resulting bond unifies the two of you as you step together into the territory of supporting the relationship and being present for all the unknowable experiences that being together in life will bring.

Committing to Grow Together

When asked what contributes to their enduring relationships, couples who have been married for decades often cite a cycle of challenge, growth, change, and renewal. Rather than feeling they've been together in the same relationship for all those years, they instead have learned to enjoy the wonder of rediscovering themselves and each other. It's as though their relationships were a series of several relationships, each reborn from the ashes of the last.

It is easy to commit to what you know and find familiar. You get together and everything moves along according to plan. Good jobs, nice home, healthy children, friends, early retirement, travel—the hallmarks of a long, healthy life. Though this is comfortable, there's not much to challenge the commitment you made in the beginning of your relationship. But real life doesn't often run according to plan—not *your* plan, anyway. As the saying goes, "Life is what happens when you have other plans." More often than not, as your relationship progresses, you'll find yourself dealing with issues and situations you didn't know about when the relationship started.

Your capacity to use the unknown to confront yourself and discover what is really going on behind the scenes helps you to be unconditionally present with your self and to contact what the Buddhists call your ground of being and what modern psychology refers to as the essential self. This is the soft, open, and tender place that meditators touch into and cultivate. We touch into our ground of being when we stop spinning our mind's stories for a moment and instead simply experience the sweet silence of our essence.

When you can offer real compassion to yourself and touch into your essence, you can hold a space for yourself and your beloved as you move through the unknown together. Your journey might take you to the discovery that you have little to say to one another once the kids are grown and gone, causing you to question whether to stay together. Or to the admission of an affair and the tumult of old, unexpressed feelings that are still unresolved. Whatever challenges confront your relationship can be a source of growth that leads to real commitment—the pledge to be honest and loving with one another no matter what the outcome.

What's in a Name? My Significant Other, My Life Partner, My Spouse ...

Does it matter what you call the one to whom you commit yourself? In some respects, no—what matters is not so much the label but the meaning. As relationships have gone through the upheaval and redefinition of recent years, many people have looked for ways to "call it like it is." Finding the designation of husband, wife, or spouse too restrictive or not appropriate for the relationship, we've seen terms such as "significant other" and "life partner" infiltrate our conversations.

The most formal form of commitment in nearly every culture remains marriage. Though the definition and institution of marriage differs among cultures, there are a number of constants. Whether the ceremony takes place in the presence of the requisite number of witnesses or before an audience of several hundred friends and relatives, the couple vows publicly and to each other that they will honor and cherish the bond that unites them. To say, "This is my husband/wife/ spouse," establishes boundaries of both ownership ("He/she belongs to me") and obligation.

In nearly every culture, Eastern and Western alike, a married couple has social, civic, and legal status greater than that of an unmarried couple. Marriage legitimizes children born of the union, grants property and inheritance rights, and defines responsibilities and duties. Though many Western cultures have moved significantly away from rigidity in their views of what marriage means, tradition remains compelling.

Kama Knowledge

The word *spouse*, which had gained popularity in modern times as a gender-neutral noun for a married person, has its origins in an ancient Greek word that meant "to pour a drink for the gods." The Latin variation, *spondere*, means "to betroth," or commit to marriage. The contract between a man and a woman who agreed to marry was called a *sonsalia*, though in keeping with the masculine and feminine word forms of the Latin language, the two partners were designated by gender. The man was the sponsus and the woman was the sponsa. By the thirteenth century, however, people were using *spouse* to designate a married person, either man or woman.

In Vatsyayana's India, what you called your partner identified the nature of your relationship. A married man was a husband. A married woman was a wife. In marriages where the husband had several wives, the elder or chief wife, generally the first woman he married, had more status than the other wives. A man, married or not, could also have an extended relationship with a courtesan, and might even live with her for periods of time as though she were his wife. Courtesans had status different from that of either wives or single women in ancient India. While prostitutes had brief consorts with men who were strangers, a courtesan had an ongoing relationship with a man she met and liked, even though he paid for her favors with money and gifts.

A Self-Quiz: What's Your Commitment Quotient?

Many couples drift into long-term relationships without giving much thought to commitment. As a result, commitment may have different meanings for each partner. This self-exploration can shed some light on how you define commitment. Circle the response that best describes how you feel or act.

1. I keep information from my partner to avoid rocking the boat.

    a. Often   b. Sometimes   c. Never

2. I keep my options open to leave if things get bad.

    a. Always   b. Sometimes   c. Never

3. I have secrets that I don't share with my partner.

    a. Many   b. Some   c. None

4. I flirt with other men or women when I'm out alone even though I know it bothers my partner.

    a. Always   b. Sometimes   c. Never

5. I flirt with other men or women when I'm with my partner even though I know it bothers my partner.

    a. Always   b. Sometimes   c. Never

6. I tell my partner where I'm going, who I'll be with, and when I expect to be back.

    a. Seldom   b. Sometimes   c. Usually

7. I call when my plans change or if I'm going to be late.

    a. Seldom   b. Sometimes   c. Usually

8. I am sexually faithful to my partner.

    a. Never   b. Sometimes   c. Always

9. I've introduced my partner to members of my family, my friends, and other people who are important to me.

    a. No   b. Only by chance   c. Yes

10. I've kept my relationship with my partner a secret from friends and other people who are important to me.

   a. Yes   b. Some people know   c. No, everyone knows

11. I secretly fantasize about leaving my relationship.

   a. Often   b. Sometimes   c. Never

12. I have a secret romantic friendship/online relationship.

   a. Yes   b. Not right now   c. No

13. I complain to my friends about my mate but don't tell my mate what is bothering me.

   a. Often   b. Sometimes   c. Never

14. I run up bills that I keep secret from my partner.

   a. Often   b. Sometimes   c. Never

15. I have a lot of thoughts about my life, our relationship, work, and sex that I don't share with my partner for fear of upsetting her/him/the relationship.

   a. Often   b. Sometimes   c. Never

Add the number of As, Bs, and Cs that you circled. If you circled eight or more As, commitment appears to be an issue for you. If you marked eight or more Bs, you might be uncertain about your relationship—you seem to be sitting on the fence. If you circled eight or more Cs, odds are good that your relationship has a strong foundation based on trust and truth.

Kama Knowledge

It looks like four, not seven as in the "seven-year itch" popularized by Hollywood, is the magic number when it comes to challenging years in a marriage or long-term relationship. Researchers have discovered somewhat of a contemporary correlation to the pattern of four-year monogamy some scientists believe existed in early human couples. Statistics collected in the United States in recent years suggest that most relationships that break down do so in the fourth year, though it might be several years later when the couple actually separates.

Commitment Anxiety

The thought of commitment sometimes frightens people who perceive it as being "locked in" to a relationship with someone else. This fear can come from the perception that being in a committed relationship precludes change. Nothing could be further from the truth.

In fact, the only way a committed relationship can survive and thrive is when each partner supports and encourages the other's growth and development so the relationship itself can evolve. Change, as the saying goes, is the only certainty. Relationships that ignore or deny change stagnate, and can indeed feel more like traps than treasures.

Sometimes people enter into a relationship and are then afraid to deepen their commitment because they like things the way they are. They don't want things to change. They fear that if things change they will be left or asked to do more than they want to in the relationship. Partners do sometimes change in ways that draw them apart. There's no denying this. But avoiding change will almost certainly do the same.

Commitment doesn't have to be of the "forever and always" variety, especially early in your relationship. Commitment, like the relationship itself, can deepen and grow with time and nurturing. Here is a list of commitments some of Dr. Josie's clients have made to each other:

◆ I commit to stop blaming, judging, and criticizing you.

◆ I accept our relationship is a teacher about myself, and I commit to learning how to be loved and loving in all my interactions with you.

◆ I commit to clearing up anything that keeps me from being present and loving with you and myself.

◆ I commit to loving intimacy and to letting go of being right.

◆ I commit to creating a balance of closeness and individual time and to learn about my needs for both.

◆ I commit to telling the truth about what is bothering me, including my feelings, fantasies, and actions.

◆ I commit to taking full responsibility for myself, my life, my happiness, and my defensiveness, and to not blaming you for the problems in my and our life.

> **CAUTION**
>
> **Out of Touch**
>
> If you have, or are, a partner who attempts to shut down the other partner's connections with friends and activities outside the relationship, take heed. This is not commitment. Instead, it could be a warning sign that your relationship is headed for serious trouble. Such behavior indicates an inappropriate need for control that is often the basis of abusive relationships.

- I commit to choosing to be happy especially when I feel that I have every right to be defensive and righteous.

- I commit to learning to love myself.

- I commit to making quality time for us to be together without structured activities.

- I commit to making time for extended lovemaking.

- I commit to cooking you dinner once a week.

Keeping the "U" in "Us"

Some people fear commitment because they fear they will lose their individual identities. Rather than inspiring a sense of closeness and bonding, "the two become as one" stimulates an urge to flee. One partner may worry about being swallowed up in the other partner's life. The best relationships, however, are almost a triad—there's you, there's your partner, and there's the relationship as an entity of its own. Such a triad can exist only when you and your partner maintain a strong sense of who you are as individuals. Then you can bring your individuality to your partnership.

> **Sutra Sayings**
>
> A relationship that develops naturally and without interference deepens over time. From compatibility comes friendship, and from friendship grows passion. Love becomes everlasting.

It is important, to you and to your relationship, to maintain a strong sense of who you are and what your place is in the world. While togetherness fosters closeness and intimacy, it can also smother and stifle. Share interests with your partner—hobbies, activities, music—but nurture your own interests, too. If you've always loved jazz but your partner prefers country, treat yourself to a jazz concert now and again. Go alone, or with other friends who share your enthusiasm.

Sometimes a couple's circle of friends changes after they become a pair. This is fine if you are both satisfied with your friendships. But it's important for each partner to establish and maintain independent friendships, too. Your friends help give your life a more complete sense of fulfillment. Often, spending time with your separate friends brings you back to your relationship recharged and relaxed. However strong and happy it is, a marriage or other long-term relationship requires time and effort to keep it running smoothly. Taking a break now and again gives you a pleasant respite.

The Many Faces of Relationships

We tend to think of commitment and relationships in a rather stereotypical model of a man and a woman pairing (and often married). This is similar to viewing all trees as green. Certainly the larger proportion of trees in the world has green leaves. But there are various species that have leaves of different colors—silver, burgundy, yellow. Even those that do have green leaves sport a spectrum of shades. Some even change colors with the seasons. You get the picture.

Relationships and commitments come in many forms, too. A couple can be man-woman, man-man, or woman-woman. Some relationships have more than two partners. There might be one man with several women, one woman with several men, or several men and women. We generally refer to these relationships as *monogamous* or *polygamous*.

Sutrology

Monogamous is the condition of having one mate. **Polygamous** is the condition of having more than one mate. Though these terms have legal implications (polygamy, or being married to more than one person at a time, is against the law in the United States and many other countries), we tend to use them to more loosely refer to partners without regard for marital status.

Relationships and commitment are important to all couples. Here, man to man.

(Hrana Janto)

Monogamy: One on One Through the Ages

Monogamy has been the formal relationship structure endorsed by most Western societies and religions for centuries. Until the seventeenth century, monogamy meant marriage to only one person in a lifetime. Since that time, it has come to mean marriage to one person at a time. Until the early 1900s, the only way a spouse could remarry was if the other spouse died. Divorce was not permitted, either by law or under most religious doctrines.

By the later half of the 1900s, more relaxed attitudes and laws regarding divorce and relationships and longer life spans gave people the freedom to leave unsatisfactory partnerings. A couple might partner for a time, then part ways and each pair with someone else. *Anthropologists* dubbed this pattern *serial monogamy*. By the year 2000, 50 percent of first marriages and 80 percent of second marriages ended in divorce.

> **Sutrology**
>
> An **anthropologist** is a scientist who studies the origin, nature, relationships, societies, and living environment of human beings. Serial monogamy describes a pattern of relationship in which the partners commit, one person at a time, to a number of other partners throughout their lifetimes.

The Fidelity Factor

A common misperception is that, among humans, monogamy and fidelity are the same. This isn't necessarily the case. The *Oxford English Dictionary* defines monogamy as "the condition, rule, or custom of being married to only one person at a time." Fidelity, on the other hand, is the state of being faithful to each other. While the partners in a monogamous relationship (marriage) are ideally faithful to each other as well, sexual relationships outside marriage are common throughout the world (and even acceptable in some cultures). Partners who are monogamous are not necessarily faithful to one another, though we tend to use the terms interchangeably.

In zoology, monogamy has a broader definition. It generally refers to an exclusive mating relationship between one male animal and one female animal. However, it doesn't appear that many species in the animal world are faithful, either. Scientists once speculated that some species of whales and birds formed lifelong relationships. Further study revealed that while some animals do remain in partnership with each other for life, the partners occasionally wander off for sex with others.

Is Monogamy a Natural Human State?

There is some discussion about whether monogamy in humans is a natural state or one imposed by social structures. The benefits of monogamy for animal species are unclear.

The role of sex, after all, is to perpetuate the species through reproduction. Monogamy appears to benefit the female in fulfilling this mission in much the same way scientists believe it benefited early human females. Males, however, seem to best carry out their end of the mission by spreading their seed to impregnate as many females as possible.

Some researchers believe that monogamy evolved in early human couplings as a response to the need to protect the female through the first four years of a child's life. During this time, breastfeeding was the child's primary sustenance, making the child exclusively dependent on its mother. It became the responsibility of the male—responding to the drive to procreate and protect his offspring—to meet the mother's needs for water, food, shelter, and safety. This helped ensure the child's survival and thus the perpetuation of his genes.

During the child's dependency years, some scientists theorize, the man devoted all of his attention to his mate. Once the child was no longer breastfeeding, the woman was free to resume her participation in hunting, gathering, and other activities. This freed the man and the woman to seek other mates with whom they would then repeat the process.

> **Sutra Sayings**
>
> The couple who learns the 64 arts, and learns them well, will always satisfy each other in sexual union. They may be together each night, yet every night feel as though they are with another lover.

Polygamy: Extending the Commitment

Though polygamy technically identifies a marriage of multiple spouses, we tend to use the term to more loosely refer to less formal relationships. The terminology, like the relationship, gets a little complicated. Polyandry defines one woman and multiple men. Polygyny defines one man with multiple women. The majority of polygamous relationships are polygynous. Most of the information available about polygamous arrangements is about the one man and multiple wife variety.

There certainly have been cultures through history that have allowed, encouraged, and even sanctioned polygamy. The harems and polygamous marriages of ancient India, though primarily the realm of the wealthy and the royal, are a good example of this. Fewer children lived to their first birthdays than died in infancy, so having more children increased a man's chance of producing offspring who would grow to adulthood. Even in such multiple pairings, however, there are standards of behavior that include commitment.

Group Marriages and Communes

The Western approach to polygamy has often been based in religious doctrines (early, though not contemporary, Mormons) and alternative social structures such as communes. While we tend to think of the sexual revolution of the 1960s when we think about communes, these group-marriage–based communities have been part of the American social landscape for over 100 years.

One of the best-known of these was the Oneida community, founded by John Humphrey Noyes as an attempt to create a Christian utopia. The group settled in Oneida, New York, and lasted until 1881. There were at one time over 500 women, men, and children living and working together. Each adult had her or his own room in one large building. Everyone shared everything else, including clothes, sex partners, and children.

Noyes viewed romantic love as selfish, and in the commune's early years he banned reproduction. While all adults were encouraged to have sex with each other, men were not permitted to ejaculate as a means of birth control. Even though Noyes discouraged people from falling in love, many did and formed secret pair bonds with one another. A climate of friction and hard feelings grew among the community. The commune came to an end after Noyes was accused of raping several pubescent girls and fled.

Eighty years later the communal utopian vision resurfaced. The climate of openness and experimentation of the late 1960s and early 1970s birthed many forms of group living, including group and nonexclusive marriages. Many people experimented with some form of multiple partners. Whether it was having more than one lover at a time, being married and openly having additional lovers, or forming a group marriage that involved several couples or singles, the experimental interest of the time radically affected relationships.

Margaret Mead once said, "No matter how many communes anybody invents, the family always creeps back." The experimentation of the '60s and '70s gave way to a reconsideration of relationship. Most of us want the stability, security, and continuity that a committed partnership affords. Most people also prefer the focused intimacy and trust that comes only as you work through the challenges and difficult times in a relationship. All this takes time and energy, and most people don't have enough of either to work at several relationships at the same time.

> **Sutra Sayings**
>
> The man who marries many women should treat them all fairly. Particularly, he should not speak badly of one to another, or allow his wives to do the same. He should have a secret with each, and tell her not to share it with the others. And he should have sexual union with each equally though he may become fatigued.

Is Polygamy "Right" for Some People?

Still, there are those who are hard-wired to want more than one lover. There are those who feel strongly that being with one person is a limitation of their capacity and desire to love, and that monogamy is a denial of some essential part of themselves. And there are those who find themselves thrown by circumstances into situations where they are happy with their mate and also loving another person. The varieties of loving forms are not new.

The Kama Sutra says a lot about how to deal appropriately with multiple liaisons. This tells us that people have been trying to balance the desire for both variety and security for centuries. Vatsyayana urges men to think twice about taking more than one wife. It is very difficult to satisfy many wives equally, he observes, which can create tension and dissension among the wives. The Kama Sutra nonetheless offers a number of sexual positions for multiple unions. Polygamy was fairly common in ancient India as well as many other cultures of the time.

It's Not Always Opposites that Attract

Most experts believe that about five percent of American men and a smaller percentage of American women are sexually attracted to same-gender partners. Many form long-term, committed relationships that, gender aside, are no different from heterosexual partnerships (though legal marriage between same-sex partners is not permitted in the United States). Homosexual men and women fall in love, form bonds, and mate. They also break up and continue to look for love again. Gay men and women experience the same sensations, desires, romance, and love that heterosexual people report. We all struggle with the same challenges of our romantic longings regardless of sexual orientation.

Dr. Josie Suggests

Many people experiment with same-sex relations at some point in their lives, usually when they're younger. The majority go on to form relationships with opposite-sex partners.

Homosexuality has existed throughout history. In ancient India, as in most ancient cultures, sexual loving between partners of the same gender was both common and accepted. The Kama Sutra considered those who found the same gender more attractive than the opposite gender to be of the "third sex." In some circumstances, same-sex lovemaking was a safe way to accommodate sexual needs when a partner was away for an extended time. Women in harems often had sexual relationships with each other as well, both as a way to teach the ways of love that the king or other royal husband enjoyed and to meet their own needs while the husband was unavailable.

We tend to think of homosexual behavior as a uniquely human occurrence. However, it is quite common in nature, among both males and females. In fact, homosexual behavior is so common in other species and occurs in so many circumstances that human homosexuality appears rare by comparison.

In the company of women.

(Hrana Janto)

The Least You Need to Know

♦ Humans need and desire committed relationships to provide comfort, security, and love.

♦ Commitment doesn't have to mean forever, though it does require intimacy.

♦ People grow and change, and so do their relationships.

♦ The challenges and joys of relationships can teach us a lot about ourselves.

Great Expectations

In This Chapter

◆ How we develop our sense of our bodies

◆ How do you feel about your body? A self-quiz

◆ What men and women worry about when it comes to their bodies

◆ Learning to enjoy shared nakedness

◆ Adapting to physical changes

What do you think about your body? Are you satisfied with what you see when you look in the mirror? If so, you're in the distinct minority. In recent surveys, four of five women and one of two men said there is at least one thing they would change about their physical appearance if they had the opportunity.

Much of your sense of yourself is tied to the image you have of your physical appearance. People who like the reflection they see when walking down a street of shop windows or past a mirrored wall generally feel more confident about themselves and their abilities than people who look away when passing their reflections. Our American culture emphasizes physical appearance almost to the exclusion of other attributes. It's much better to be good-looking, as defined by an arbitrary and often unrealistic (and unhealthy) standard, than to be kind or intelligent. The "supermodel" look so popular today, however, is in stark contrast to the anthropological model of attractiveness that seems to drive sexual attraction for both men and women.

Shaping Your Body Image

Body image starts long before you give it any conscious thought. From birth, your environment shapes your sense of how your body should look—and how it does look. Relatives and strangers alike feel compelled to offer their observations. "You're skinny as a rail!" "My, what chubby little legs!" "Such a husky young man." "A moment on the lips, forever on the hips." What others say about your appearance has a tremendous effect on how you feel about how you look.

By the time they reach school age, kids dread looking different from their friends and peers, whether in form or fashion. As we become adults, we tend to exchange this need to look like everyone else for the need to look like the ideal man or woman. The problem is, the ideals we have in mind often exist only in our imaginations.

The Super Body Complex

Eight million Americans suffer from eating disorders; seven million of them are women. The vast majority are young women, in their teens and early twenties, with *anorexia* or *bulimia*. These potentially life-threatening conditions were nearly unheard of 30 years ago; today, they affect as many as one in five college-age women.

Many experts blame the surge in these body image disorders on the pervasive media message that thin is beautiful. The supermodels whose bodies adorn the covers of magazines and sell everything from cosmetics to underwear are typically lean and lanky. While this body type occurs naturally in fewer than five percent of American women, nearly 95 percent of them want the look anyway.

In 1960, the typical supermodel flaunted curves, not lines. Her looks weren't so far out of reach—she weighed only about eight percent less than the average "regular" woman. Today's typical supermodel weighs nearly 25 percent less than the average woman (who weighs what health experts consider normal). Women who aspire to this superhuman appearance find only disappointment and disillusion.

Sutrology

Anorexia is self-induced starvation. Those who have this disorder have a distorted self-image and view themselves as fat no matter how thin they really are. **Bulimia** is also known as binge and purge—those who have this disorder eat normally or even overeat, and then force themselves to vomit.

Health experts estimate that at any given time, one of every two women is dieting. In just over 20 years, the diet industry has exploded into a $35 billion megamarket to cater to their desires. Rather than morphing their more-curvaceous figures into the slim, boyish lines of their supermodel and TV star idols, however, most women instead play a potentially hazardous game of yo-yo—they lose and gain, lose and gain, lose and gain, often ending up gaining more than they have lost. The process of dieting is proving ineffective for losing and maintaining weight loss. What works the best is learning to eat sensibly, combined with exercise and a good sense of self.

Men are not immune from this obsession with body shape, either. In the 1980s, male supermodels took on a lean, sculpted look. While only a small percentage of men have the body type that can support such a long torso and washboard abs look, many more hope they can aspire to it by working out constantly. Some health experts believe that men who spend an inordinate amount of time at the gym may be suffering from a distorted image disorder similar to the one that results in anorexia in women. These men, who may work out five or six hours every day, are never happy with their body bulk or definition.

The most valuable way to improve self-image is to accept our bodies as the vessels of spirit that they are. No matter how perfect or imperfect our bodies seem, they are only temporary homes for our spirits. Sometimes we can put the body-perfect quest into perspective by remembering that our bodies serve us well, give us pleasure, give life, and carry us from here to there no matter what they look like. Feel your body's softness, firmness, curves, and muscles. Relish the feel of the air on your skin. These simple joys are the natural pleasures of the flesh that we can enjoy no matter how much or how little there is of us. Of course, exercise and healthy eating habits are important for maintaining your body in the best condition possible. But eat and exercise for health, not to fit your body into someone else's standard of how you should look.

Kama Knowledge

Throughout much of history, artists have portrayed the female body as full-figured and voluptuous. No artist brought this to the level that German painter Peter Paul Rubens (1577–1640) did in his work. The Baroque period in which Rubens lived was a time of opulence and richness, which his paintings captured and reflected in a blend of symbolic and representative images. In one of Rubens's most famous paintings, "Presentation of the Portrait of Marie de Medici to Henry IV," men, too, flaunt fleshy, abundant bodies. These were the ideals of the time, ascribed to mortals and gods alike in their artistic renderings.

The Shifting Influences of Culture and Fashion

Body image has always been a public matter, of course. Throughout history, the fashionable few have held undue influence over the less fortunate masses. The bustle dominated fashion from the 1600s to the late 1800s, accentuating what women today try to minimize—their backsides. Corsets focused attention on busts in the late 1800s as bustles finally faded from interest, giving way to bras in the decade of decadence, the roaring 1920s. And in the 1960s, the flat-chested Twiggy soared to supermodel-dom and nearly put an end to the bra (not to mention the curvaceous figure).

Accompanying these fashion shifts were corresponding adjustments in body image. During the time of the corset, big backsides were in. When the hipless Twiggy debuted, nothing but flat would do. These kinds of extremes are equally distressing to the majority of women who cannot achieve them.

Such unrealistic ideals are far less common in Eastern and other cultures where thinness is not desirable. In cultures where people may struggle to get enough (such as parts of China, the Middle East, and Africa), a strong, healthy body with perhaps a little extra on it is considered attractive.

Thinness is stylish only in industrialized, well-fed cultures such as ours, which are more likely to emphasize physical characteristics in both men and women that researchers define as the anthropological ideal. Such features are more related to childbearing (women) and protection (men) than to fashion. Women with broad hips and larger breasts are seen as more fertile, while men with strong muscles and a lean build are seen as more capable of protecting and providing for the family.

Not that Eastern cultures overlook ideals of physical appearance, however. Every culture has its standard of beauty for both women and men. The Kama Sutra advises men and women alike to seek features in each other that are similar to their own physical traits.

> **Sutra Sayings**
>
> A man should seek for his wife a woman who has good hair, teeth, nails, eyes, and breasts. These features should be of the proper size and look, with none lacking or in excess. The man should have these same traits himself.

What's Your Type?

Not every body has the ability to mold itself into a desired image. People are generally born with one of three body types—ectomorphic, endomorphic, or mesomorphic:

◆ The ectomorphic body is small-boned, with slight muscles and a slender build. Most supermodels are of this body type.

◆ The endomorphic body features a larger frame and a rounded shape, and is more likely to carry extra body fat.

◆ The mesomorphic body is a body-builder's delight, with a sturdy build and well-defined muscles.

Proper nutrition and adequate exercise are essential for any body's health, regardless of its type. But hours in the gym are not going to change an endomorph into either an ectomorph or a mesomorph, an ectomorph into a mesomorph, or a mesomorph into an ectomorph. Your body is what it is.

Common body types.

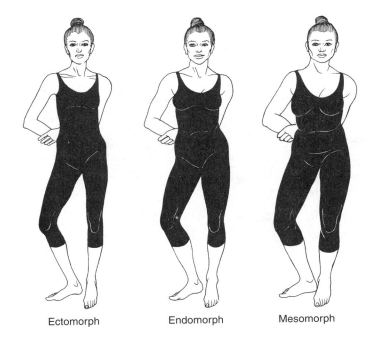

Ectomorph   Endomorph   Mesomorph

The Body Beautiful: A Self-Quiz

What body parts do you worry about? What do you think others worry about? Check your assumptions with this quick self-quiz. For each statement, choose true or false.

1. Men prefer blondes.

   True _____   False _____

2. Women prefer men with big, bulging muscles.

   True _____   False _____

3. Women are just about as likely to have their breasts reduced as they are to have them enlarged.

   True _____   False _____

4. The physical feature men find most attractive in women is big breasts.

   True _____   False _____

5. The one physical feature men most often want to change about themselves is their hair.

   True _____   False _____

6. The one physical feature women most often want to change about themselves is wrinkles.

   True _____   False _____

Let's see if you're in for any surprises. Here are the answers, as reported by various surveys and studies:

1. **False.** Though about 80 percent of women believe men prefer blondes, most men prefer women with the same color of hair as theirs. So while blonde men might prefer blonde women, those golden locks do little to stir the interest of men whose hair is another color.

2. **False.** You wouldn't know it by looking in the window of a health club near you, but women tend to prefer men who look fit and trim without a lot of extra bulk (in the way of muscles, that is).

3. **False.** Though the number of women wanting to reduce the size of their breasts is steadily increasing, those who want to build a bigger bust line still outnumber them nearly two to one. In 1998, 132,000 women had their breasts enlarged compared to 70,000 who had them reduced.

4. **False.** Despite the amount of coverage given to breasts in everything from advertising to television, men tend to find backsides and legs more appealing.

5. **True.** America's 40 million bald men spend about $1.3 billion each year trying to restore lost hair or cover the evidence.

6. **True.** Though research shows that women grow more comfortable with their bodies as they age, more than 160,000 American women went under the knife in 1998 to tighten and smooth their faces and eyelids. Most were between the ages of 35 and 64.

What Worries Men About Their Bodies

Women tend to believe men don't worry about their own appearance. Yet American men spend more than $5 billion a year to improve their appearance through cosmetic surgery, personal care products, and hair loss treatment. They also fork over more than $3 billion a year on fitness equipment and health club memberships. Men worry most about height, hair, and build.

With the first two of these concerns pretty much out of their control (though some hair loss treatments are helpful), many men focus their attention on building a more muscular physique. Some work out at the gym, and others turn to cosmetic surgery for assistance. Liposuction leads the way, accounting for nearly 20 percent of the cosmetic procedures performed on men in 1998.

Men also worry about penis size (some enough to surgically enhance their appearance with penile implants). Though there can be considerable variation in the size of flaccid penises, erection is a great equalizer. While not everyone measures exactly the same, the vast majority of men find their erect penises function just fine.

Kama Knowledge

The typical American man envisions his ideal body as at least 5'11" tall, broad-shouldered and narrow-waisted, and weighing in around 175 pounds. In reality, the average man hits the weight, but is an inch shorter and wears a 34-inch belt. The typical woman envisions her ideal height as 5'5", weight 125 pounds, and dress size 6. In reality, the average woman is 5'4", weighs 140 pounds, and wears a size 14. Though estimates vary, it's likely that 10 percent or less of the American population meets these ideal standards.

What Worries Women About Their Bodies

Just as surely as a man checks his hairline when he sees his reflection in a window or mirror, a woman checks her backside. In one survey, two-thirds of the women polled said the physical change they feared most as they got older was an expanding rear view. From an anthropological perspective, wide hips signal fertility. Many scientists believe this is a genetically programmed turn on for men, whether women like it or not.

In fact, body fat in general worries women who fear their partners will find them less attractive if they gain weight. Feeling they are fat makes it hard for many women to enjoy being in the nude. They often dress to mask their size (whether or not they're truly overweight), which increases their anxiety at the thought of disrobing or appearing naked in front of a lover.

Women also worry about the size and appearance of their breasts, as evidenced by the high number who have surgery to make desired alterations. An increasing number of women who had breast implants first done 10 or 20 years ago are now having them replaced, since newer implants are made of more pliable and resilient materials for a more natural look and feel. Many people also report that they "hate" their stomachs. They feel ashamed that they are not perfectly flat or that they have stretch marks.

A Self-Exploration: What Do You Expect?

What physical characteristics do you find appealing in a long-term lover? Studies suggest that what we think we want in a committed partner often turns out to be irrelevant when we find our soul mates.

This self-exploration can help you identify what matters to you and what doesn't. You can respond to these statements or questions by yourself or with your partner. You'll get the most from this self-exploration if you discuss your responses with each other.

1. When I was a child, I envisioned my wife/husband/life partner would look like …

   _____

   _____

2. When I look at my wife/husband/life partner now, the features I find most appealing are …

   _____

   _____

3. Disrobing in front of my partner makes me feel …

   _____

   _____

4. I would feel more comfortable about being in the nude if I could change just this one body feature …

   _____

   _____

5. When my partner and I are naked together, my body feature that he or she most enjoys looking at is …

   _____

   _____

6. When my partner and I are naked together, his or her body feature that I most enjoy looking at is ...

_____

_____

7. I wish my partner would look more at my ... and less at my ...

_____

_____

Unwrapping the Package

Exposing your body to someone you love can fill you with anxiety. What if he doesn't like what he sees? What if she doesn't see what she likes? Even couples who've been loving partners for a long time may not be comfortable the first few times they bare all to each other if shared nakedness is new to their relationship.

Being naked implies a sense of vulnerability and exposure that, in some respects, can be even more intense than what we feel when we open ourselves to each other emotionally and spiritually. Most adults have plenty of experience building walls to protect and defend themselves against emotional revelations that take an unexpected turn and which result in hurt instead of bonding. When you stand naked before your lover, it's hard to recover.

This physical openness is yet another dimension of intimacy. Just as we must take risks to let our minds and souls develop closer bonds, we must, too, take the risks of physical exposure to let the completeness of our beings draw together. A committed relationship based on mutual trust and love finds this new dimension of intimacy both exciting and affirming. As a couple, you share yourselves—fully naked—in body, mind, and soul.

Dr. Josie Suggests

Clothing can be incredibly arousing, especially when you're taking it off. Turn the process of undressing into erotic play. Kiss and caress body parts as undressing reveals them. Loose, flowing garments are easier to remove in stages than are items with buttons and zippers. For a different spin, slowly take off your own clothing instead of each other's.

What's Under the Covers May Surprise You

Couples who are accustomed to making love under the covers, in the dark, or partially clothed may not necessarily be unhappy with the level of intimacy and bonding they feel. Some partners slip into the habit of making love this way, and aren't aware of how different their experiences could be if they uncovered. Others are self-conscious about their bodies, and reluctant to show them because not seeing means they don't have to think about their insecurities.

But opening yourself to the full use of all your senses—including sight—may make you wonder why you've resisted. Sharing your body fully with your partner can give you a new level of confidence and comfort that will make sexual loving a deeper and more fulfilling experience for you both. Your imagination has already been fueling your desire; the real thing can be even more arousing.

Take care in what you say and how you respond, particularly when nakedness is a new experience for you and your partner. Show loving appreciation for your partner's willingness to share his or her body with you. Tell your lover what you like about what you see, and what excites you about his or her body. And above all, keep a sense of humor. Sometimes bodies look and act in unexpected ways that a gentle laugh can put in perspective.

> **CAUTION**
>
> **Out of Touch**
>
> Nakedness can be intimidating, especially if you're not used to seeing each other's bodies. If you're uncomfortable, stop for a moment to talk with your partner about what's bothering you—but keep it simple. Often simply saying what is so for you lets you refocus on the pleasure. See if that happens, then continue only if you both want to.

People often worry about how to respond if they're disappointed when they finally see what's been under cover for so long. First of all, most committed couples aren't disappointed. Anticipating the moment of revealing themselves to each other has heightened the sexual tension between them, and they savor every aspect of discovery—the expected and the unexpected.

Even if what you see isn't quite what you expected, there's usually a joy in what you do see. If you do feel a sense of disappointment, try to figure out why. Did your partner misrepresent himself or herself somehow? Did your imagination get carried away? Often there's an unrealistic ideal at the basis of your reaction. Once you identify what it is, you can step beyond it.

The following exercise lets you visually explore each other's bodies in a gentle and honoring way. Be sure to take your time and enjoy the experience.

Exercise: Looking at Each Other's Bodies

1. Light candles and put on some soft music. Arrange the bed for love play with clean sheets.

2. Bathe together, then lie together looking into each other's eyes for a few minutes as you gently harmonize your breathing.

3. Ask if you can look at your partner's genitals. Sit up and gently admire your partner's genitals. Tell him or her how beautiful they are and how much pleasure you receive from them. It is intimate and erotic to look. Be reverential.

4. If you like, you can do this with touching, too. Ask your partner, "Can I touch you here?" "Does this feel good?" This is a good way to learn what pleasures your partner. Keep a playful, reverential tone without being silly.

Are You Ready to Lose Your Inhibitions?

Physical openness is amazingly freeing. When you and your partner are naked with each other, many barriers dissolve. You forget, when you're at the height of pleasure, about your belly or your thighs or whatever body part ordinarily bothers you. It just doesn't matter how big or small you are when you're in the middle of a great orgasm. You see each other for who you are physically, not as a dream ideal but as real lovers. Take the time to explore each other's bodies (and your own, too). Activate all your senses, and stay aware not just of how your body feels of but how your partner's body feels and responds, too.

Some people have inhibitions about nudity that are difficult to overcome. Unfortunately, if from the time we are little children we're told to cover our nakedness, this becomes a deeply ingrained pattern. Breaking free from inhibitions about being naked can take time.

Create an environment where you feel comfortable being nude, where no one is going to walk in on you, and where there are no intruding distractions. Turn the lights down low, or burn candles. The most important thing is to feel relaxed and open to your partner. For those who feel more comfortable with a little bit left to the imagination, there is nothing quite so lovely as a silky Japanese kimono, or a batiked sarong. You can be nearly naked and show off the parts you want seen and hide the rest.

Loving Looking at Your Body (and Your Partner's, Too)

Reverence for each other's bodies, asking for permission to look, saying what a miracle the body—and all of its parts—is, lingering with a loving and even adoring glance, not just sneaking a peak, can take your relationship to another level. Rather than removing the mystery, it enhances the marvel. The human body really is a work of art, in all its many shapes and sizes. Try looking at your partner as though he or she is indeed a great work of art.

How Do You Think Your Partner Feels About Your Body?

Most anxiety about being naked together arises from the prospect of uncovering the unknown. You get all worked up, worrying about what your partner will think when she sees that your erection curves to the left or he sees that your nipples sink in a bit when you lie on your back. Odds are, neither of you really notices these things—and if you do, you find them to be endearing characteristics.

Out of Touch

Don't ask questions that lead to no-win answers. "My butt's too big, isn't it?" leaves all but the most skilled communicators wondering how to answer without getting thrown from the bed.

If you like, take turns telling each other what you love about the other's body. Start by saying, "What I love about your body is …." Go back and forth with this until you've each had five turns. Then you can say, "What I'm most self-conscious about in my own body is …." Again, take five turns each.

How Does Your Partner Actually Feel About Your Body?

In most committed relationships, partners are satisfied with each other's bodies. Variations from the ideal don't matter all that much to most people. Part of this is the comfort of familiarity—your bodies feel good when they connect, or even just lie in bed together. You've learned, through the repetition of your experiences together, what works for you. You've adapted and adjusted for discrepancies and differences.

Still, many long-time lovers who aren't used to talking with each other about their bodies may find it uncomfortable to start doing so. Try to honor your partner's willingness to be honest and open rather than responding with defensiveness and anger to shared information that isn't quite what you had hoped it would be.

How Do You Feel About Your Partner's Body?

Frequently the things that bother you about your partner's body have a hook into your past. Perhaps your partner simply doesn't fit your love map. Or maybe something about your partner is triggering something in you and you're projecting your discomfort with your own feelings onto your partner.

You might feel that your partner's body is too big and in fact he or she takes up more of the bed than you'd like. Try to pay attention to how you feel when you're most bothered. Do you feel crowded out, like there isn't enough space for you? You might notice if that is a theme in your relationship with your partner or in your past. Rather than withdrawing or becoming angry with your partner for being too big, you can just ask your partner to be aware of the amount of space he or she is taking and to be more aware of your need to have enough room to be comfortable.

The Kama Sutra Can Help You Make Love to (and with) Your Body

The Kama Sutra spends a great deal of time counseling couples to take as much pleasure from the unwrapping as from the sexual union. Vatsyayana goes into great detail explaining the subtleties and nuances not only of using your five senses to enjoy one another, but also of uncovering the mysteries of your bodies and how they both invite and respond.

Body language and verbal language don't always convey the same message, Vatsyayana observes. The body often speaks truer, displaying your feelings and desires in ways words can't convey. While it's important to listen to the words, particularly if one of you is saying "no" or "stop," letting your bodies do the talking can make for new and exciting lovemaking.

Loving Changes

Surprise! Your body changes—with pregnancy and childbirth, with aging, possibly with injury or illness. Such changes need not put an end to the joy you feel in seeing and exploring each other's bodies. Instead, let them lead you to new discoveries and pleasures. And keeping up with your body's changes can influence them in subtle and obvious ways. Exercise keeps muscles toned, joints flexible, and bones strong. Healthful eating gives your body the nourishment it needs to transition through life with grace and beauty.

Several studies show that most people feel more comfortable and confident about their bodies as they grow older, even though their bodies have likely drifted even further from the idealized "norm." Some of this is maturity—as you grow older, you come to accept many things that would have troubled you when you were younger. Some of it is experience—you've spent several decades, as an adult, housed in this package and you're finally becoming accustomed to it. And some of it is reduced pressure, usually subconscious and from within, to mate and reproduce—particularly for women past menopause, for whom pregnancy is no longer a worry.

Dr. Josie Suggests

Physical attraction is only one aspect of what draws two people together. Much of what we view as desirable in the opposite sex is framed long before we're aware of such attractions, in the love maps that we formulate based on early childhood perceptions. (See Chapter 5.)

Some changes are not those we want. You may no longer be as limber, with arthritis limiting your movements. A woman may lose a breast to cancer, a man may join the "zipper club" (open heart surgery). These are most often changes over which we have no control. Accepting them and moving on to the best relationship they allow can be difficult but ultimately rewarding. Chapter 23 explores ways to keep sexual loving as an integral aspect of your relationship no matter how old you are.

The Least You Need to Know

- ◆ Being naked together and enjoying each other's bodies are important elements of an intimate, committed relationship.

- ◆ The worries and fears partners have about what the other thinks are often unfounded.

- ◆ Most committed partners enjoy and appreciate each other's bodies for what they are, and don't think about how they might differ from the ideal.

- ◆ Change is a normal and inevitable part of life. The changes your body goes through can offer you opportunities you might otherwise not have had to experience deepened pleasure in sexual loving.

Chapter 8

Navigating Troubled Waters

In This Chapter

- ◆ How brain chemistry and romantic love are linked
- ◆ Where we get our expectations about sex
- ◆ Examining your relationship: a self-quiz
- ◆ What goes wrong in relationships and how to fix them

When two people first fall in love, the rest of the world disappears. They are totally absorbed in the details of each other—the lingering scent of her perfume, the scratch of his beard against her cheek, the harmony of their laughter. They can't stand to be apart, and call each other when they are— just to hear each other's voices.

They feel so good together, they extend their commitment—move in together, get married. Things are great for a while, then slowly but surely the sizzle fades. Before they know it, what they swore would never happen to them has—they go to work in the morning, come home in the evening, and fall into bed at night with a perfunctory kiss. There are bills to pay, toilets to clean, maybe even kids to shuttle around. All their friends nod knowingly … welcome to Real Life.

What happens to relationships?

Affairs of the Heart ... or the Brain?

Symbolically, we associate romantic love with the heart. The heart is the seat of emotion, of caring, and of compassion. Our deepest, most meaningful conversations come straight from the heart. Figuratively speaking, the heart is the doorway to human conscience, where we identify with the finest qualities of the human character, and where we experience emotion through the depths of joy and suffering.

The ancient Egyptians believed the heart was the center of the mind. In China there is a term that refers to the thinking heart, feeling mind. Modern scientists would say they just had it backwards—the mind is actually the center of the heart. Or to be more precise, the brain is the seat of love. Scientific studies suggest that much of what we know as romantic love is actually the effect of natural chemical substances in the brain.

The brain's *limbic system* produces a number of natural substances that chemically behave much like *amphetamines*. These substances cause a feeling of excitement and exhilaration. During the early stages of romantic love, or infatuation, the level of these substances rises. Researchers don't know quite why or how this happens, though some believe it is a psychosomatic process reflecting an interaction between the emotions (the mind) and physiology (the body).

> **Sutrology**
>
> The **limbic system** is a ringlike area in the center of the brain that plays a role in the feelings and expression of emotion. **Amphetamines** are chemicals that stimulate the nervous system.

But as good as this stimulation feels, the brain can't sustain it forever. Gradually, over about 18 months to three years, the levels drop off. And just like that, the honeymoon's over. Researchers believe more calming substances replace the stimulation, helping the brain to settle down and the mind to settle into a sense of comfort.

Sexpectations

As confused as we often are about what to expect from relationships, we're even more puzzled when it comes to expectations about sex. As we mentioned in Chapter 1, what passes for sex education in most Western cultures barely scratches the surface of biology. Classes cover puberty and hormones and morphing body parts. No one teaches, or even talks much about, the pleasures of bringing those parts into alignment with one another.

The expectations about sex that most people bring into their adult relationships typically represent a hodge-podge of ideas pulled together from what they see (and don't see) between their parents and other adults in their childhoods, locker room bragging or slumber party gossip, and backseat explorations. These snippets and snapshots fit within a narrow frame: Boys like sex, girls don't.

The Hazards of What We Think We Know

Unfortunately, what we think we know often isn't so. In reality, men and women have about equal desire for sex (as first established in the 1950s through the extensive studies known as the Kinsey report and subsequently supported by other studies). Girls don't get pregnant from toilet seats, boys don't suffer "blue balls" if they get sexually aroused but don't climax, and parents do have sex.

Despite the profusion of sexuality in the media and our professed openness about sex, today's young people know far less about sexual love than did their counterparts in India 2,000 years ago. There is no modern version of the Kama Sutra to guide the sexual awakening of couples or stir the passions of spouses. Without knowing what to expect, it's difficult to feel satisfied with what you get.

How Good Should Sex Be?

Well, how good do you want it? How good can you stand it? Sex should be as good, and as fun, as you and your partner want it to be.

In some respects, expectations are limiting. Some of the problem is pleasure anxiety—people tend to think that something as pleasurable as sexual loving shouldn't be so enjoyable. So they reduce their expectations around sex. They fall into the mindset of "common wisdom" that says married couples (or couples who have been together a long time in a committed relationship) don't make love that often. And when they do, they don't enjoy it that much.

Says who? Yet many couples accept this image of marriage, cutting themselves off from the intimacy and joy of limitless sexual loving. Without a model such as the Kama Sutra to show them that what they see isn't necessarily how things should be, these couples fall back on the collages they've constructed for themselves.

Sutra Sayings

The man and the woman should be well-versed in the elements of lovemaking, so they may enjoy the pleasures of sexual loving to the fullest. When they do not know these elements, their marriage will struggle or fail.

Does Familiarity Breed Discontent?

Couples commonly believe that a decline in lovemaking is a normal result of becoming familiar with each other. Part of the excitement of new love, after all, is the joy of discovery. Once you've explored every nook and cranny, what's there to do but roll over and go to sleep?

Use what you've learned about each other to give each other pleasure! Bodies, attitudes, desires, and tastes all change with time. Go re-exploring. Rediscover each other. You might be surprised to learn that, once again, what you know isn't quite so.

The mundane details of everyday life can put a crimp in anyone's love life. All couples experience an ebb and flow of desire and longing for each other that comes from many sources. It isn't always easy to look upon your partner with romantic eyes when you've just paid bills or washed laundry. But it is important to realize that you don't have to act like every married couple you once swore you'd never be like.

Kama Knowledge

A recent study shows that not everyone believes sex is an essential aspect of marriage. About a third of the women and a sixth of the men surveyed identified themselves as happily married yet not interested in sex. Another survey shows that the longer a couple is married, the less often they have sex. Nearly half of couples married less than two years make love three times a week or more, while the same percentage of those married more than 10 years have sex one to three times a week.

Why Relationships Get into Trouble

People are often shocked and confused when their relationships begin to unravel. The partner who once seemed to love you without reservation now suddenly likes hardly anything about you. The lover who once found endearing everything you said and did, who laughed at every little quirk of your nature, now finds your traits a constant annoyance, inconvenience, and burden. What happens to turn a love nest into a bed of nails?

Relationships get into trouble not because partners fight or disagree about issues, not because they have different styles of dealing with money or attitudes about child rearing. After all, how long would someone who was a carbon copy of you hold your interest? Relationships get into trouble because partners shrink each other into little boxes and stop seeing each other as the individuals with whom they fell in love originally.

Does Everything Have to Be About Sex?

When a relationship goes bad, the first thing that suffers is the sex. It's easy to blame bad sex for a faltering relationship, but this is upside down. Like the deceptive rise of an iceberg above the water line, problems in the bedroom hint at much deeper and bigger issues below the surface.

So yes, just about everything ends up being about sex—both good and bad. Sex carries all the emotions for the whole relationship. If partners are not talking about the things in their lives that are bothering them—finances, kids, jobs—they begin to retreat into their own separate lives. It's very hard to have good sex when you can't communicate about anything else. After all, sex is a form of communication.

People tend to think sex problems are just about sex, but in fact they are about the relationship. Sex problems are symptoms. If sex is not working in your relationship, then usually something is not working in your life. Look at yourself first. What's making you unhappy? Are you fulfilled professionally or are you staying at a job you dislike? Have you given up the activities you once enjoyed "for the relationship"? The kind of sex that most of us want is possible only when we are fulfilled in our own lives. Withheld communication is not conducive to erotic feelings. When you're withholding feelings, they backlog. Your partner reaches for you, but you don't respond because you're mad about how your partner is spending money. It becomes difficult for you to be immediate and present, which is what good sex is all about, so you stop trying.

Sometimes sex is also about power. Some people feel that letting themselves lose control during lovemaking causes them to lose, at least temporarily, themselves and the power they hold in the relationship. Conscious role playing that explores power and surrender can be exciting and erotic, and is different than unconsciously using sex to feel powerful and in control.

The real power is in giving. Giving openly and generously to your partner inspires the same in return. In such an environment, control issues evaporate, at least for the moment. There is a comedy routine about the power of being next. Everyone jockeys to be first, thinking this will gain control. But the real power belongs to the person who is next, who can control who becomes first by letting the person behind go ahead. In putting yourself aside, you free yourself from the struggle.

The Pain of Betrayal

Many people seek comfort and solace outside the relationship, looking for affirmation that it's not their fault that things have fallen apart. They seek sexual relationships with other lovers, betraying the relationship through infidelity. This makes it look even more like sex is the problem, when in fact sex is just a symptom.

Issues of betrayal are difficult to overcome in relationships. It's often not even so much about the sex act itself as it is about the partner taking time, energy, love, and attention somewhere else. The betrayal is really the lying and whatever is going on emotionally that the partner is withholding that makes the partner want to stray in the first place. The closeness and intimacy couples thrive on evaporates.

Sutra Sayings

When there is trust, fear and worry dissolve into pleasure. The heart knows only love and happiness. The couple that has trust will know the joy of increasingly pleasurable sexual loving.

Betrayal doesn't always take the form of an affair. One partner can feel betrayed when the other engages in activities that keep them apart. Pouring all your energies into your work, spending too much time going out with the guys (or with the girls), retreating to the basement every night after dinner to build a model train empire, spending your evenings watching television or cruising the Internet in the other room ... these are all actions that couples may use to avoid intimacy.

Setting Boundaries

There is a tendency for people to want guarantees when they go into new relationships. It's impossible, however, for someone to promise something will or won't happen when events and circumstances are not within their control.

It's important for you to create safety for yourself. Neither your lover nor anyone else can do this for you. You do this by knowing what your boundaries are and how you want to live in a relationship, rather than trying to elicit promises that people might not be able to keep.

A Self-Quiz: How Is Your Relationship Doing?

The pressures of everyday living take their toll on the best of relationships. It's easy to take your partner for granted when there are so many other demands for your time, attention, and affections. Couples who share a solid bond of intimacy can generally weather the ups and downs of their relationships. Sometimes, though, the bond loosens. Unless the partners notice and take action, the relationship can slip away. Respond "true" or "false" to these statements to see how your relationship is doing.

1. My partner knows, or should know, that other commitments sometimes come first.

    True _____   False _____

2. My partner and I find it hard to agree about things like where to hang pictures and how to arrange furniture.

   True _____   False _____

3. I'd like to put more zest in our love life, but it's difficult for me to be adventurous in bed when all I can think about is work or kids or bills.

   True _____   False _____

4. Fifteen minutes of foreplay sounds like a luxury.

   True _____   False _____

5. I feel like our relationship is more work than play.

   True _____   False _____

6. It's hard for me to listen when my partner talks to me.

   True _____   False _____

7. I don't feel I can ask my partner to do things for me sexually.

   True _____   False _____

8. There are things I'd like to do for my partner sexually, but I'm afraid to try them or even ask if my partner finds them appealing.

   True _____   False _____

9. My partner does things during love play that I don't particularly enjoy, but he or she seems to enjoy them so I never say anything.

   True _____   False _____

10. I sleep on the couch or as far on the edge of the bed as possible when I'm mad at my partner.

    True _____   False _____

If more of these statements are true than false for you, you might want to take a closer look at how you and your partner communicate. You may have issues of power and control in your relationship, or use sex to punish or reward. You also may have too many competing priorities, making it difficult for you to find time to nurture your relationship and your partner.

Rediscovering Desire by Rediscovering Yourself

Psychologist and sex therapist David Schnarch theorizes that couples lose sexual desire when they lose themselves in the relationship. A relationship, says Schnarch, is a balancing act. We need the right amount of individuality blended with enough togetherness to maintain a healthy connection to our own path in life, while finding fulfilling intimacy in the relationship. This is no easy task.

For passion to be rekindled, individuals need to tend to themselves, rediscover their own lives and truths, and find the meaning and creativity in themselves that they are instead seeking from their mates. And—this is the important part—they need to stand up for themselves and their truth while keeping the balance of connection to their partner.

Relationships ask people to grow, to become aware of how past wounds rise up in little and not-so-little ways in current relationships. As a result, people often overreact, misinterpret, or go into a foggy trance.

It's important to stop blaming your partner or the relationship for what really are personal problems and look to yourself and what is and is not working in your life. Each partner needs to take responsibility for living his or her own hopes, dreams, and power.

When you can do all this, then you again become the person your beloved fell in love with, rather than the critical, blaming, withdrawing person you became in the muddiness of your confusion and pain. In this climate passion blooms again.

Kama Knowledge

Even with the Kama Sutra to guide them, lovers in ancient India sometimes struggled with sexual loving. Friends, relatives, and attendants were all sources of information and encouragement. It was common for a friend to intervene between lovers who were having trouble. It was the friend's task to discover the concerns of each partner and convey the information to the other. The friend served as a therapist and advisor, offering suggestions and support. The approach often had the desired effect of reuniting the couple.

Do You Need Sex Therapy?

Many people want better sex. (In all likelihood, that's one reason you're reading this book.) Their relationships are fairly strong and solid, and they generally feel the sex is pretty good. But they feel their lovemaking could be better somehow, perhaps more exotic or more adventurous. Both partners agree they'd like to explore themselves more intimately through sexual loving. For these people, the Kama Sutra is waiting.

The Kama Sutra is not a replacement for sex therapy, however. Some couples have more serious challenges in their sexual relationships. They might be struggling to manage low sexual desire, premature ejaculation, lack of orgasm, or incompatibilities they haven't been able to resolve such as frequency or styles of lovemaking. Some people are facing gender identity issues.

For these people, there is some form of therapy. Couples or sex therapists are clinical specialists (usually an M.A, Ph.D., or M.D. with specialized training in sex therapy) who can help couples identify, isolate, and repair their relationship issues. Sometimes therapy breaks through barriers in a relatively short time. In other situations, therapy can extend over many months or years.

What Therapy Can Do to Help

There are many ways therapy can help couples whose relationships are in trouble. Therapy can …

- Show you how to get off the cycle of criticizing, judging, blaming, and withdrawing and how to communicate with compassionate understanding.

- Help you to reinvision your relationship.

- Help you to get in touch with your own truth and to speak it in ways that your partner can hear.

- Help you to understand how the old hurts and patterns from your childhood affect your relationship.

> **CAUTION**
>
> **Out of Touch**
>
> If you're considering sex or couples therapy, ask about the therapist's training and perspective in working on the issues you are facing. If you're uncertain whether a therapist is a "good fit" for you, interview several until you find one you feel comfortable with. Ask each therapist what his or her perspective is on the issues you want to deal with.

Therapy can also be a place for you to …

- Learn new ways to relate.

- Learn about yourself and your partner.

- Learn how to open to intimacy and closeness and vulnerability.

- Clarify whether or not to stay together.

- Learn new skills and approaches that deepen communication and intimacy.

What Therapy Cannot Do for You

As much as therapy can do to help troubled relationships, it has its limits. Therapy cannot …

◆ Get your partner to be more like you want him or her to be.

◆ Give you "great chemistry" if you don't have it.

◆ Guarantee your relationship issues will be resolved.

◆ Keep your partner from leaving.

What to Expect from Therapy

People entering therapy often hope that the problems they are facing will disappear. Unfortunately, this is generally not what happens. Often people don't enter couples therapy until they are considering separation and the therapy begins by helping them sort out whether or not to stay together. Once they have made a decision to stay in the relationship, and have determined that their intention is to improve upon the way they relate, a period of hard work follows.

The good therapist helps each person to look at himself or herself and at the issues and patterns the relationship is triggering. Some therapists focus on teaching the skills of better communication, resolving conflict, and learning to fight in nondestructive ways. They might suggest reading, homework, and workshops.

 Dr. Josie Suggests _____

Friends are a good resource for therapy referrals, or consult a professional listing of couple's and sex therapists. If you are calling a therapist for the first time, ask for a telephone interview (these are no charge). Briefly share your reasons for seeing the therapist, and ask about the therapist's training and approach to working with the issues you are facing. Trust your intuition about whether the therapist feels like a good fit for you.

Some therapists focus on helping couples become more expressive and less antagonistic. Some therapists recognize that there are issues from childhood influencing the way partners relate to each other. They help couples to use those issues as a way to assist each other to become more whole through the process of relating with one another.

Other therapists feel that relationships are powerful vehicles to become more whole spiritually as well as psychologically. While these therapists focus on helping clients to function better, resolve issues, and alleviate symptoms, they also encourage people to use the challenges they face as a means of growing emotionally, personally, interpersonally, and spiritually.

Choosing a Therapist

Choosing the right therapist is itself a process of creating a relationship. A good therapist can intuit, draw on psychological wisdom, and even bring in complementary approaches such as body-oriented therapy, guided imagery, art therapy, and more.

Ask people you know for a recommendation, then interview the therapist. Explore the therapist's point of view on the issues you are facing. This is especially important if you are in a nontraditional relationship. Even though therapists are trained to hold an objective position, they are human beings with limits and biases.

A therapist is professionally trained to work with the issues you bring and can offer a fresh perspective. A wise and skilled relationship expert looks at you and your relationship from a perspective you do not have and that can be valuable. It is going to take some time to change old patterns, so ask your therapist about his or her approach and see if it works with your budget and schedule. And if after a few sessions you don't feel like you are in the right hands, don't hesitate to look elsewhere.

Unfortunately, the insurance system frequently covers only a few sessions with a therapist—usually too few to make a real difference. If you are not prepared to pay for counseling out of your pocket or you are on a limited budget, you might want to look into the counseling program at your church or social service agencies (check your local telephone directory under "counseling"). Many therapists offer workshops for couples, which can be an intensive way to learn in a weekend what might take many sessions in private therapy.

Sex, Marriage, or Family: What Kind of Therapy Is Right for You?

Sex therapists focus on sexual functioning and issues in relationships related specifically to sex. These include issues that relate to performance, difficulty with erection, ejaculation, orgasm, and low sexual desire. Sex therapists also deal with gender issues and issues around sexual orientation (straight, gay, bisexual).

Marriage and family therapists specialize in family and marital issues. They may or may not have taken additional training in sexuality. Some marriage and family therapists focus on the couple's relationship and never talk about sex. A sex therapist starts with the sexual aspect of the relationship. Psychologists may not specialize in relationship or sexual issues.

There are also people who are sex and relationship educators, teachers, and people who work as sexual surrogates. A surrogate works in conjunction with a therapist and a client. The surrogate acts as a hands-on teacher of all aspects of sex with his or her client. While intercourse is frequently a component of work with a surrogate, the emphasis is on all aspects of sexual education and function. Intercourse may or may not happen and is not the focus or goal.

Dr. Josie Suggests

Letting go of the past is an important step toward the future. Sometimes when couples create a ritual for saying goodbye, they discover a shift develops within each of them that lets them see each other in a different light. They can release the old relationship they shared and start a new one.

It is important to find out if the therapist you're considering is knowledgeable and capable of addressing the issues you bring. Call and ask questions of the therapist on the telephone. And as a matter of practicality, if you expect to be filing insurance claims, find out if the therapist accepts your insurance (and if your insurance plan accepts the therapist).

Restoring Your Relationship

What does it take to restore a relationship once you have gotten to the point of no return? Well, first of all, there is no point of no return. Some couples who don't seem to have any chance of staying together manage to turn themselves and their relationships around in the final stages.

The couples who are most likely to renew and restore their relationships are those who can do the following:

♦ Shift out of their personality-driven issues and truly establish themselves in heart-centered caring.

♦ Give up hurtful and defensive relationship habits, and pledge themselves to loving that is bigger than themselves and their fears and insecurities.

♦ Let go of the limiting past and recreate a relationship based on respect, equality, and a shared vision that supports the individual's growth as well as the couple's.

Other couples will end their relationships because they no longer can live with who they have become in the relationship. They've lost the loving good will that makes relationships thrive, and they have lost hope. The friendship that bonds individuals is lost and separation is the inevitable outcome.

How the Kama Sutra Can Help

In ancient India, couples turned to the Kama Sutra for needed counsel and advice about matters of the heart and relationships. One reason this was often successful for them is probably that the Kama Sutra provides a protocol for behavior.

Certainly the Kama Sutra doesn't offer much instruction in deep communication (though it recognizes and honors the need for it). But sometimes couples in trouble need to go back to the basics, back to the niceties of courtship, to rediscover their attraction for one another.

The Kama Sutra encourages couples to treat each other to little gifts and surprises, to listen to each other's stories, to laugh together, and to be attentive to the other's needs and desires. These are courtesies and pleasures that can benefit nearly every relationship.

Remember, you and your partner originally got together because you enjoyed each other. You had fun together, and you just liked being together. It's important to continue this as your partnership grows and evolves. Couples need to laugh together, even in bed, because when you're laughing, you're not arguing or pouting or retreating. When you're laughing, you're having fun.

The Least You Need to Know

- ◆ Relationships and sex require attention and effort.

- ◆ Sex is often part of the problem in relationships.

- ◆ Sex can be as good as you can bear it to be.

- ◆ The key to fixing problems in your relationship often lies in fixing the problems of your life.

Part  3

Friends and Lovers

Trust. It's such a scary thing, many people never really try it. At least not with other people. But trust is the foundation of intimacy—and intimacy is the core of sexual ecstasy according to the Kama Sutra. To truly surrender in love, you must trust another as well as yourself. With trust, we can ask for—and receive—what we desire.

For some people, the asking is the hardest part. So we don't. We expect our partners to magically know what we want and need, then become frustrated and even angry when they don't. These chapters take you on the inside of communication, so you can see how sharing through conversation builds trust and intimacy.

Chapter 9

The Importance of Trust

In This Chapter

◆ The different meanings and levels of trust

◆ An exploration of what trust means to you

◆ How to safely restore damaged trust

◆ How the Kama Sutra promotes trust between partners

For all that we talk about trust, many of us aren't quite clear what trust actually means. Oh, we say things like "You can't have love without trust," and "I'd trust her with my life." But what do we really mean?

Trust exists in layers or levels, and grows and evolves as two people get to know one another. Since it's an impossible task to decide that someone is for all situations trustworthy, trust is not black and white, which further complicates understanding. You might trust another person enough to share laughs at lunch, but not quite enough to divulge your most vulnerable secrets. Trust requires that we take risks, give up control, and allow life to support us rather than hovering over every detail and managing every interaction with another.

Defining Trust

The dictionary defines trust as a "firm belief or confidence in the truth, integrity, reliability, strength, and character of another person or thing." In relationships, trust means feeling confident that it's safe to be who you are when you're with your partner, and believing that your partner cares about you and your well-being. Trust also implies that we feel confident and relaxed enough to have faith that the future will turn out well.

Trust is the essential foundation of any relationship. You don't want to confide your hopes, dreams, and fears in another person without feeling that you can trust him or her to handle with kindness and respect the information you share. When you entrust your deepest feelings and emotions to a committed partner, you're putting your life in that person's care.

The Three Faces of Trust

As we've said, trust exists on several levels. As psychotherapist John Amodeo points out in his book *Love and Betrayal, Broken Trust in Intimate Relationships* (Ballentine Books, 1994), there are three primary layers of trust—trust of *self*, trust of *others*, and trust of *life*. This is a progression—to trust life you have to trust others, and to trust others you have to trust yourself.

When you trust yourself, you live easily within your skin. You are comfortable with your body and your emotions. You know how to care for, validate, and soothe yourself. You feel capable of dealing with the challenges you face in life. You have confidence in your abilities to make decisions and take risks.

When you trust others, you feel expansive and contented around them. When you're in the company of people you trust, you feel safe and at ease to be yourself. You feel free to laugh or cry, lounge around in your sweats, or even work up a sweat. You have faith that your trusted coworkers, friends, family, and partners appreciate you and enjoy being with you. You feel safe being who you are with them even if you are occasionally grumpy.

> **Sutra Sayings**
>
> Neither husband nor wife should give the other cause to be jealous. Those who feel betrayed become despondent and distrusting of each other and of men or women in general.

When you trust life, you recognize that life supports us. You accept that there is a mysterious force greater than you that guides you toward fulfillment and well-being. You are confident that your life is moving you forward without your willing every little detail. Trust life and you know you can't, nor do you have to control, every aspect of life. Trusting life does not mean, however, that you can coast along without making choices, taking responsibility, and contributing. Life, as the saying goes, is not a spectator sport.

Trust, Intimacy, and Relationships

Many people enter into relationships believing they trust each other. But as often as not, they haven't really talked about what this means to each of them. To one partner, trust might mean remaining monogamous and faithful. To the other, being trustworthy could mean showing up on time for a dinner reservation.

Partners who don't share a common understanding of trust, or who trust too quickly, often end up hurt and disappointed when they realize the other isn't really who they thought or expected. This is what we often call "blind trust"—leaping ahead to what we think we know. Such trust is also often naive—we see what we want to see rather than what is actually there.

There is a close relationship between trust and intimacy. To some extent, one cannot exist without the other. Trust requires honesty where we reveal ourselves and see others as they really are. Because most adults have become quite skilled at revealing only what they think others want to see, honesty is the necessary risk that builds trust.

What Trust Means to You: A Self-Exploration

Trust often means different things to partners. What does trust mean to you (and your partner)? Your answers to these questions might give you some interesting insights. Be honest—there are no right or wrong answers.

1. Trust in marriage or a committed relationship means …

    a. Till death do us part.

    b. Shared visions, hopes, and dreams.

    c. Knowing where my partner is and who she or he is with.

2. If my partner had an affair …

    a. I would be devastated and probably leave the relationship.

    b. I would be angry and hurt at first, then try to figure out what wasn't working in our relationship.

    c. I don't know what I would do. I've never thought about it.

3. The worst thing that could happen to the trust in my relationship would be …

    a. My partner has an affair.

    b. My partner says he or she is going shopping but instead goes to meet friends for drinks.

    c. I have an affair.

4. My trust in my relationship grows stronger when ...

  a. My partner does what he or she says he or she will do.

  b. My partner confides in me.

  c. My partner and I confront an issue and work through it to reach an understanding or solution that pleases us both.

5. I lose trust in my partner when he or she ...

  a. Says one thing to me and something else to friends or co-workers.

  b. Asks me to stop calling at work.

  c. Consistently can't pick me up at the airport or stop at the store for me on the way home from work.

6. It wouldn't bother me that my partner was late if he or she ...

  a. Called to let me know.

  b. Brought me a gift to apologize.

  c. Never did it again.

7. The most important element of trust is ...

  a. Shared chemistry.

  b. Common goals and interests.

  c. Regular dialogue and discussion.

Share and discuss your responses with your partner. Sometimes two or even all three choices may seem to fit with your view of trust.

Your Relationship's Foundation

Some people wander into relationships guided only by their attractions and fears of being alone. For a relationship to endure over the long term, you and your partner must be friends as well as lovers. Your partner needs to be a trusted ally, someone you can count on to be there for you in good times and bad, a person who tells you the truth with compassion.

Sometimes people expect things from a relationship and a partner that neither can provide. Your partner cannot take away your pain or prop up your poor sense of self. Your relationship cannot put an end to loneliness or life's frustrations. These are tasks only you can perform for yourself.

Building Trust

We establish trust incrementally as we go through experiences with each other. If your partner promises to meet you at a restaurant at 7:30, you trust he or she will be there. If, however, your partner is consistently 20 minutes late, you might begin to judge your partner as flaky, take it upon yourself to show up under the wire at 7:50, or you might get plugged into your own unresolved issues from childhood. Let's say that you were often neglected as a child, left to wait for parents who were working late. Your partner's lateness can reawaken powerful feelings that have their roots in your childhood experiences. Sharing how trust gets broken is the first step in rebuilding trust. Being late is annoying and eats away at the good feelings in a relationship, but it does not break trust in the same way as an affair.

Dr. Josie Suggests

Often couples who have differing views of trust don't realize the other's view is different. Talking about trust and discussing times when you feel your partner has betrayed your trust can help both partners understand the other's perspective.

When your partner is repeatedly late, the experience teaches you that your partner views this kind of commitment differently than you do. You have several options for dealing with this difference. You can alter your definition of being on time to accommodate your partner's habitual tardiness. You can become angry and resentful each time your partner violates your trust. Or you can talk with your partner about why this lateness bothers you and how it affects your level of trust.

People who show up when they say they will, who do what they promise, and who demonstrate that they value the other's feelings and well-being establish themselves as trustworthy. The experience of knowing someone will show up when promised carries forward to other aspects of life. You expect such people to stay true to their word, whether they promise to meet you at a certain time or vow their commitment to you. It's harder to trust someone who is inconsistent in keeping promises.

Many people who grew up in families where trust was abused carry their distrust into their adult relationships. Children are small people who deserve to be protected and respected. When they are treated badly, abused, and neglected, they do not learn self-respect or who they can safely respect and trust.

Dr. Josie Suggests

Real trust comes from trusting yourself, from knowing that you have the power to make choices and direct the course of your life. Talk with your partner about how you are learning to trust yourself more and how that is affecting your relationship with each other.

People who have experienced betrayal frequently have trouble trusting and often think they can create safety for themselves by demanding elaborate, detailed agreements from others. Rather than protecting them from hurt, premature promises of commitment often set them up for disappointment when the promises are impossible to keep. This only reinforces distrust and a pattern in which people see themselves as victims in relationships. It's more effective to make smaller, simpler agreements. If circumstances change, or you change your mind, talk honestly with each other about what is happening.

Can Friends Be Lovers and Lovers Be Friends?

People who begin their relationships as friends have an advantage in knowing each other without the illusions that typically accompany intense romantic attraction. Research shows us that the best foundation for a good committed relationship is friendship. When sexual chemistry colors our decision-making abilities, we are more likely to choose to be with someone with whom we don't have the kind of overall real compatibility that a good relationship requires. Starting a relationship as friends allows us to get to see each other in a number of situations and to grow a strong foundation for commitment.

Treating each other with the kind of respect that we give friends, and as we have suggested throughout the book, talking to each other as friends, is a healthy way to relate. Some of us treat our friends better than we treat our partners. A partner sometimes becomes a surrogate parent in your mind, and you react to him or her as you did to your parent who, it might seem, was trying to control you. We usually give people who are "just friends" a bit more slack in allowing them to be who they are, flaws and all.

It's not uncommon for formerly married couples to find themselves drawn together again. Sometimes they unite just once for "old time's sake," sometimes they become occasional lovers. And sometimes they rekindle their love. How they fare the next time around depends on well they have understood and healed the issues that split them apart.

Kama Knowledge

Studies show there are nearly half as many divorces as marriages in the United States each year. While about 25 percent of couples who divorce site sexual infidelities as among the primary reasons for the split in their relationships, nearly 80 percent place significant blame on money problems. The odds of second and subsequent marriages succeeding are even more bleak—as many as 80 percent break up. The older the partners are, however, the more likely they are to stay together.

Expressing Emotions

Many people believe venting their feelings is healthy for them and for their relationships. This is a qualified truth—it *is* healthy and productive, if you express your emotions without hurting your partner. (Or you could beat up a pillow or scream into the wind, which may help you feel better for the moment but doesn't do much to resolve the problem.)

Usually the emotions one partner expresses are only slightly about the other partner. Couples bring childhood wounds into their adult relationships, old hurts that they buried beneath the surface but haven't really healed. Some of us may not have been listened to with caring and respect. People often unconsciously expect new partners to make up for the shortcomings of parents and previous partners, to hear their complaints, and to validate their perspectives. Even though the history of these hurts doesn't exist in the new relationship, partners expect each other to somehow respond and "fix" it. When they can't, anger, frustration, and other emotions erupt.

When tension heats up between partners, both people can become overwhelmed by the intensity of their own and the other's emotions. This is called flooding. Research shows that men become flooded more easily than women do.

It's a good idea to learn to recognize when you and your partner become flooded. You know the emotional water's rising when …

◆ You get short of breath, your heart races, and your body temperature rises.

◆ You become defensive and start to recycle words or repeat the same point.

◆ You stop being able to hear what your partner is saying.

◆ You stop being present, feel confused, or find yourself or your partner tuning out.

When you notice any of these warning signs, you are emotionally flooded. This is a good time to take a break. Most likely, everything and anything you say will only make the situation worse anyway. At this point it's very easy to say things you'll regret later—it's best to acknowledge how you're feeling and suggest a time out.

> **CAUTION**
>
> **Out of Touch**
>
> When you are in a difficult situation with your partner and feel yourself becoming angry, confused, or overwhelmed, take a time-out. Tell your partner you need a few moments, and go for a walk, take a hot bath, or do some other activity you find soothing. Come back when you've calmed down and feel you can talk about your feelings without becoming defensive.

Make sure you check back in at a specified time, though. An hour might be long enough, or you might need longer. It is important to communicate your need for more time, so your partner doesn't feel like you've just disappeared or are refusing to deal with the issues.

Sometimes what you say is less the problem than how you say it, what you don't say, or what your body says on your behalf. Scowls, frowns, rolled eyes, clenched fists, and tensed muscles give off the message of contempt and anger. A contemptuous tone belies otherwise innocuous words, turning language into a weapon.

When Trust Is Threatened

Opening up and rebuilding trust after it has been broken in a relationship takes time, gentleness, and commitment. For some people, sex is the language that draws them back into the circle of love. They are able to turn the emotional intensity of sex into a healing and cleansing ritual. Other people must rebuild trust with words and deeds before they can put aside their hurt and venture into the intimacy of sex. Trust is necessary if two are going to truly join together in sexual embrace. In sex, our boundaries melt we as become tender, vulnerable, and less defended.

Concern Without Confrontation

The first step in repairing broken trust is to confront yourself instead of your partner. Did you commit to something that you cannot live with? Were you afraid that if you revealed the truth of your feelings that you would be abandoned? Remember, this is about you, not about your partner.

The next step is to gather courage and practice what psychologists Gay and Kathlyn Hendricks call "telling the microscopic truth." You reach this truth by opening yourself to your deeper feelings and thoughts, and sharing them with your partner. You might use anger to hide hurt or fear. When you can instead tell your partner, "It scares me to think you might leave me if you see how much I need you," you become vulnerable in a way that makes you easy to hear. You are also speaking a truth that is impossible to refute.

When people get to know and accept their vulnerable feelings and learn to share them impeccably with each other, they create an environment where love and trust grow.

Dr. Josie Suggests

Rather than blaming, criticizing, withdrawing, or freezing your partner out in icy silence, learn to express your emotions cleanly by taking 100 percent responsibility for your feelings. Use "I" talk. Rather than saying, "You are so inconsiderate!" try saying, "I feel unseen and used." This helps you separate the emotions of the moment from past baggage, and helps you end the blame game.)

Trusting Again

Human beings are remarkably resilient. We bounce back, time and again, from despair and disillusion when a relationship sours, to joy and renewed faith when a new stage of loving or a new relationship begins. Togetherness and intimacy are basic human needs (remember Maslow's hierarchy from Chapter 5), and we cannot help but seek to fulfill them. The key to moving forward instead of grinding circles into your soul is to learn from broken trust. With awareness comes understanding, and with understanding comes compassion. Use your awareness to break the cycle of negative patterns and behaviors. Use your understanding to forge new patterns of interaction. And use compassion to forgive yourself for your imperfections.

Sutra Sayings

A man and a woman who have been together a long time occasionally quarrel. When their fury separates them, they should calm each other with affectionate words and embraces so they may reconcile their love. When they come together in desire, theirs is the union of loving.

Here's an exercise to encourage communication and trust between you and your partner. Sit with your partner in a place and at a time when you won't be interrupted. Each of you should take 10 minutes to talk about what's going on in your lives.

Exercise: Talking as Friends

1. When you are the talking partner, talk about what is working and what is not. Talk about hopes, fears, dreams, and desires. Talk about how you feel about your life and your relationship with your partner.

2. Be as specific, personal, intimate, and vulnerable as you can be. Reveal yourself to your partner. Do not blame, judge, criticize, or seek solutions. Open your heart and speak as you would to your dearest, most trusted friend.

3. When you are the listening partner, just listen. Don't interrupt, agree, disagree, or judge. Listen with genuine curiosity and kindness.

Embracing Trust with Your Partner

Only when two people trust each other, says the Kama Sutra, can they be comfortable and open with each other. In sexual loving, trust is especially important. Partners give themselves to each other—they don't take from each other. In giving, they then receive.

In addition to stirring the erotic fires, the elements of sexual loving nurture and support trust between partners. One reason ancient Indian couples studied the Kama Sutra was to learn the progression of these elements, so they would know what to expect and how to please each other. The woman had great faith that the man well-versed in the elements of sexual loving would follow the appropriate progression, which was intended to make the experience as enjoyable for her as for him. As he did so, her trust in him grew, as did her faith that lovemaking would give her great pleasure.

Tenderness and caring between the couple taught each to respect the needs of the other. It was no arbitrary determination that newlyweds not only had to wait 10 nights after their wedding before consummating their marriage, but also were expected to engage in prescribed acts of sexual loving on each of the days leading to sexual union. By the tenth night, both ardor and trust ran high and the two were truly ready to unite in body, mind, and spirit.

The Least You Need to Know

◆ Trust and intimacy are interconnected—intimacy requires trust, and trust leads to intimacy.

◆ Couples sometimes have different views of trust. It's important to understanding your partner's perspective.

◆ When talking with your partner about your feelings, focus on how you feel, not what your partner says or does that induces your feelings.

◆ Moving progressively through the elements of sexual loving as the Kama Sutra teaches helps couples to build the trust between them that allows them to open themselves to each other.

Chapter 10

Tell Me What You Want

In This Chapter

- ◆ The different styles of communication
- ◆ How to ask for what you want
- ◆ How making love and making conversation are alike
- ◆ Enriching your relationship through the Kama Sutra

We tend to take the components of conversation—talking and listening— as givens. After all, we learn to talk when we're just two or three years old and practice for the rest of our lives. As children, we get messages from the environment that let us know when it is safe to speak and when it is not. As a result, many people become cautious and self-conscious about speaking their own truth.

Learning to listen is a slower process. A lot of people tend to view listening as the passive aspect of conversation, something we can do while doing other things, like watching TV or cleaning up the kitchen. In reality, listening requires a lot more effort and concentration than talking. It requires our full attention and presence, even though we don't always give them.

We all know when someone is listening to us and giving us his or her full attention. We also know when a friend or partner is distracted or preoccupied by formulating a rebuttal. Really listening to another challenges us to get into their experience, thoughts, and feelings and out of our own fears and agendas. This kind of listening makes partners feel loved, cared for, and understood in a way that deepens trust and intimacy. It also gives us the freedom to relax, safe in knowing that we don't have to argue or prove a point. We can be ourselves.

When you listen to your partner unconditionally, you are curious to understand his or her point of view even if you don't agree, and you can empathize with what he or she is feeling. Both of you can relax, and no longer feel the need to be on the defensive. Listening in this way doesn't mean you have to agree with what your partner says. It just means you are putting aside your opinions, judgments, biases, and preferences to listen to your partner's perspective. You try to understand what your partner's truth is, whether or not you agree.

Looking Out from Within

Have you ever noticed how you tend to view others from within your own framework? If you're an outgoing and talkative extrovert, you may automatically approach others as though they are the same way. You may not even notice when they're not. If, on the other hand, you're a quiet and reserved introvert and find casual conversation challenging (or pointless), you may find a talker to be quite annoying and even overbearing.

And while most of the time it's perfectly fine for you to be the way you are, intimate relationships require that you make some adjustments to communicate clearly with a partner whose style differs from yours. It's important for you to put yourself in your partner's shoes, and to listen to what your partner is really saying.

Most people have the best of intentions when they generously ignore habits and behaviors in their partners that they in fact find annoying. After all, each of us has our little quirks and idiosyncrasies. Your partner is likely just as tolerant of yours, in the beginning. You may even find these traits somewhat endearing at first.

Sutra Sayings

Whether bold, shy, wise, or trusting, those who make an open presentation of their feelings encourage love and attention. From this can develop a strong and lasting relationship. To understand each other's meanings and intentions, lovers must study and know each other.

Unfortunately, this tolerance eventually fades. Hinting, nagging, and making demands take its place, and suddenly partners find themselves wondering how they virtually walked on water last week, yet this week can barely float. Learning how to listen to each other opens the door to conscious communication. Here is an exercise to help couples develop listening skills and compassion.

Exercise: Learning How to Listen

1. Repeat what you heard your partner say as closely as you can. Speak in thought "chunks" that aren't too long for your partner to remember.

2. Validate your partner's point of view. Say, "That makes sense." You don't need to agree; simply getting into the other's experience and seeing how it is true for them is the point.

3. Empathize with your partner by guessing at what they must be feeling: "I guess you are feeling angry, hurt, disappointed, used …"

Learning How to Say It

There is no single right way to say something. Your particular style might work for you and your partner and be entirely wrong for another couple. In fact, what's right for you today might be wrong next week! Research shows that happy couples can laugh at themselves and the repeating issues in their relationship. While humor can soften the hard edges and difficult places in a relationship, inappropriate humor (especially if it's really masked sarcasm or veiled passive aggression) can wound people and erode trust and safety.

It's all too easy to blurt out what you're feeling without regard for how you want your partner to receive your message. Learning to be sensitive to another takes a lifetime of paying attention. "Hey! That's not a handle!" sounds quite different from "Let's try a more gentle touch." The former will likely end the evening's sexual adventures, while the latter could spark a night of incredible ecstasy.

Make your request a "do" rather than a "don't." Most people instinctively react by thinking they are doing something wrong and pull back in the face of "don'ts," viewing them as criticisms and complaints. A "don't" becomes a stop order that gives your partner no alternative direction, effectively shutting down your sexual loving.

A "do" encourages and offers direction, telling your partner what he or she can do instead to give you pleasure, which expresses your interest in expanding and deepening your lovemaking. "Don'ts" take your attention away from the activity, causing your partner to start wondering. "Do's" keep you on track and in the present, focused on what feels good. The best sex happens when you are present.

Positive Substitutions

Rather than Saying ...	Try Saying ...
You never listen to me	What I'm about to say is really important to me, and I'd like to have your full attention
You don't make sense	I don't understand
Don't do that	Try touching me here, like this
Stop criticizing me	I'd love it if you would compliment me about something
You never act like we're a couple when we go out together	I'd like for us to hold hands, sit close, and kiss now and then when we go out together

Learning How to Hear It

It can be disheartening to hear that what you've been doing to pleasure your partner isn't what he or she wants. Flicking a nipple with your tongue may have sent a former lover into throes of arousal, but only irritates your current partner. Your partner may be open enough to tell you this early in your relationship, or may not feel comfortable "threatening" your lovemaking until your touch becomes unbearable.

Many people are likely to withhold their true feelings, not wanting to hurt the other person. When your partner finally does say something, particularly if you've been lovers for a while, you may feel more hurt than if he or she had said something in the beginning. Try to hear your partner's comments as an effort to help you both enjoy more pleasurable sexual loving.

Let your partner finish talking before you say anything. Listen for the real message behind the words—your partner loves you, loves making love with you, and wants the experience to be as fulfilling as possible for both of you. Your partner is not telling you that you're a bad lover. Your partner is simply saying "this doesn't do much for me."

If you feel yourself becoming defensive, take a deep, slow breath before responding. Rather than countering with, "Why didn't you say something sooner?" or "I thought you liked that," ask your partner what he or she would like instead (if your partner hasn't already told you). Then try it. You might like it as much as your partner does. Continue to solicit feedback—gently and lovingly—from your partner.

Kama Knowledge

The masculine style of communication is informational, involving lots of facts and details about how things can be done. The feminine style of communication is feeling-oriented and relational. These styles are generalizations, of course—a man might have an emotional/feeling style, and a woman an informational style. The two different styles can be jarring to the other. Recognizing different styles can be the first step to understanding one another.

Silence Can Speak Louder than Words

Westerners grow up with aphorisms of their own, some of which are of limited value. "If you can't say something nice, don't say anything at all" is one of dozens we learn in kindergarten. While following this corollary to the Golden Rule might work fine at parties, it can harm a more evolved relationship. Saying nothing is almost always worse than the concern or problem hiding behind the silence. Silence leaves interpretation wide open. Silence can imply approval, disapproval, criticism, or indifference.

Staying quiet also eats at you, the keeper of silence, when you have something to say but feel you can't say it. Your unspoken words fester beneath the surface. If you keep them there, they will erupt when you least expect it—and often not in the way you would choose. However difficult you find talking about what's bothering you, it's the only way to clear the tension.

Silence clouds lovemaking, too. Some people are uncomfortable making sounds or talking during sex. They may fear being overheard, or may have had unpleasant experiences in previous relationships. Women especially may feel it's inappropriate to express pleasure through noises or words.

Sex is an energetic as well as a sensate and emotional event. Psychiatrist Wilhelm Reich theorized that pleasure and orgasmic sensations begin in the genitals and spread throughout the body. When they reach the throat, allowing sounds to come forth actually increases the pleasurable feelings. Your words, sounds, and noises not only communicate your joy to your partner, but also intensify your sexual pleasure.

A Self-Quiz: How Well Do You Communicate with Your Partner?

Do you say what you mean and mean what you say, or do your comments and actions leave room for (mis)interpretation? Read through this quick self-quiz to see how your communication skills measure up. Choose the answer that best describes how you typically behave or respond.

1. You're on a long trip in the car, and the first exit in 150 miles is approaching. You'd really like to stop. You say to your partner …

   a. Let's take this exit. I'd like to stop.

   b. Do you feel like stopping? This is the first exit we've passed in almost three hours.

   c. Are you hungry?

2. You've had a long, hard day at work and you really want to go to sleep. Your partner, however, is feeling particularly amorous and wants to make love. You say to your partner …

   a. I love you, and I love making love with you. But I've had a tough day and I'm very tired. Can you hold me while I fall asleep?

   b. C'mon, can't you see I'm tired?

   c. Nothing—you just roll over and pretend to be asleep.

3. Your partner shows up wearing jeans and a sweatshirt for your dinner reservation at a fancy restaurant you've never been to before. You say to your partner …

   a. The restaurant is very formal. Let's go somewhere else tonight, and come back another time.

   b. Didn't you know this place was dressy?

   c. How could you show up dressed like that? You never listen to what I tell you!

4. Your partner likes to begin lovemaking by caressing your thighs, but that doesn't do much for you until you're more aroused. You say to your partner …

   a. I love that you're touching me and it feels better when you start our love-making by kissing the side of my neck by my ear.

   b. I'd rather you didn't start with that.

   c. Don't do that! It drives me nuts!

5. You're both tired and neither of you really knows what you want for dinner. You say to your partner …

   a. Because nothing in particular strikes us, good or bad, let's have Chinese delivered. Someone else can do the cooking, cleaning up is a snap, and we can just relax and unwind.

b. Just make a decision—it doesn't matter to me.

c. Fine. I'll get myself something to eat. You're on your own.

6. You are at a dinner party with your partner and you were seated next to a man/woman you found attractive. On the way home you say to your partner …

a. It was great to feel attracted to another person knowing I would not choose to act on it. I feel so connected and attracted to you and I love being committed to you.

b. Wow, that new friend of our host's sure was sexy. And what a beautiful body! I think he/she was attracted to me.

c. When I see someone that great-looking, I wish we had an open relationship.

7. Your partner is stroking your genitals and you would like him or her to use a firmer touch. You say to your partner …

a. I love that you're touching me. What would feel just great to me is if you did that harder.

b. That isn't really turning me on. Could you do it harder and faster?

c. This just doesn't do it for me [and you pull away].

If most of your answers are a's, you generally express your needs and feelings clearly yet kindly. If most of your answers are b's, your comments might sometimes hurt your partner's feelings or leave your partner unsure about how you feel. If most of your answers are c's, your communication skills need improvement and could cost you your relationship.

Shifting Gender Roles

Fifty years ago, an American woman's place was in the home. The man left for work each morning and returned each evening. In between, he earned the family's income and she managed the children and the household. The woman took care of the man's needs, from fixing dinner and ironing shirts to satisfying his sexual desires. Men were men and women were women, and their roles and responsibilities were both clear and distinct from one another.

Today's environment is very different. As many women as men are in the American workforce. Dinner is likely to be something someone picks up on the way home from work. Kids and homework may compete for time with togetherness and sharing as a couple. There are few lines between men's work and women's work. When both partners have jobs and careers, both must also share in household tasks. Increasingly, couples are caring not only for their children but for the needs of their aging parents as well—the so-called "sandwich generation" of care-givers.

Sutra Sayings

When passion is high, it is the body that speaks. It is no longer bashful but seeks union with the lover's body. It at once relaxes and tenses, and presses to the lover's body those parts that bring the most joy.

Boundaries in the bedroom have blurred, too. Today, a man is as concerned as a woman is about meeting his partner's needs. A woman is just as likely as a man is to initiate lovemaking. While many couples enjoy this environment of freedom and openness, others find it confusing and even intimidating. Life sometimes looks easier when the lines around roles and rules are solid and strong.

She Said, He Said: The Fine Art of Dialogue

Is it really possible that men and women speak the same language yet express different meanings? While certainly there are some differences in the ways men and women communicate, we're not really from different planets.

Just Like Sex, Conversation Is an Exchange of Energy

What if you viewed conversation with your partner in the same way you view love-making? Would it change how your conversations start, progress, and end? Actually, conversation is much like lovemaking. Many people initiate a conversation for functional reasons—to discuss the day's plans, who's picking up the kids, what to have for dinner. When the exchange of information is complete, the conversation is over. We might liken this brand of conversation to obligatory sex—each person strives to satisfy his or her needs, but the experience isn't particularly fulfilling.

Memorable lovemaking, on the other hand, generally starts with each partner present in his or her body and attentive to each exchange between them. There is a continual dance of stroking, kissing, caressing, embracing, laughing, talking, and sometimes tears of intense emotion. Both partners are totally engrossed in each other, giving each other their full attention. Bodies, minds, and souls unite in a crescendo of delight as the exchange reaches its peak, then remain entwined as it gradually diminishes. The giver and the receiver become one and lovemaking is no longer a matter of who does what to whom but mutual play in pleasure.

Ah, wouldn't it be grand if conversation could have the same intimacy and connectedness? It can, if you pay it the same attention.

The word "conversation" comes from a Latin word that means "to turn around." By definition, a conversation involves two or more people who "turn around" an exchange of ideas. Conversation takes mutual participation—you can't do it by yourself, or with only one party contributing (that would be a monologue). The best of conversations are those that generate an energy of their own—the flow of ideas that start the discussion leads to new ideas that result from the discussion. Each party leaves the conversation feeling somehow heard, nurtured, enlightened, satisfied, and understood.

Ahhh … now that's more like it!

Asking for What You Want

Many people have a clear sense of what they want in an ideal relationship, yet feel their desires are not practical in real life. Why? Is it because what they want is so outrageous or bizarre that they dare not mention it? Is it because they feel no one could possibly deliver on their request? Is it because they believe they have no right to expect the ideal in a real relationship?

Childhood factors often come into play in our adult relationships. As a child, you were told to keep quiet, not ask for things, not be selfish. Perhaps your requests resulted in feeling humiliated or rejected. At any rate, the message was clear: Wanting is bad. So you decided to be self-sufficient and not depend on others to fulfill your needs. Unfortunately, when we decide that wanting will make us feel too vulnerable and don't ask, we don't get the closeness and love we desire.

It's common for people to believe that your partner should understand you well enough to know what you want, without you needing to spell it out. In many relationships, partners feel that they have an intuitive link between them and they often do sense each other's needs and desires. If this works with movies and ice cream, shouldn't it work with sex? Unfortunately, no matter how sensitive we are to each other, we are not full-time mind readers. If you want to be sure your partner knows what you want, you have to ask.

The sexual conversation is a sensitive story. Making love is an intimate exchange between two people. While intuition (sensing what pleases each other) and experience contribute to your pleasure, they aren't always enough to make sexual loving as fulfilling as it could be. Asking for what you want—in a caring and sensitive way— empowers both partners in getting their desires fulfilled, especially if you're yearning for something different than what is happening.

Dr. Josie Suggests

When you ask for what you want, be specific and positive. Instead of asking your partner to display more affection, ask your partner for a hug when he or she comes home from work. This turns an ambiguous desire into a doable action.

Take care not to present your request as a demand, however. Especially when asking for what you want is a new approach for you, it's easy to be demanding. Soften your requests with, "I like it when you …" or "I'd like to try …." Your partner may choose not to fulfill your request, of course, but at least you've opened the door of communication a bit further.

Tendering Response and Feedback

Asking for what you want is only one step in the dance of communication. Without response and feedback, you and your partner really don't know whether the request has been fulfilled. If you've asked your partner to try something and he or she agrees, let your partner know how it feels. Is it what you expected? Would you prefer the touch be a little softer, a little firmer, a bit to the right or more to the left? The dialogue of sexual loving requires participation from both partners for true communication to take place.

Response and feedback can take the form of dialogue, body language, and unspoken sounds—or a blend of all three. Some people find it more spontaneous to "ooh" and "ahh," while it's more natural for others to say "yes" or "that's good." Lift or move your body in response to your lover's touches. And if it's not so good or not what you had in mind, gently refine your request. "That feels good, and it would feel even better if you rubbed a little harder." Ask your partner if you can guide his or her hand to show what you had in mind.

Give yourself time to learn new touches and experiences. The first time you try something new might not be quite the thrill it is in your imagination. Much of the pleasure in sexual loving comes from exploring each other's desires and responses. This is as true when partners who have been lovers for a long time try something new as it is for partners who are new lovers.

Who Has the Power?

Sometimes in a relationship that's struggling, communication becomes a battle of control and power. Defensive retorts and contemptuous sarcasm replace thoughtful answers and curious inquiries. When criticism, blaming, contempt, and icy silences color communication, open communication is impossible. Sexual loving suffers when this happens. Rather than being an exchange of loving energy, sex becomes a weapon in the arsenal of the power struggle.

Control issues often surface in a relationship when one partner is afraid that his or her needs are being overlooked or unattended. Fear can drive us to issue ultimatums or attempt to establish new rules for the relationship. The other partner might retaliate with anger, *passive-aggressive behavior*, or *withholding behavior*, and the power struggle is on in full.

Breaking the cycle requires both partners to acknowledge their parts in the situation and become vulnerable—that is, rather than acting tough and indifferent, they share their pain and hurt over the loss of closeness. Then they can begin to confront their dissatisfaction and work collaboratively toward mutually agreeable solutions. Sometimes their behaviors have become so firmly entrenched that they need the help of a marriage therapist.

Sutrology

Passive-aggressive behavior is behavior that indirectly expresses your feelings, such as sarcasm, little jokes, and indirect jabs, and asking "What do you want" rather than expressing your own desires, thoughts, and feelings. **Withholding behavior** is withholding thoughts, feelings, and your body when you are angry or hurt.

Does Control Really Matter?

Control is a response to feeling afraid and vulnerable. It is so frequently a matter of contention and conflict within relationships that we have given it a title—the power struggle. While the power struggle is an unavoidable and normal phase in a couple's relationship, it is not fun. The struggle not to lose one's self while being in a close, committed relationship sets up a recurring cycle of struggle and resolution as couples grow into new levels of intimacy and individuality. Each completion in the cycle leads to a new level of personal growth and the potential for greater intimacy.

It is the *ego* that seeks control. In contemporary East/West psychology, the ego is viewed as your sense of self or the "I" dimension of who you are. The ego tries to establish itself by identifying itself as separate, unique, and special. It is always a little insecure, so it seeks to make itself solid and safe by establishing boundaries. Because the ego feels insubstantial and insecure, it builds itself a safe and solid fortress of accomplishments and achievements to reassure itself that it is okay. Then it can say to itself (and show the outside world), "I can take care of me, I can function in the world. I am not defective or bad."

When we are small we get our sense of self from the others in our lives. Our parents and caregivers give us messages that form our sense of self or ego identity. If these caregivers chastised us for being independent or worried excessively about us getting hurt when we went out to play, the message we got was that our desire for independence wasn't good or safe. To get along we all adapted somewhat by becoming what others expected.

If who we were and what we wanted was "bad," we developed the appropriate behaviors and eventually began to believe we were those behaviors. We then believe we are this false self.

The false self or the ego looks for validation from the outside to prove that it exists, since it has lost touch with its true nature and adapted to what is expected. The never-ending desires of the ego or personality are fueled by the sense that it (the ego) is not enough. No matter how much we accomplish or attain, our egos cannot be satisfied.

Sutrology

In contemporary East/West psychology, the **ego**—the false self or personality—is the aspect of the self that seeks to protect itself through control. The **essence**—the soul or true self—is the spiritual aspect of the self that knows absolute acceptance and unconditional love. The ego and the essence coexist in a dance of balance and counterbalance.

Counterbalancing the ego or personality is the *essence*, or the soul (spiritual) dimension of who you are. The essence is consistent and never changes. It exists in the realm of nonduality, and its basic nature is openness, trust, and warmth. It is aware, compassionate, and able to experience without judgment. Our true nature is the spiritual dimension of who we are, always have been, and always will be. The Buddhists say that our essence is basically good and whole. Meditation can help you to cultivate a relationship with your essence or your basic goodness. Unlike the ego, which needs continual reinforcement and support, the essence doesn't need to be built up or protected.

A Delicate Balance

The dance between the ego and the essence exists on an individual level as well as on a relationship level. A person whose ego is well fortified but lacks contact with his or her soul appears strong and solid, though he or she might be rigid and inflexible and lack openness and fluidity. A person who is in touch with his or her spiritual side can appear flexible, mutable, and open, yet lack the grounding that comes when the sense of self is well developed.

Our culture's emphasis on performance and achievement reinforces the ego and personality development. This emphasis has led us to an abundance of material success, while at the same time leaving us feeling that there is still something lacking in our fast-paced and frantic lives. We need to balance a strong, grounded presence in our lives with a sense that we are more than flesh, accomplishments, and desires. Relationships become the arena where we can learn to work with both sides of the self and with another. This process creates balance and growth.

Relationships are fertile ground for the personality and the soul to evolve. Our conflicting needs for both independence and togetherness drive our quest for new levels of awareness and balance. We need to go through these cycles in relationships to grow as partners and as people. The challenge of learning to work with the ego's fear and the soul's longing in a committed relationship pushes us to become more whole and connected.

Intercept and Decode Mixed Messages

One of the most common complaints partners have is that the other sends mixed messages. Words may say one thing but mean something else. Body language might send different signals. The result is confusing and frustrating for both partners. While sometimes you are intentionally vague, more often you don't realize you're sending mixed messages.

A mixed message indicates some kind of conflict or ambivalence. Part of you is saying yes and part of you is saying no. A relationship can help bring the conflict to life, so that you can become clear about the conflicting feelings you're having. "Yes, I want to make love with you, but I'm upset with you because you're having an affair and I feel betrayed and hurt and my body doesn't want to unite with you."

Sometimes mixed messages are about smaller things, but still reflect the need to talk. But usually the little things don't cause ambivalence. Deeper issues do. It's an inner turmoil that causes you to give mixed messages. If it only happens once in a while in a relationship, it's no big deal. But if it happens all the time, it's significant. Picking up on mixed messages takes awareness. It also takes time in the relationship to detect each person's pattern of response. Couples who have been together a long time sometimes seem to have an entire level of communication between them that only they understand. From the outside, this might look like intuition— a connectedness that takes place without any apparent effort on their parts. If you could peek inside such partners, however, you'd likely see a degree of awareness of what the other is feeling and doing.

CAUTION

Out of Touch

Keep the meaning of "no" clear during sexual loving. "No" should always mean "no." It's too easy for someone to get hurt or frightened when a partner ignores the message to stop doing something.

Some couples consciously develop and cultivate that awareness, and it serves them well. Other couples have established patterns that sabotage their relationships. Sarcastic jokes, one partner rolling his or her eyes in response to what the other has said, contemptuous remarks such as "Oh, he's always late," are often unconscious messages that undermine the relationship.

When approaching a conversation about a mixed message, ask your partner if he or she is open to hearing your feelings. Take responsibility for what you are feeling; that is, don't start in by accusing, blaming, or analyzing your partner. You might begin by saying what you're feeling. "When you say you're looking forward to having a night alone with me and then arrive late and sit down and read the paper until 10:00 and then come to bed and want to make love at 11:00, I feel unimportant and mistrustful. I don't trust that you will keep your word, and as a result I don't feel good about making dates with you."

Talking to each other about contradictory signals is an important step in making your relationship more conscious and requires sensitivity. It's important to practice listening and being curious about your part in this. The more undefended and open you can be to what your partner has to offer you, the more you can learn and the more likely you will resolve contradicting signals.

What Do You Want to Change?

Just about everyone has something to say when you ask what they would change about their partners. Many can reel off lists of "don'ts" and "doesn'ts"—he doesn't do this, I don't want her to do that. It's easy to focus on dissatisfactions—somehow they're more obvious.

Yet it's the pleasures and satisfactions that drew you and your partner together in the first place, and that hold your relationship together now. How often do you think of those positive attributes? How often do you tell your partner what he or she does that makes you happy and that you *wouldn't* change?

To a great extent, you are who you are. You're not likely to change your personality to please someone else—nor would you want someone else to change personalities just to please you. Shy or bold, outgoing or introspective, virtues and flaws, you have a personality that is inherently yours.

What you can shape and change, however, is the way you express your personality. Just as clothes present your physical image to the outside world, actions and words present your personality. And just as you can wear different styles of clothing, you can use different actions and behaviors to change the way you present yourself to others.

When you and your partner are open, honest, and listen to each other nondefensively, the feedback that you give and receive adds to your self-awareness. After all, your partner wants the best for you and sees you from a vantage point that you don't have, so a partner's insight can be a valuable reflection. Perhaps your partner has a habit of finishing other people's sentences. This affects not only you but everyone with whom your partner has a conversation. Kindly and gently making your partner aware of this habit and its consequences helps your partner see himself or herself as others do. He or she can then decide whether or not to change.

Notice there's a point of decision here, and it's not yours. The only behavior you can change is your own. While you can encourage and support others in their efforts to change, they must make the changes themselves. You can, of course, change the way you feel about your partner's behavior and the way it affects you.

Using the Kama Sutra to Improve Your Partnership

The Kama Sutra teaches couples to pay close attention to what pleases the other. In so doing, they will also please themselves. By observing each other's reactions and talking with each other about what gives pleasure and what doesn't, partners maintain an open dialogue that strengthens the bonds of their relationship.

There is a tendency to blame relationship troubles on less than satisfactory sexual loving. Struggles in bed are usually more symptom than cause, however. Even with its focus on sexual loving, the Kama Sutra recognizes this. It counsels couples to establish good communication before engaging in sexual activity. This is a valid lesson even 2,000 years later.

The Least You Need to Know

- Listening is an activity that is at least as important in conversation as talking.

- Asking for "dos" is more effective than demanding "don'ts" when you want your partner to change.

- Remaining silent is almost always worse than saying what you feel, even when your feelings aren't very positive.

- You're far more likely to get what you want if you ask for it than if you wait for your partner to figure it out.

Chapter 11

Keep the Fires Burning

In This Chapter

- My partner, my best friend
- How to extend passion and intimacy beyond the bedroom
- How much sizzle is in your sex life? A self-quiz
- How to manage kids, careers, and other responsibilities of your life and still have time for each other
- Using the Kama Sutra to recharge your sexual loving

In the beginning when we connect at a soul or essence level, we feel like we've met someone who, at long last, really sees us and appreciates us for who we are. We can let down our guard. Falling in love is an opportunity for the ego to experience a reprieve from having to build, defend, and prove itself. Basking in new love, we relax in the acceptance of another person. There's a kind of magic in being able to easily share who we are with another person. Even if you've done this before with another person in a different relationship, it's new each time. Throw good chemistry and good sex into the mix, and you've got a heady brew!

When we enter into a committed relationship, we hope we can continue this connection at a soul level. It feels so good—the chemistry, the sex, the intimacy, the sense of acceptance and appreciation. Your values are similar, you feel that the two of you could live life better together than alone. So you commit. You can't imagine it could be any better with anyone else.

Then the ego suddenly awakens, reasserts itself, and says, "Wait a minute! What happened to my safe and established life? Who's taking care of my fortress?" All the safe places your ego had to hide out in are now gone because that witness to your joys and sorrows is now there all the time. Where once you felt open and sharing, you now feel exposed and vulnerable. Ambivalence surfaces, and power struggles begin. Don't panic! This is a normal stage in the life cycle of your relationship—and it repeats itself in various formations throughout the relationship. The good news is that as you become conscious of these patterns, you also become better-equipped to navigate the twists and turns along the way.

More than Just Partners

Couples today ask more of each other than couples in any generation before. Not only do we ask that our partners be lovers, helpmates, playmates, co-parents, best friends, and confidantes, but we want them to be equals, too. And we want to be partnered by our partners. We want our partners to engage and meet us on all of life's fronts—financially, emotionally, erotically, intellectually, and spiritually. This is a tall order.

We all have conscious and unconscious expectations that our partners must treat us better than the role models who have helped us shape our expectations—parents and all the other caregivers who formed our images of how relationships work. This ideal is also influenced by the images you've gathered from books, movies, and television. But then along comes a real person who floats Oreos in milk and eats them with a spoon, snores all night, and has a first-thing-in-the-morning look that could scare the monsters back under the bed. How do you keep the fires of passion burning when your day starts with a cold shower and a challenge to the pictures of ideal love you've long cherished?

The good news is that when you start telling the truth to each other, the realness in your relationship grows and offers you the potential for true authenticity and intimacy.

Life and Love in the Real World

There are many phrases to describe today's Western lifestyles—life in the fast lane, the era of instant gratification, the generation of change. These are exciting and inspiring times, with tremendous technological and medical breakthroughs unlike any in history. Computers speed through complex tasks, rapidly accelerating the amount of work one person can do in a day.

While the price for this lifestyle isn't quite the Shakespearean pound of flesh, it can be high. We struggle to manage careers, finances, families, and households. More often than not, what we give up first are our selves and our relationships. Playing the guitar gives way to helping with homework. Fixing dinner replaces yoga class. And date nights surrender to late nights at the office. We lose our selves in the frenzy of trying to make it all work. And when we lose our sense of self, we lose the energy and ability to be present in a relationship.

You've Lost that Loving Feeling?

When you first fall in love, there is a sense that life is wonderful and generous. Making time for long walks, talks, and hours of lovemaking takes priority over life's other responsibilities. None of the details that now preoccupy you seemed important then, and if they did, they certainly weren't as all-consuming as they are now.

In the beginning, being together was the most important thing. So you extended your commitment or got married, started a household and maybe a family, and now you go to bed early only when you're sick. What happened to those wonderful lusty feelings? Odds are, they're still there. They just don't get much exercise these days (perhaps not unlike other parts of you). Your challenge is to dig them out and dust them off, and put them to good use once again.

> **Sutra Sayings**
>
> To keep affection and adoration for each other strong, couples should read poetry to each other, talk of the arts and the sciences, and share in conversation. They should confide secrets to each other, and enjoy loving sexual union.

The Kama Sutra invites couples to learn about each other—in and out of the bedroom.

(Hrana Janto)

The Kama Sutra stresses the importance of continuing a sense of courtship in marriage. It advises couples to learn about each other's tastes, likes, and dislikes, and to present each other with small gifts that show their love and affection. Interestingly, though the Kama Sutra does describe positions of sexual union for those whose passion is intense, it consistently counsels against that variation of sex we know as the quickie. Lovemaking, counsels Vatsyayana, is better delayed than rushed.

Rekindling Desire

Rekindling passion in your relationship often means going back in time a bit. Not literally, of course—though it might be nice if you could. Just time-travel in your mind for a few minutes. What first attracted you to your partner? Did you leave little notes or buy small gifts for each other, extend touches just to be in contact, telephone for no reason other than to hear the other's voice?

Over time, these loving gestures tend to drop out of the relationship. This happens not because you love each other less, but more often because your confidence with your partner's love and the commitment of your relationship leads you to believe you no longer need them. You've built the bonds that connect the two of you, and feel safe in their strength. Making love becomes a staple rather than a treat in your relationship. Taking each other for granted is not erotic.

Dr. Josie Suggests

While gifts and tokens of affection are usually welcome by your partner, nothing fuels the feeling of intimacy as much as sharing with your partner about yourself, what is going on behind the scenes in your hearts and minds. Remember to talk as friends and listen with an open and curious mind.

What's often missing in a relationship that's lost its sizzle isn't the sex act itself but the whole experience of sexual loving and its requisite elements of passion and intimacy. These elements extend far beyond the union of bodies. Many couples understand this extension in the context of foreplay—the kissing, caressing, and embracing that arouses sexual excitement before sexual union—and of afterplay—the kissing, caressing, and embracing that affirms the union of bodies and souls following sexual union.

Remember those gestures of affection that drifted out of your relationship as you and your partner became more confident of each other's commitment? As simple as they seem, they are much more than basic preliminaries. They make up the ongoing and extended foreplay that keeps the romance alive in relationships. Love notes, small gifts, phone calls for no reason other than to say "I love you," saying thank you, a surprise dinner in or out, going out of your way to get the concert tickets you know your partner would enjoy, holding hands, sharing tastes of food. All the little actions we typically associate with courtship are in fact ways to continue foreplay and afterplay. They mattered in the beginning of your relationship because they showed you how valued and important you were, and helped you establish intimacy and passion between the two of you. They matter now because they continue to renew your relationship.

It's About Time

In the early stages of a relationship, spending time together is a priority. You part company with great reluctance, and rush home from work to be together again. But then something shifts, and almost without notice the situation reverses. You rush from the house in the morning for early meetings, and may not see each other until bedtime, if then.

You really didn't have more time when your relationship was young, even though it seems that way. You made decisions and choices about how you spent your time that focused on your partnership. There is an element of necessity to this early on, when you're not sure of your partner and the nature of your relationship. You want to "give it all you've got" to see if it will work. When it does, you begin to relax and once again allow other interests to reclaim pieces of your time and interest.

It would be nearly impossible, in fact, for most people to continue their relationships at the same level of intensity that they had in the beginning. We all need to settle down and tend to our own pursuits and interests. In addition to the passion and intensity of the early days together, most of us want our relationships to provide us with a certain amount of comfort and security. We also want the freedom and support to fulfill our own purpose, if that relationship is to become a long-term commitment. We all must find our way to balance how much time we spend together and how much time we need for our own lives. Too much togetherness, and we become flat and undifferentiated; too much autonomy, and we stand the chance of slipping away from each other.

> **Dr. Josie Suggests**
>
> Talk with your partner about how much time you want to spend together, and how you want to spend it. Typically, couples come up with an evening together in the middle of the week, and then extended time over the weekend, with perhaps time off during one of the weekend days for individual errands, sports, or other interests.

Think honestly about how much time you want to spend with your partner. Do you envision yourself spending two, three, four nights together sharing intimately, having dinner out with friends, attending plays, or reading aloud to each other by the fire? Do you feel like you'd really like less time with your partner doing parallel activities like the grocery shopping or running errands so you can pursue your own interests?

Consider the time you need for your responsibilities and the activities you do that revitalize you—work, kids, exercise, shopping, meditation, sports, reading, and crafts.

A Self-Quiz: What's Your Sizzle Quotient?

How do you use the time you have together, or make time to be together? Answer the questions of this quick self-quiz for a little insight into your time management skills.

1. It's Saturday night, and amazingly the kids are at overnights with their friends. Suddenly you and your partner have the house to yourselves. What do you do?

   a. Share a long, luxurious shower or bath. Put a thick quilt and pillows on the floor in front of the fireplace, light the candles, put on soft music, and indulge each other.

   b. Try new Kama Sutra unions in different locations around the house.

   c. Fall asleep together on the sofa while watching the late movie.

2. It's Monday morning, and you've awakened an hour before your alarm is set to go off. You roll against your partner and feel an unexpected surge of arousal. You …

   a. Gently wake your partner with kisses and caresses. What could be a more perfect way to start a new week!

   b. Whisper your partner's name to see if he or she wakes up. If so, you make love. If not, you curl against your partner and drift back to sleep.

   c. Roll away and go back to sleep for what's left of that last hour.

3. You have a regular date night with your partner and your tennis club decides to have an all-day tournament and evening dinner.

   a. You wouldn't think of mentioning changing the date and tell the club director you can't be there.

   b. You tell your partner you are sorry to miss your regular date night and ask to switch to another night.

   c. You forget to mention it to your partner and then start complaining about something else. A fight follows.

4. You've been turned on by your partner all week and have made several sly innuendoes that your partner hasn't picked up on.

   a. You tell your partner how attracted to him or her you've been and suggest that you have a Saturday night date to practice some positions from the Kama Sutra.

b. You complain to your partner that he or she is unresponsive.

c. You withdraw and hold your partner in contempt, thinking she or he has always been unavailable for sex.

5. You'd really like to make love, but you've got a hectic week and no time in sight to connect with your partner.

a. You say, "I want to make love with you and I just don't have the time I'd like to give to being with you. Can we have a quickie now and a longer time on Sunday morning?"

b. Have a quickie.

c. Dismiss the idea for lack of time.

6. The romantic weekend with your partner that you've been planning is just two days away. At a staff meeting, your boss asks you to step in for a colleague who has a family crisis and can't make a big presentation in a distant location.

a. You say sure, as long as the company will pay for your partner to accompany you.

b. You tell your boss you had plans for the weekend and you'll have to get back to her. Then you leave the meeting to call your partner to discuss the situation.

c. You pick up your travel voucher and stop on the way home to get a gift for your partner.

7. You and your partner are working opposite shifts and seldom share a day off.

a. You leave loving and suggestive notes for each other, occasionally surprise each other with shared meals, and plan loving liaisons that make the most of your limited time together.

b. You divide up chores and household responsibilities so you can spend as much of your shared time together as possible.

c. You both complain to your bosses and to each other about the unfairness of your situation.

Sutra Sayings

Husband and wife should not blame the other excessively when there is wrongdoing, but rather use gentle language in their rebukes. They should not scold each other in public or give each other sulking looks, but instead go to a place to be alone until feelings of kindness and generosity return.

If you have five or more As, you're hot! If you have five or more Bs, your flames could use a little fanning. And if you have five or more Cs, it's time to check your sexual pulse!

Letting the Kama Sutra Carry You Away

So you might be wondering, if you can't even find time for a quickie now, how on earth will you find time for lovemaking Kama Sutra style? Unfortunately, not even the Kama Sutra has a way to make more time. But it does have dozens of ways to help you make the most of the time you have together.

The problem with sex for the sake of sex, or the quickie as it's familiarly known to thousands of couples, is that it becomes more about getting it done and over with so you can get to sleep, so you can get on with your day, or because the kids are at the bedroom door—pick your favorite excuse. Not to say that these challenges are less than valid. Today's lifestyles, as we all know, are increasingly hectic. A quickie is itself sometimes a luxury.

If you are not present during lovemaking—whether quick or extended—your body and your mind may well be disengaged from each other. While your body strains toward orgasm, your mind may have wandered to unpaid bills or your grocery list or even the report waiting for you on your desk at work. You could be thinking about whether the kids are really asleep, whether you set the timer on the coffee maker, or if you locked the garage door. In the meantime, your body moves and responds and sweats and spasms but your soul is elsewhere.

Sex Kama Sutra style brings minds, bodies, and spirits into union.

(Hrana Janto)

Sex Kama Sutra style brings the body, mind, and spirit into contact and into shared focus. Yes, this takes more time than basic stimulation, tension, and release. But the dimension the Kama Sutra brings to sexual loving—being aware and present—changes your expectations. The union of your bodies is no longer just an exercise in sex but instead becomes an experience of intimate communion and sharing.

Kama Knowledge

Children were a very important aspect of relationships in ancient India. While it was the wife's responsibility to care for the children, the husband was expected to play with and entertain them. Most fathers in Vatsyayana's India were devoted and involved parents who took seriously their responsibilities to begin educating their children in the acquisition of the three values of life—dharma, artha, and kama. Middle- and upper-class families had trusted servants who functioned as nurses, much in the same fashion as modern-day nannies. This allowed parents to spend more time with each other as well as to participate in the many social activities expected of them according to caste and status in the community.

Do the Kama Sutra with Kids in the House?

It's hard to feel comfortable abandoning yourself to the throes—and sounds—of passion when in the back of your mind you're wondering if the kids can hear you. Young children are both curious and demanding—they want to know what you're doing, and they want your attention and presence. Older children, on the other hand, know enough to know what you're doing (even if you think they don't) and may feel uncomfortable and embarrassed about it.

Economy of space has become the defining characteristic of modern houses and apartments. Seldom do you find long hallways separating bedrooms. Larger accommodations may place the master bedroom suite on a different level or in a location somewhat distanced from the other bedrooms. But most homes are pretty efficient, which means rooms are close together. Sound may travel better than you'd like, especially at night. How do you let yourself go, Kama Sutra style, and still maintain the privacy you need and desire?

The best, though not always most practical, solution is to have bedrooms that are separated from each other by some distance. When this is not possible, try using various forms of "white noise" to create natural sound barriers. Fans and low music are common ways to do this, and have the added advantage of helping kids fall asleep. Draperies, carpets, and wall coverings can make rooms more attractive and can also absorb sounds.

Easier Said than Done?

Children, it seems, have a sort of radar that goes into high gear as soon as you start making love. Though sound asleep when you checked on them before tiptoeing into your bedroom and closing the door without even a click, your child cries or wails, "I need a drink!" just as things get hot and slippery.

If you're the parent who responds, it's difficult to maintain the momentum of the moment while you tend to your child's needs. The mommy or daddy part of you takes over (as it should), and you become nurturing and comforting. When you finally get back to bed, your sexual tension is pretty slack. The mood has cooled and threatens to slip away. Unfortunately, there aren't any easy answers for this—which is especially frustrating if you've carefully planned your nightcap for after the kids are asleep but before you both are too tired to play.

Sometimes you end up just snuggling and falling asleep. Though disappointing, this isn't necessarily a negative—you enjoyed intimate contact, and now share the warmth of sleeping in each other's arms. If you still feel like making love, there's no reason to abandon your desire. Just accept that it's changed. Even if your original passion has dimmed a bit, you can still get the fire going. Rather than trying to get back to where you were, head for the direction you want to go.

And let go of the idea that love play has to lead to intercourse! Holding, kissing, and fondling don't have to culminate in orgasm. Both men and women—when they don't feel sexually deprived—report that sex play without intercourse can be truly satisfying, especially when you both know that down the line your lovemaking will include intercourse.

> **Dr. Josie Suggests**
>
> When you're a parent, you're "on duty" all the time. Plan to spend a certain evening each week with your partner, and let your children know this is your special time together. Not only does this help you find time for each other, but it shows your children that this is a normal aspect of a loving adult relationship.

Handling the Inevitable Interruptions

There's nothing more disconcerting than to be deeply involved in the sexual pleasures of each other and suddenly feel or hear the presence of your child. The emotions that flood through you in the instant of recognition can leave you feeling panicked, embarrassed, and fearful. Take a deep breath. It happens to every parent, and it won't scar your children forever. Just stay calm.

When your child walks in on your lovemaking, resist the urge to yell at the child to get out. Instead, calmly but firmly tell your child this is private, and to please shut the door on the way out of your room. Later, talk with your child about the importance of respecting closed doors and address any concerns your child may have about what he or she saw. You don't need to go into great detail, though you do need to assure younger children that everything is fine and you were having fun, not being hurt. Sex, to young children, can look and sound violent.

The need to find privacy doesn't have to squelch spontaneity and your joy in the pleasures of sexual loving. It can become part of the adventure of making love. Planning your romantic trysts or clandestinely arranging to meet in another part of the house can add anticipation to the mix of sensations you're already feeling, making your union all the more exciting when it finally can take place.

CAUTION   Out of Touch

Stay calm when your child walks in on your lovemaking. Young children especially find it frightening to see their parents engaged in sex, believing they are hurting each other. Without yelling, ask your child to leave the room and shut the door, then talk with him or her later to address any fears or concerns. Let your child know you were enjoying and loving each other the way adults do.

Staying Lovers While Being Parents

Parenting is a time-and-a-half job. You're on duty roughly 14 hours each day, and on call for the remaining 12 hours. Well, 10, really, though it certainly feels like you need at least two more hours in the day to keep up. Most parents also work outside the home, crunching even more into those 24 hours. Time and energy are critical factors—you don't have enough of either.

Despite the challenges and pressures of everyday life, it's essential for the health of your relationship for you and your partner to remain lovers even as parenting consumes most of your attention. It's easy to overlook each other's needs when there are so many other demands to meet. You tend to assume your partner sees how busy you are, and can wait for his or her share of you.

Dr. Josie Suggests

Children need to know that sexuality is natural and normal. They are naturally curious about differences between your bodies and theirs, and about the changes that take place as they grow and develop. When your child asks a question about sex, just answer it. Give a simple answer to start, and get more detailed if your child keeps questioning.

Become proactive. Schedule dates with each other. Hire a sitter and get away, or arrange for your kids to spend the night with friends or relatives. If evenings are just too difficult, try meeting for lunch one day a week. Take walks together—it's good exercise, too. Each night talk as friends. Intimacy grows when you reveal your hopes, fears, and dreams to one another. This need not take a long time. Five minutes each with no need to respond other than "thanks." This goes a long way toward bridging the connection even in your busy life.

Encourage older children to use weekend mornings to exercise their independence by fixing their own breakfasts and finding activities to engage themselves, such as reading, playing quietly, or even watching a video or selected television programs. (Be sure to lay down clear and explicit ground rules to establish the necessary limits!) Then stay in bed for an extra hour or so. You can just cuddle and talk, or let passion take over.

Some partners are afraid to show that there is passion between them in front of the kids. While lovemaking ought to be private, it's important for your children to see their parents in loving contact. Remember, perceptions about what it means to be committed to loving another form very early in children and come from what they observe around them. Hugging, kissing, holding hands, and snuggling on the couch together are all ways that you can show your children that loving touches are among the many dimensions of marriage.

Restoring Compassion

A challenge for many couples is remembering how to relate to each other as friends. Though our relationships grow from a basis of friendship, we tend to feel once we become lovers, friendship doesn't matter so much any more. Not true! Numerous studies identify friendship as the single most important factor in determining whether a relationship will last. Yet most couples treat each other differently—usually with less kindness and compassion—than they treat their friends.

> ### Kama Knowledge
>
> The Kama Sutra contains dozens of recipes for potions and aphrodisiacs, some involving exotic ingredients. One such concoction mixes various powdered plant roots and monkey excrement, which, if applied to a woman, causes her to love only the man who applied it. Another boils together the seeds of several plants, the juices of other plants, and oils to make an ointment that, when rubbed on the lingam, causes it to stay enlarged for a month.

Here's an exercise to help you and your partner reconnect as friends. Choose one day a week when you can go to your bedroom after dinner and close the door. Tell the kids this is your time together, and the only acceptable interruption is a genuine emergency (wanting to know if there are more cookies in the cupboard doesn't qualify!). Then try the following steps.

Exercise: Talking as Friends

1. Taking 10-minute turns, talk without offering any feedback other than "thanks." During your turn, don't blame or criticize. Make it about you—your frustrations, joys, hopes, and dreams.

2. Kiss and cuddle, and touch without it leading to intercourse. Do not talk about money, kids, or work.

Stoke the Coals

A fire requires attention to keep it from dying out. Feeding it plenty of fuel keeps the flames hot and high. But a fire can't burn its hottest for long before burning itself out. It needs to cool down and smolder, to form the coals that can keep it burning indefinitely.

Passion is the same way. Lovemaking does its part for keeping passion hot. But after the fire flares, it needs to form the coals that will keep the passion alive. These coals are all the little things you do for each other that remind you of your love and commitment. When your desire rekindles your passion, those coals are hot and ready to again support the fire of your love.

You won't always be in the mood for sexual loving, of course, or able to take advantage of it when you are. But properly tended, your romance and passion will be there for you when you want to bask in its warmth and light.

The Least You Need to Know

- More than ever before, we ask that our partners be our lovers, helpmates, playmates, co-parents, best friends, and confidantes, as well as our equals.

- Few people have enough time to do all the things they want to do. What matters most is using the time you do have to support and nurture your relationship.

- Planning to make love helps you set aside time for each other. The anticipation of waiting to enjoy the pleasures of sexual loving can intensify your desire.

- Children need to see that sexuality is a natural dimension of adult relationships.

- The most powerful aphrodisiac is intimacy, which arises from regular sharing and communication.

Part 4

Bodies Beautiful

We have worshipped the human body since the beginning of human existence. Even primitive drawings in caves that were once home to our ancient ancestors detail human images engaged in various activities of everyday life, from hunting to making love. The ancient Hindu drawings of the Kama Sutra so beautifully evoke the mystery and power of sexual loving.

But how do our bodies work, and how can we use them to unleash the divine pleasure they contain? The chapters in this section take you on a tour of the male and female bodies, peeking into functions you may have only heard about in whispered locker room conversations. Your tour concludes with a look at what happens when bodies unite in sexual ecstasy.

Chapter 12

Her Body

In This Chapter

- ◆ The yoni myth
- ◆ Getting to know your body: a self-quiz
- ◆ Understanding the woman's body and how it works
- ◆ The Kama Sutra's three yonis

In Hindu mythology, Yoni is the mother-goddess. Hers is the kingdom of fertility and creativity. The lotus flower in full bloom, a powerful symbol of life, death, and rebirth (the lotus blossom opens with the sunrise and closes at sunset), often represents her. The lotus also symbolizes knowledge and compassion.

In Tantric systems such as the Kama Sutra, a woman's genitalia are known collectively as the *yoni*. Much Hindu art overlays the image of the lotus onto the image of a woman with her legs spread wide. This depiction honors the yoni as the portal from spiritual existence to human being. Through it the seeds of new life enter, and the form of a new person returns.

Femininity, Fertility, and the Kama Sutra

Ancient India revered fertility. Sexual union, while certainly a pleasure worth indulging solely for enjoyment and intimacy, had a greater mission—to join the seed of the man and the seed of the woman to create another life. Procreation was an essential dimension of a person's divine mission in his or her earthly existence. Failing to produce new life meant failing to fulfill this mission. This had serious ramifications for the afterlife.

In the Eastern view, the sexual union that produced a child strongly influenced the child's physical and emotional make-up. Vatsyayana and his contemporaries believed that a child conceived during a sexual union of great passion and love between the partners received the best of its parents' genetic material. Such a child would have a strong body and a strong soul, and was destined for a happy and fruitful existence. On the other hand, a child conceived from an unemotional union received hereditary dregs and would have a weak existence.

Sutrology

In Sanskrit, yoni means womb. In common usage, **yoni** typically refers to the collective female genitalia.

The Kama Sutra honors the yoni, the female genitalia, as the portal from spiritual existence to human being; it is the gateway of life.

(Hrana Janto)

By exerting every effort to make sexual union joyous and pleasurable, the man and woman demonstrated their commitment to this divine mission. Their success meant a happy and prosperous existence in this life as well as in the next.

A Self-Quiz: How Well Do You Know Your (or Her) Body?

Most of us believe we know our bodies pretty well. And if you've been making love to the same body for a long time, you probably feel you know that body pretty well, too. Here's a quick self-quiz to see how much you really know. Choose the correct answer from the options.

1. The clitoris is one of the most highly sensitive parts of a woman's genitalia.

    True_____   False _____

2. A woman can ejaculate during orgasm.

    True_____   False _____

3. It takes about 15 minutes, at a minimum, to arouse a woman to orgasm.

    True_____   False _____

4. Some women just can't have orgasms.

    True_____   False _____

5. Large breasts are better than small breasts for breastfeeding.

    True_____   False _____

6. Sexual intercourse during menstruation causes cramps and increased bleeding.

    True_____   False _____

7. There are certain times during a woman's monthly cycle when there is no way she can become pregnant.

    True_____   False _____

Let's see how well you know the female body. Here are the correct answers.

1. **True.** The clitoris could well be called the organ of orgasm (the ancient Chinese called it the "pleasure place"). But this doesn't mean it's an orgasm switch or button that when touched instantly ignites the flames of passion. The clitoris is extremely sensitive, and must be handled with great care. Men: Think of the clitoris as a small and *very* sensitive penis.

2. **True.** Though still controversial, research shows that the fluid a woman ejaculates in orgasm is chemically closer to seminal fluid than urine and probably functions as additional lubrication. Female ejaculate is usually odorless and evaporates quickly. In ancient India people believed that drinking a woman's ejaculate was life-enhancing.

3. **True** for many women, and many women would prefer even longer love play to intensify the climax.

4. **False.** Every woman can reach orgasm. Most women who don't are not receiving enough, or the right kind of, stimulation. It's important to share with your partner what feels good and how long you want it to continue. It takes practice to understand each other's needs and desires.

5. **False.** The size of your breasts has little to do with whether you can successfully breastfeed, or for that matter receive pleasure from having your partner stimulate your breasts. A woman whose nipples are deeply inverted (poke in instead of out) may have difficulty nursing because the baby may have trouble getting a good "lock" on the nipple. And some women who've had cosmetic or reconstructive breast surgery may have damaged milk ducts, which would keep the breast from making enough milk. But size is not an issue.

6. **False.** In fact, the opposite is more likely to be true, particularly if you reach orgasm. Sexual stimulation increases the flow of blood into the tissues of the pelvic area, helping to relax the muscles (including the uterus). This relieves cramping and allows the menstrual flow to leave the body more freely.

7. **False.** This would be true only for a woman who's had a tubal ligation or hysterectomy and can no longer become pregnant. For a fertile woman, there is no such thing as a safe time.

Kama Knowledge

The controversy around whether or not women ejaculate during orgasm has settled in favor of saying the copious fluids ejected during a woman's orgasm, often with great force, constitute female ejaculation. The origin of these fluids is still not clear, but they are expelled through the urethra, which led to the misconception that the woman is urinating during orgasm. Like urine only in that it is carried through the same organ, the composition of a woman's ejaculate is unique and unlike either urine or the other lubricating fluids her body makes during arousal and orgasm. Women report that orgasm coupled with ejaculation is particularly intense and pleasurable.

Yoni and Company: Female Body Parts and How They Work

Tantric systems view the yoni as the container for the energy of Shakti, the yin force. The core or center of this energy resides inside the yoni, in the area we call the G-spot. Love play awakens the Shakti, which then grows in force and intensity until it culminates in the ecstasy of orgasm. Rather than viewing sexual loving as a function of physiology, the Tantric perspective integrates body and energy.

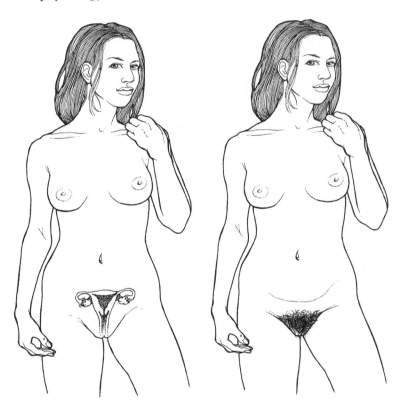

The energy of Shakti, the yin force, lies in the female reproductive organs.

In Western terms, the female sexual organs reside in the woman's lower abdomen. The cornerstone of their structure is the uterus, a hollow muscular organ that sits like an upside-down pear just above the pubic bone. To each side are short tissue stems at the end of which bloom the ovaries, which produce both eggs and hormones. A fallopian tube hangs down from the upper corners of the uterus, one for each side, to channel an egg into the uterus. At the bottom of the uterus are the cervix and the vagina. In combination, these organs make both sex and reproduction possible.

Ovaries, Eggs, and Fallopian Tubes

The ovaries are two rather small glands, a little over an inch long in an adult woman, located one on each side in the lower abdomen. A baby girl starts her life with the full complement of eggs, or ova, that she'll have as an adult—nearly two million between both ovaries, though fewer than 300 ova will ever be released and have the potential to produce new life.

Each month after a woman reaches sexual maturity, the ovary releases a ripened egg. Barely visible to the naked eye at the size of a pinpoint, the egg floats into the abdominal cavity. Fingerlike extensions sway gently at the opening of the fallopian tube, ushering the egg into the channel that will take it into the uterus.

If sperm have managed to make their way as far as the fallopian tube by the time the egg gets there, conception takes place. A single (usually) sperm penetrates the tough outer core of the egg, fertilizing the egg and initiating the sequence of events that will eventually produce a baby. The fertilized egg proceeds up the fallopian tube and into the uterus, where it burrows into the blood-rich uterine wall.

If there are no sperm present, or fertilization fails to take place, the solitary ovum continues its now futile journey. Rather than settling in for a nine-month stay, the unfertilized egg keeps going. It takes with it the thickened lining of the uterus, now also without a purpose. The body flushes this residue out through the vagina to clean house for the next cycle.

The ovaries also produce the hormones that give a woman her sexual characteristics and make the entire cycle of fertility possible in the first place—estrogen and progesterone. (More on hormones a little later in this chapter.)

The female reproductive organs.

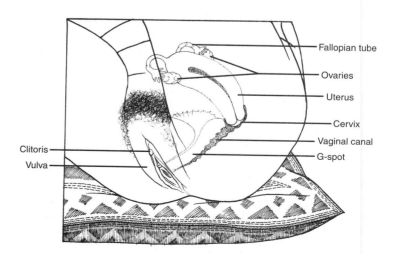

Uterus and Cervix

The pear-shaped uterus lies in the lower abdomen, just above the pubic bone, between the bladder in the front and the bowel in the back. Broad side up, the rounded top of the uterus tips forward slightly. In a woman who's not pregnant, the uterus is about the size of a fist—3 inches or so long—and weighs 2 to 3 ounces.

A hollow muscle, the uterus can expand to nearly 100 times its original size during pregnancy. When pregnancy reaches full term and it is time for the baby to meet its parents, the bulked-up uterus propels its contents into the birth canal with tremendous force.

A rich, soft layer of tissue, the endometrium, carpets the interior of the uterus, presenting a nurturing environment for a prospective tenant such as a newly fertilized egg. The endometrium thickens in anticipation. If there is no fertilized egg, the excess tissue sloughs off and leaves the body as the menstrual period.

At the base of the uterus, where the stem would be on an upside-down pear, is the cervix. It's rather like a muscular passageway controlling the opening between the vagina and the uterus. Except during childbirth, this opening, called the *cervical os,* is no larger than the tip of a ballpoint pen. During childbirth, powerful contractions pull the cervix open to a diameter of about 4 inches so the baby can pass through. It then returns to its normal size, which is just large enough to allow menstrual flow to leave the uterus or semen to enter.

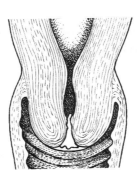

The cervix at its normal size, just large enough to allow menstrual flow to leave the uterus or semen to enter.

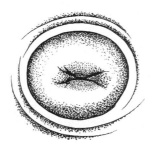

Mucus coats the cervix, serving two purposes. One is to keep the cervix from drying out. The other is to create either a welcoming or a hostile environment for sperm. The type of environment depends on hormonal activity throughout the menstrual cycle. Sperm can still penetrate the cervical os when the hormonal conditions are less than ideal, even during menstruation when many women assume sex is "safe." Though pregnancy is highly unlikely when adverse conditions exist in the cervix, it can still occur. An ovulating, fertile woman should always consider the possibility of pregnancy, no matter where she is in her menstrual cycle when she has sex.

> **Sutrology**
>
> The **cervical os** is the opening in the cervix and literally means "mouth of the neck." **Mucus** is a slippery, somewhat thick fluid that sensitive internal tissues secrete to keep themselves moist. A **pap smear** is the collection of cells scraped from the cervix that is examined under a microscope for signs of cancer.

When the ovary releases an egg, this sends a chemical signal that causes the woman's body to alter the proportion of estrogen and progesterone. Though the balance shifts ever so slightly, it is enough to initiate a series of changes in preparation for a potential pregnancy. The cervical mucus thins, making it easier for sperm to get through the cervical os.

Though the cervix isn't particularly sensitive to the touch (which is why your gynecologist can take a *pap smear* without sending you through the ceiling), it does respond to pressure. Too much pressure, such as can occur with deep penetration during sexual intercourse, can be painful.

Vagina and Vulva

The vagina is a muscular channel leading from the cervix to the outside. From a Latin word meaning "sheath," the vagina varies from about 2½ to 4 inches in length. The vagina's muscular walls have ridges and a rich supply of blood and nerves. At rest, the walls of the vagina touch each other. When a woman is sexually aroused, the vagina's walls engorge with blood. This both intensifies their sensitivity (particularly near the opening) and causes them to pull open.

> **Sutra Sayings**
>
> Passion and desire cause the man and woman to seek sexual union. The pleasure they experience from being present and consciously enjoying each other is what becomes their ultimate satisfaction.

During arousal, the walls of the vagina secrete a clear fluid that provides lubrication for the penetrating penis. (Two sets of glands located near the vagina's opening, Bartholin's and Skene's glands, also produce a lubricating secretion.) Certain areas of the vaginal wall are highly sensitive in many women (what Westerners call the G-spot), the stimulation of which can lead to intense pleasure and orgasm. Located on the front wall of the vagina, generally about three inches inside, the G-spot is an area of sensitivity more so than an anatomical structure.

Kama Knowledge

Named after Ernst Grafenberg, the German gynecologist who first described it, the G-spot seems to be a cluster of nerve cells buried deep within the vaginal wall that responds to pressure. Because the G-spot is close to the urethra, stimulation causes some women to feel an urge to urinate. Most women experience intense arousal with G-spot stimulation that produces deep, full body orgasm, though some feel discomfort or even nothing special at all. Pleasure generally intensifies as arousal heightens. Postures of sexual union in which the lingam rubs against the G-spot can give the woman great pleasure, especially when thrusting slows to allow more extended pressure. Many women enjoy having their partners rub the G-spot during oral lovemaking as well.

Despite the perceptions of ancient Indian lovers, the vagina is extraordinarily flexible and can pleasurably welcome a variety of penis shapes and sizes. The vagina is also the birth canal. During delivery, it stretches, flexes, and contracts to help push the baby through. Following birth, it returns to its usual size.

Just inside the entrance to the vagina is a small circle of tissue that has achieved an odd fame (some would say infamy) through the centuries, the hymen. Why this membrane flap exists is anyone's guess—it doesn't appear to have any anatomical or physiological function. In young girls, the hymen often has a small opening.

Kama Knowledge

In ancient Greek mythology, Hymen was the god of weddings. He was rumored to be the son of Apollo and the muse Calliope. As a young man, Hymen rescued a group of women taken captive by pirates. Among them was the woman he loved, and as a reward for his efforts the gods gave the woman to him in marriage. Hymen and his beloved lived happily ever after. The word *hymn* as we use it today evolved from the Greek word *hymnos*, which means "wedding song."

Tradition has long viewed the hymen as irrefutable evidence of a woman's virginity. It's long been believed that only a penetrating penis could alter the hymen. While it's true first intercourse can and often does tear or stretch the hymen, we now know various events can cause this opening to enlarge—from inserting tampons to horseback riding, bicycling, and other strenuous physical activities.

Many women do experience slight bleeding and even pain with their first sexual unions, as the hymen further stretches or tears. Others do not. Once stretched or torn, the hymen becomes just another little flap of tissue.

"Vulva," from the Latin word for womb, refers collectively to the tissues just outside the vagina, also known as the external genitalia. These include the mons veneris, labia majora and labia minora, clitoris, and perineum.

CAUTION

Out of Touch

A medical condition called vaginismus, in which the muscles around the vagina spasm and contract involuntarily, can make sexual intercourse very painful or even impossible. There are various causes for vaginismus, including infections and psychological trauma. Medical evaluation nearly always leads to successful treatment.

The mons veneris is the soft pad of tissue over the pubic bone, from which the pubic hairline starts. The fleshy, liplike folds that extend from the mons to the perineum (the area between the vagina and anus), surrounding the vaginal opening, are the labia. The outer pair is the labia majora, which serve to protect the more highly sensitive labia minora beneath them and also to secrete fluids for lubrication during sexual arousal. The labia minora, which lead to the vaginal opening, join just below the mons veneris to form a protective covering over the clitoris called the clitoral hood.

The vulva.

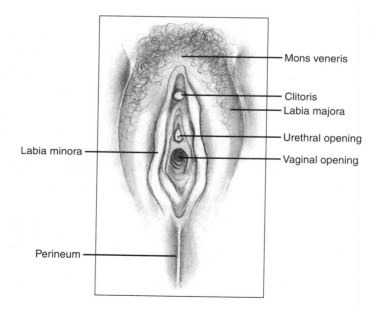

The clitoris is a small organ that's quite literally a bundle of nerves. So extremely sensitive that it spends most of its time hooded, the clitoris has an exclusive mission: sexual arousal. Stimulating the clitoris typically produces orgasm, though some women find direct contact to be too intense to be pleasurable, particularly in the early stages of love play. The clitoris contains erectile tissue similar to that found in the penis, and swells when aroused.

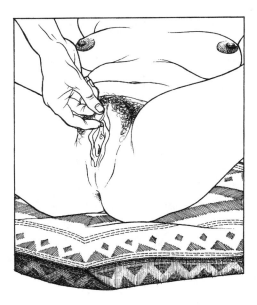

To explore the clitoris, first lubricate your own or your partner's clitoris with oil or a water-based lube. Then gently begin to touch the clitoris and the shaft. Breathe and relax as you receive the touch. Pay attention to what places are the most pleasurable. Many women find that one side or the other (10 o'clock or 2 o'clock on the clitoral shaft) has a place that feels great.

Breasts

Medically speaking, breasts are mostly fatty tissue. They come in an endless variety of shapes and sizes. Many women notice that one breast is slightly larger (or smaller, depending on your perspective) than the other. Other breast tissue includes the nipple, areola, and milk ducts.

Breasts really serve two purposes. One is purely functional—they provide nutritional sustenance for babies. Large breasts are not necessarily any better than small breasts for breast-feeding—it's one of the many miracles of the human body that breasts generally can meet their functional obligations regardless of size.

Breasts are also sexually arousing. Many women find it pleasurable to have their breasts stroked, kissed, sucked, and caressed, and nipples lightly bitten. The partner doing this usually finds it arousing, too. (Such actions are among the elements of sexual loving the Kama Sutra presents as pleasures for both partners to enjoy in the early stages of loveplay.) Some women have large nipples and small breasts, others have large breasts with small nipples. Nipples and the skin around them, the areola, can be dark or light in color, and not very or highly sensitive.

CAUTION **Out of Touch**

The sudden appearance of lumps, dimples, or discoloration in a breast can be a sign of cancer or other health problems. If you notice something suddenly different about your breasts, follow up with your doctor immediately.

The breast is both an organ of sexual arousal for women and men, and of nutritional sustenance for their babies.

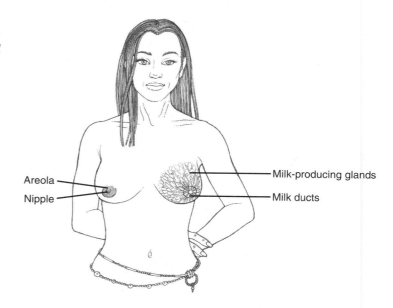

Areola

Nipple

Milk-producing glands

Milk ducts

Breasts change. They change during a woman's monthly cycle, in response to changing hormones. They may become tender and even a bit swollen just before your period. They change during pregnancy, as they prepare to nourish and sustain the life within after its birth. Nursing breasts change even more, enlarging as the milk ducts go into full production mode. And breasts change after menopause, when the body's hormone levels again shift.

It's important to become familiar with the normal changes of your breasts, so you can detect changes that are not normal. Some changes may signal a need to see the doctor, since they can be signs of infection or cancer.

The Mystical, Magical Orgasm

Orgasm is an intricate combination of physiological and emotional reactions that lead to an intensely pleasurable release of sexual tension. Every woman experiences orgasm differently, and each woman may experience different kinds of orgasms. Many women have multiple orgasms during a session of sexual loving.

Clinically speaking, orgasm is a release of sexual tension that occurs when the nerve endings of sensitive body parts such as the clitoris, G-spot area, and breasts are so stimulated that they cause involuntary muscle spasms. A woman can feel an orgasm just in her pelvic region or throughout her body. How extensive the feeling gets depends on the intensity of sexual peaks of tension that develop during lovemaking, and the ability to relax and allow the pleasure to build and spread throughout her body.

Women who have difficulty reaching orgasm may be unknowingly tense during love-making, preventing sexual pleasure from building to the peak where it begins to discharge. Sometimes a woman doesn't know quite what it would take to bring her to orgasm, or is afraid to ask her partner for specific stimulation. Sometimes her partner doesn't know she hasn't reached orgasm, because either she doesn't tell or she leads her partner to believe she's satisfied.

This is a distinctly Western view of sexual pleasure. In the Eastern view, each partner pays close attention to the other's arousal. Partners also guide each other in pleasuring, so the love play is mutually and deeply satisfying. The Eastern view emphasizes joy and pleasure over climax. Rather than orgasm being the goal of sexual loving, it becomes yet another dimension of lovemaking.

Dr. Josie Suggests

Remember the sensory exercises in Chapter 4? Now that you know more about your body's parts, go back and try the exercises again. Watch your body, and your partner's, as you enjoy pleasuring each other. Talk with each other about what you like and what feels good. This will help you identify and describe what you want when you make love.

Deer, Mare, and Elephant: The Three Yonis

The Kama Sutra shows that ancient Indian lovers had a pretty thorough understanding of how things worked. Vatsyayana and other writers keenly observed that deep arousal made sexual union both pleasurable and possible. What could not be done with unprepared organs, Vatsyayana observes, became most desired when arousal was strong.

Though scientific knowledge of the body's inner organs and their workings was fairly limited in ancient cultures, curious couples did quite a bit of exploring to understand the parts within their reach. They astutely observed variations in both female and male genitalia. Ancient India classified women into three types according to yoni depth and style (the corresponding types of men are discussed in the next chapter):

◆ The **deer** or **doe** is a woman of slight build and gentle temperament. The deer yoni is narrow and not very deep, and best accommodates a man who is a hare (whose erect lingam (Hindu word for the erect penis) measures six finger-widths in length, or about 3 inches).

◆ The **mare** is a woman of sturdy build, with a flare to her appearance and personality. The mare yoni is full and sensuous, best suited for a man who is a bull (erect lingam measures eight finger-widths in length, or about 4 inches).

◆ The **elephant** woman is tall and large-boned, with a ruddy complexion and harmonious demeanor. The elephant yoni is cavernous and deep, best able to enjoy a man who is a stallion (erect lingam measures 12 finger-widths in length, or about 6 inches).

Sutra Sayings

When love play begins, the woman does not desire and cannot accept vigorous penetration. As her passion increases, she thinks no more about her body and willingly, even eagerly, accepts her lover's thrusts.

Vatsyayana strongly recommends, consistent with the beliefs of his contemporaries, that the most satisfying sexual unions are those that take place between matched types—deer with hare, mare with bull, elephant with stallion. The ancient sage also astutely observes that people aren't always attracted to others who are perfect matches (anatomically speaking). The Kama Sutra describes a number of sexual unions intended to accommodate unequal matches.

Female Hormones: What They Are and What They Do

The human body, through the action of the endocrine system, produces dozens of chemical substances called hormones. Hormones regulate hundreds of specific body functions from metabolism to sexual development. The ovaries produce the key female hormones, estrogen and progesterone. The adrenal glands, located above the kidneys, and the placenta in a woman who is pregnant also produce estrogen.

The female endocrine system.

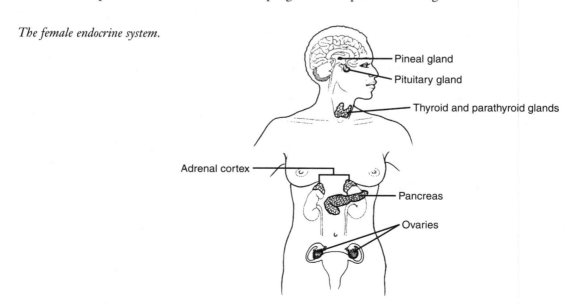

Pineal gland
Pituitary gland
Thyroid and parathyroid glands
Adrenal cortex
Pancreas
Ovaries

Most women identify female hormones with the menstrual cycle. Changing hormone levels cause the uterus to build up its lining (when estrogen levels rise) and then shed it (when estrogen levels drop). Some women dread their periods, while others welcome them as affirmation of their femininity.

Hormones also take the blame for the mood swings some women experience during their menstrual cycles. While there isn't much you can do to alter your hormones (unless a doctor tells you there is a medical problem), you can make life a little easier for yourself by cutting back on sugars, salt, caffeine, and alcohol if these substances are part of your diet.

While some women (and their partners) don't feel much like enjoying sex during their periods, there's no reason not to. It can be a pleasurable and loving experience. The tissues of the vagina are somewhat swollen during menstruation, which provides a different sensation for both woman and man during intercourse.

Arousal and orgasm often relieve cramping and muscle tension by increasing the flow of blood to the vagina and other structures. In the Kama Sutra, Vatsyayana advises couples to avoid positions of deep penetration, as these could cause the woman pain.

In ancient cultures, menstruation was closely linked with fertility and was viewed as a special time. During her period, a woman was treated with extra kindness and caring. After her period, a woman was considered renewed and refreshed. In the Tantric view, a menstruating woman is in a place of existence between the earthly and the heavenly worlds.

> **CAUTION**
>
> **Out of Touch**
>
> Don't skip the birth control just because you're having your period. Though unlikely, it is possible to become pregnant even during menstruation if there is still an egg in the fallopian tube. Menstruation does not prevent sexually transmitted diseases (STDs), either. (See Chapter 15 for more on STDs.)

Loving Her

The erotic sentiment in the East paid attention to the woman's rhythms, cycles, responses, and emotions. The teachings of the Kama Sutra indicate that Vatsyayana understood well how fulfilling a woman's pleasure was important to the whole family. In the East there is a saying that comes from China. When the small river of yin flows (the lubricating juices and ejaculate that flow from a sexually fulfilled woman) the couple's union is happy. When the medium river of yin flows, the family is harmonious. And when the great river of yin flows from the woman, the entire community is blessed. In the West, we have had things turned around. Until recently, the emphasis was set on a man meeting his sexual needs and the woman was there in service to him. Then the tables turned and she was entitled to an orgasm. Now, we know that her response and way to orgasm is a longer, slower road than his. A woman takes longer to reach fulfillment and her capacity for pleasure is unlimited. She can go from peak to peak of pleasure for as long as she likes.

Granted, this can be daunting for a man who is focused on the goal of bringing his partner to orgasm so he can then have his. The idea of giving pleasure to a woman whose capacity is unlimited can be intimidating to the uninitiated. A woman's capacity to continue to orgasm after the first release, experiencing wave after wave of pleasure and opening, is unlike anything men who have not themselves experienced multiple orgasms have known. A deeply satisfied woman is like a vessel that, when full, spills over ever so generously, and gives back to her partner abundantly.

The Least You Need to Know

- Every woman's body, though similar in design, is unique.

- Partners need to communicate with each other about what they find pleasurable.

- Eastern cultures honor and revere the feminine.

- A fulfilled woman is a generous woman.

His Body

In This Chapter

- The mythology of the lingam
- Getting to know your body: a self-quiz
- Understanding the man's body and how it works
- The three kinds of lingams according to the Kama Sutra

In the beginning, according to ancient Hindu mythology, there was Shiva, the god of all-being. Shiva holds the opposite pole of his partner and lover, the feminine principle Shakti. All powerful, Shiva created and ruled the air, water, wind, fire, earth, sun, moon, and cosmic spirit. Shiva is India's foremost deity and worshipped most often in the form of a "lingam." Because they are of Shiva's creation, all men contain these same eight elements. The lingam symbolizes Shiva's power as the creator of all existence.

Today, throughout India's cities and villages are shivlinga—literally, Shiva's lingam—of every size imaginable. Fresh flowers and ocher powder are reverentially placed around Shiva's lingam in a demonstration of the sacredness that still surrounds this deity.

Masculinity, Virility, and the Kama Sutra

In the Tantric teachings, the *lingam*, or *phallus*, is the source of all life. In most Hindu art, the lingam takes a symbolic phallic shape that bears little resemblance to an actual erect penis. When appearing on a figure, the lingam is often the dominant and disproportionately large feature, symbolizing its power and potency. Many sculptures present the lingam alone, honoring the symbolism of the organ's life-giving power. Other art shows the lingam and the yoni together, symbolizing their interdependent nature.

The Kama Sutra honors the lingam and yoni: the life-giving power of the male genitalia and the gateway to life of the female genitalia.

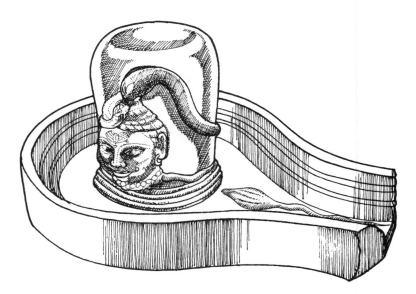

The time and society of the Kama Sutra were male oriented. Men owned property, established careers to bring them wealth and status, and participated in civic activities. Men were the merchants, teachers, priests, scholars, and rulers. All men of class, regardless of occupation or wealth, were expected to be well educated in the arts and sciences, in the religious doctrines, and in the teachings of the Kama Sutra.

Underlying all other expectations was a reverence and respect for women and the feminine. Eastern cultures such as Hindu, as you remember from earlier chapters, believe every person, man or woman, is neither purely yang (male) nor purely yin (female). Rather, their existence requires the presence of both

Sutrology

Lingam is the Hindu term for the penis, usually referring to the male organ in its erect state. A **phallus** is a symbolic and often stylized representation of the erect penis. It comes from the same Greek root as does the word "blow," meaning to flare.

yang and yin within the individual. In the East, as you recall, sexuality was not simply about procreation and pleasure—it could be a vehicle to self-realization as well. The sex act can be a way to balance the masculine (yang) and the feminine (yin) energies.

This foundation established a unique social structure for a male-dominated, or patriarchal, culture. Though men technically had all the rights and power, they could not become complete beings (as their Hindu beliefs required them to strive to achieve) without women. Though this wasn't quite equity between the sexes as the Western world of today might view it, it was considerably more so than what existed in Sir Richard Burton's society when he translated the Kama Sutra for the West in the early 1800s.

A Self-Quiz: How Well Do You Know Your (or His) Body?

You spend a lot of time with your body, and you probably think you know it pretty well. But do you know yourself (or your partner) as well as you think? Take this short self-quiz to see. Choose whether each statement is true or false.

1. A man's most erotic body part is the glans.

   True_____   False _____

2. A man can have an orgasm without ejaculating.

   True_____   False _____

3. A man can go from flaccid to ejaculation in three minutes.

   True_____   False _____

4. The larger the erection, the more pleasurable the sexual loving.

   True_____   False _____

5. A man doesn't need much participation from his partner to have a sexually satisfying experience.

   True_____   False _____

6. The only stimulation that fully arouses a man involves his penis.

   True_____   False _____

7. It's possible for a man to maintain an erection for an hour or longer.

   True_____   False _____

Well, let's see how well you can separate fact from fiction. Here are the correct answers:

1. **False.** While the glans is highly sensitive, a small area just below it, the frenulum, is even more so.

2. **True.** Orgasm and ejaculation, though they most often happen in tandem, are independent functions.

3. **True.** Not the most pleasurable experience he can have, to be sure, but certainly possible (and sadly common when partners don't know there are other options).

4. **False.** Love play and arousal contribute the most to sexual pleasure. There are sexual positions to provide pleasure for just about any combination of sizes.

5. **False.** You might think this after #3, but the most pleasurable sexual loving for either partner takes place when both participate, with full awareness and presence, in making love.

6. **False.** Though certainly the penis is highly sensitive, a man's body reacts erotically to kissing, stroking, caressing, and embracing literally all over.

7. **True.** The longer a man delays ejaculation, the longer he can maintain an erection—and enjoy sexual loving.

Lingam and Company: Male Body Parts and How They Work

As the vessel that carries the seed of new life, the lingam is a divine instrument that is not to be used carelessly or wastefully. To honor and respect the lingam is to honor and respect Shiva, the god of all-being.

Sutrology

Ejaculation is a reflex action in which rhythmic muscle contractions propel semen through the urethra and out the opening of the penis.

Tantric teachings view the lingam as the essence of Shiva, the yang force and the god of all being. Love play arouses the lingam, which swells and grows as it fills with the power of creation. The *ejaculation* that releases this power should result from thoughtful, passionate sexual loving. Because in the Eastern view lovemaking's ultimate mission is the creation of new life, sexual union provides both ecstatic release and a necessary step toward procreation. Ejaculation ejects not just physical material but also spiritual essence.

The male sex organs reside in the lower abdomen, at the base of the pelvis. The most prominent of them, the penis and the testicles, are outside the body. Internally are the prostate gland, a pair of Cowper's glands, and a pair of seminal vesicles. Linking internal with external are the urethra and the vas deferens. The urethra is a shared channel for both urine and semen (one or the other, not both at the same time). The tubelike vas deferens runs from the seminal vesicles to the testicles.

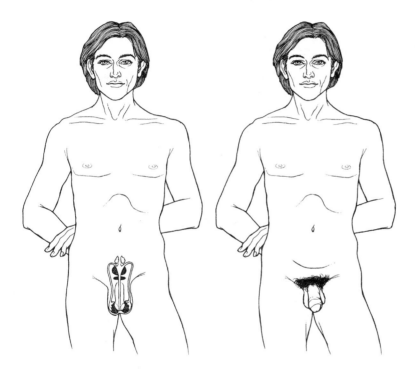

The energy of Shiva, the yang force, lies in the male reproductive organs.

Glands, Vesicles, and Urethra

The prostate gland is within the man's pelvic cavity, at the base of the urinary bladder. About the size and shape of a chestnut, it wraps around and connects to the urethra. The prostate gland's mission is to produce the secretions that contribute to semen. Some men enjoy having the prostate gland stimulated, either from the outside by firm pressure against the perineum (the area in front of the anus extending to the scrotum) or from within the rectum via anal penetration.

As a man gets older, the prostate gland typically enlarges. No one really knows why this happens—it doesn't work any harder or produce any greater volume of semen. This isn't a problem unless it interferes with urination by compressing the urethra.

Cowper's glands, located below the prostate, produce the fluid that appears at the tip of the penis during sexual arousal but before ejaculation. Though mostly semen, it can and often does contain some sperm. The seminal vesicles, a small pair of saclike glands above the prostate, produce most of the fluid that becomes semen.

The urethra does double duty as the conduit that carries both urine and semen out of the body. It passes through the prostate gland and into the penis. Except when a man is sexually aroused, the passage to the urethra from the bladder remains open. In the stages of arousal preceding ejaculation, a small valve closes to keep urine from entering the urethra and semen from passing into the bladder.

The vas deferens is another conduit in the male reproductive system. During ejaculation, it siphons sperm from the testicles into the body and up through the prostate gland where the sperm joins the semen. At this point the ejaculate enters the urethra.

The male reproductive organs.

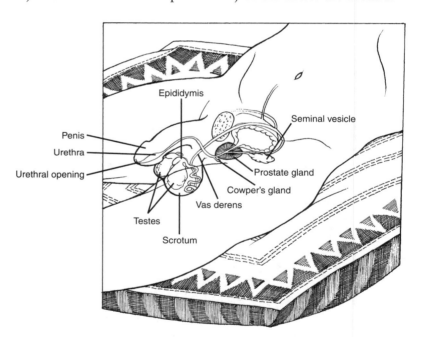

Sperm and Semen

Semen is the fluid of procreation. On this, East and West agree. The milky liquid transports sperm, which, when deposited near the cervix with a little help from the lingam, carries one-half of the genetic material to begin a new life. When the male seed joins with the female seed, the two halves become a new whole.

Many people are confused about the difference between *sperm* and semen. Think of them as seed and stream—the stream (semen) speeds the seed (sperm) to its destination. It is possible for a man's ejaculate to contain only semen and no sperm, as happens after a vasectomy. The semen/sperm mixture is sometimes called "ejaculate," because ejaculation is the means by which it leaves the man's body.

Sperm cells are visible only under a microscope. They have bulbous heads and hairlike tails, giving them a tadpoleish appearance. The head contains genetic material and a small supply of nutrients to sustain the sperm on its arduous journey through the yoni. The tail provides propulsion, whipping furiously to push the sperm through the vaginal fluids and cervical mucous.

> **Sutrology**
>
> **Semen** is the fluid of a man's ejaculation. It contains liquids produced by the prostate gland and seminal vessicles. It also contains a form of sugar called fructose, which causes the sperm to become active. **Sperm** are the cells carrying the male's genetic material.

Though it takes only one sperm to unite with the woman's egg, each ejaculation from a fertile man contains 80 to 150 million sperm. Fertilization is truly a scenario of all for one—the majority of those millions of sperm die to create a more hospitable environment for the relative few that make it as far as the woman's fallopian tube.

Semen comes from various locations within the man's reproductive system. The primary contributors are the seminal vesicles (70 percent), prostate gland (25 percent), and Cowper's glands (5 percent). Its function, in addition to carrying the sperm, is to create a pH-balanced environment as it transports sperm from the man's testicles to the woman's vagina.

In the Eastern view, semen contains not just biological building blocks but also the seed of a new soul. The soul's need to become a new being spurs the drive of erotic desire, seeking to send the semen on its quest to find and merge with the seed of the woman.

Testicles and Scrotum

Behind the penis is a pouch of tissue called the scrotum. The two testicles hang suspended within its protective covering. The testicles produce testosterone, the male sex hormone. They also produce sperm, a process that requires the testicles to be about 5 degrees cooler than the body's usual temperature. The muscles of the scrotum contract or relax to move the testicles closer to or further from body heat.

It takes about 72 hours for the testicles to manufacture sperm. Once they're mature, the sperm move to a holding area called the epididymis. Though it resembles a wad of rubber bands or string, the epididymis is really a very long, very thin, tightly coiled tube. Sperm can live in these temporary quarters for about six weeks. After that, they begin to deteriorate and are reabsorbed into the body as proteins, to be replaced by fresh sperm.

Many men like to have their testicles caressed, squeezed, and otherwise stimulated during love play. The testicles also swell during sexual arousal, and pull up tight against the body.

Penis

The tubular structure of the penis contains three cylindrical chambers, the corpus cavernosa, that fill with blood when a man is sexually aroused. This causes the penis to stiffen and swell into an erection. The tissues of the penis are somewhat spongelike, and also fill with blood during an erection. This gives the penis the rigidity it needs to penetrate the woman's vagina.

The smooth head of the penis is called the glans. The glans is highly sensitive, with nearly as many nerve endings as the fingertips. The opening in the top of the glans, which looks like a small slit, is where the urethra exits. It carries either urine or semen from the body. The urethra runs lengthwise through the penis, sheathed within penile tissue that extends along the interior of the perineum.

The penis becomes rigid to enter the woman's vagina.

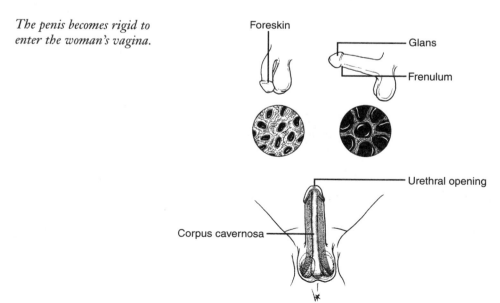

In an uncircumcised man, a rounded hood of skin called the foreskin covers the glans when the penis is relaxed. When the penis is erect, the foreskin retracts to expose the glans. A circumcised man has had his foreskin surgically removed, often in infancy. In terms of sexual performance, either works just fine as long as the foreskin of the uncircumcised penis moves freely.

When flaccid (nonerect), the penis ranges in length from 2 to 4 inches, measured from the tip of the glans to the base of the penis, and roughly one inch in diameter. An erect penis ranges in length from 5 to 7 inches, with 6 or 6½ being about average, and swells to about 1½ inches thick.

There is considerable variation in penis size, however—both in length and diameter. Some penises are long and skinny, others are short and thick. Some penises curve to one side or the other. Just as breasts vary widely among women, penises differ greatly among men.

CAUTION

Out of Touch

Partners, take your cues from your man when it comes to pleasuring the frenulum. As with the clitoris, a little goes a long way—and it doesn't take a lot to cross the line to too much.

Kama Knowledge

Where or why the practice of circumcision got its start is a great mystery. Nearly all cultures, with the exception of ancient India and some Germanic tribes, have used circumcision. In many, cutting away the foreskin is a ritual symbolizing a boy's passage into manhood. In others, circumcision marked social or religious status. Ritual circumcision typically used special knives, sometimes made of stone. (In modern Western cultures circumcision is done primarily for appearance.)

Just beneath the corona, or ring of tissue, that delineates the glans is an extraordinarily sensitive area called the frenulum. Some people refer to the frenulum as the man's clitoris, so intense are the sensations that result from its stimulation.

Unlike the clitoris, however, there are few clues to identify the frenulum. In some men the frenulum exists as a small bump, while in other men there's no physical evidence. Women often need their male partners to show them how to find and stimulate this highly arousing spot, which, like the clitoris, needs a tender and well-timed touch with fingers or tongue.

Hare, Bull, Stallion: The Three Lingams

From the beginning of time, it seems apparent, men (and women) have worried about penis size. The Kama Sutra addresses this concern in detail, describing lingams in animal terms based on size. It does so not to create insecurity in those who feel they don't measure up, but instead to provide guidance for pairing with a yoni that fits the lingam. Ancient India classified men into three types according to lingam length and thickness:

- The **hare** man has a small but lively body with a gentle voice and manner. The hare lingam measures the width of six fingers in length (about 3 inches) when erect and is most satisfyingly matched with the narrow and shallow doe yoni.

- The **bull** man is of sturdy build with a hearty temperament and an impressive bearing. The erect bull lingam measures the width of eight fingers in length (about 4 inches) and is thick in roundness. The bull lingam best matches the full and sensuous mare yoni.

- The **stallion** man is tall and firmly muscled, with a love of adventure and fun. The erect stallion lingam measures the width of 12 fingers in length (about 6 inches), and best matches the cavernous and deep elephant yoni.

Of course, such pairings reflected the ideal physical match-ups. Vatsyayana and others recognized that people are often attracted to each other for reasons beyond physical appearance. The Kama Sutra describes various unions intended to minimize disparities between lingam and yoni, so sexual loving can be a mutually enjoyable experience.

The Ecstasy of Ejaculation

Though for most men they most frequently happen together, orgasm and ejaculation are not the same event. Orgasm is the involuntary contraction of muscles in the pelvic area. Ejaculation is the release of semen through the penis.

In clinical terms, the process occurs when stimulation of the nerves in the penis reaches a level that causes a response from the spinal cord. This sets in motion a chain of events that starts when the muscles around the epididymis contract to squirt sperm up into the vas deferens. The sperm merge into the stream of semen being secreted from the seminal vesicles and the prostate gland.

The point at which the prostate gland releases this mixture into the urethra is sometimes called the "moment of inevitability," because after this happens there is no stopping the orgasm and ejaculation. Further contractions of the muscles in the pelvic area send the stream of semen spurting through the urethra and out the penis.

It is possible for a man to reach orgasm and not ejaculate. In some men, this happens when the valve that closes off the bladder during ejaculation fails to work properly. Instead of shooting through the urethra and out the tip of the penis, the semen streams into the bladder. This is called retrograde ejaculation, and is both harmless and painless. It becomes an issue only if a couple is trying to conceive, as there is no semen leaving the man.

 Sutra Sayings

A woman desires to feel the lingam deposit its seed deep inside her yoni, so she may feel pleasure and fulfillment. As part of her enjoyment, she wants lingam and yoni to remain joined, so she may continue to experience delight.

Men can also learn to consciously control ejaculation, delaying it indefinitely while enjoying riding the edge of pleasure with their partner. It is possible to become sensitive to, and approach, the point before ejaculation and then cool the energy down a little. Sometimes the penis becomes a bit less hard. You can continue love play in this way for a long time before climaxing and you can also come to orgasm but not ejaculate. Though this takes practice to master, most men can learn to recognize the subtle changes that take place in their bodies immediately before orgasm and ejaculation.

For many Western men, orgasm and ejaculation are the goals of sexual loving. It signals the culmination and release of sexual tension. In the Eastern view, ejaculation is a sacred act whose purpose is to create new life. It is often, though not necessarily, the climax of sexual loving.

Exercise: Delaying Ejaculation to Prolong Pleasure

One way to extend your lovemaking is for the man and his partner to learn the signals his body sends as he is approaching the moment of inevitability. Early signs that this moment is approaching often include shallow breathing, rapid heartbeat, and a sense of pressure in your lower pelvis.

1. When you recognize the signs of inevitability, slow down and breathe deeply to spread the sensations from the genitals throughout your body.

2. Tell your partner you are on the brink and are slowing down so as not to ejaculate. This allows your partner to synchronize with you.

3. Let your sexual tension subside a bit and continue to enjoy each other.

Dr. Josie Suggests

According to the erotic teachings of India, a man could enter a woman soft and come out hard. The method for inserting a soft penis is called stuffing. It can be highly pleasurable for both partners to feel the soft and tender penis growing full and hard inside.

Male Hormones: What They Are and What They Do

The primary hormone responsible for male gender characteristics is testosterone. The testicles produce most of the testosterone in a man's body, though the adrenal glands (located above the kidneys) produce some testosterone, too. Testosterone regulates both sperm production and sex drive.

Testosterone production significantly increases in puberty, initiating the changes associated with changing from boy to man. The penis and testicles enlarge, the voice deepens, body hair appears, and muscle mass increases. Testosterone levels reach their highest levels during a man's early 20s, then stabilize at a fairly constant level.

Testosterone levels may drop slightly with old age, as other bodily functions also tend to slow somewhat. Though it may take longer to achieve both an erection and ejaculation in your 70s than it took in your 20s, you still maintain the ability to give and receive sexual pleasure.

A man whose testicles are surgically removed (such as to treat cancer or other serious medical problems) loses the ability to produce sperm. However, he still feels sexual desire and maintains the ability to have erections and ejaculations.

Maintaining the Heights of Desire

Without control and pacing, a man can explode from flaccid to ejaculation in about three minutes. This is not as pleasurable—for man or partner—as it would be if the lovemaking lasted 10 times as long. (Or more!) Fortunately, with awareness and practice, a man can enjoy sexual loving for just about as long as it remains pleasurable for him and his partner.

Sutra Sayings

A man whose sexual excitement ends quickly is not so pleasing for the woman, whose desire is just beginning. What pleases a woman is a man whose lovemaking can last a long time and who can stay in her until she is satisfied.

There are several ways a man can extend his erection for prolonged sexual loving. Tantric teachings stress the importance of awareness, of being fully present, during lovemaking. The Kama Sutra and the love texts that came from China, Japan, and the Middle East provide directions for dozens of kisses, embraces, caresses, and sexual postures to vary and prolong sexual loving.

Many men worry that they won't be able to get an erection. At some point in every man's life, this is likely to happen. Mostly, this is an isolated occurrence that could be due to any number of reasons. The common term for this is impotence, a rather ugly word that implies a man is powerless without his penis. This, of course, is not true, though not being able to get an erection can leave a man feeling helpless and frustrated. The more accurate clinical term for the persistent inability to get erections is erectile dysfunction, which simply says something's not working quite right with the system.

A man who regularly experiences difficulty or inability to get erections should have a medical examination to identify any health problems. A number of medications, such as those for high blood pressure, can cause erectile dysfunction. Health conditions such as diabetes and peripheral vascular disease (problems with blood circulation) can also be responsible.

Today men have numerous medical options for getting firmer erections, including the pill sildenafil (known more commonly by its brand name Viagra). Though psychological factors have long been considered responsible for erectile dysfunction, new research has led doctors to realize there are physical causes in most cases.

> **CAUTION** **Out of Touch**
>
> Not every man can safely take Viagra. If you're taking medications that contain nitroglycerine or other nitrate compounds (as many heart medications do), you cannot take Viagra. Doing so could cause a severe and potentially fatal drop in blood pressure. Discuss your health condition in detail with your physician before taking Viagra or similar products (including the so-called herbal variations).

Loving Him

Men are raised to be doers and providers, which often carries over into the bedroom. It can be hard for a man to learn to receive pleasure from his partner, but this is a good way to learn to balance his yin and yang essences, or to get in touch with the feminine.

A woman's sexual appetite ignites a man's passion. Her passionate response whets his desire and he wants to please her. When a woman is filled and fulfilled in the sexual embrace, her natural response is to be generous and want to give to her partner. This give and take with lavish care given to each partner's pleasure fulfills and connects us deeply to one another physically, emotionally, and spiritually.

The Least You Need to Know

- ◆ Large or small, thick or thin, penis size is nothing more than a representation of a man's uniqueness.

- ◆ A man can learn to control his ejaculation to extend sexual pleasure for himself and his partner.

- ◆ Though orgasm and ejaculation often occur simultaneously in a man, they are separate functions.

- ◆ It is important for men to learn how to receive pleasure as well as to give it.

Chapter 14

When Bodies Unite

In This Chapter

- ◆ The mysteries of attraction
- ◆ The kinds of union, passion, timing, and love
- ◆ The importance of preliminaries
- ◆ Keeping a sense of intimacy after the lovemaking ends

For the lovers of Vatsyayana's India, the Kama Sutra was a source of wisdom and knowledge about sexual loving comparable to what couples today seek in the offices of therapists. Then, as now, loving relationships formed the basis of community and culture. The pairings between man and woman, husband and wife, represent both the present and the future of a society.

In attempting to define the characteristics a man and a woman should consider in their attractions to each other, the Kama Sutra takes into account various qualities such as personality and temperament. This, too, is consistent with our modern view of what matters in a relationship. But the Kama Sutra adds two dimensions we often overlook or even view as unimportant—the compatibility of genitals and passions.

Perhaps you haven't consciously approached relationships thinking about whether or not your genitals fit well with the one you desire. But there's a good chance that you noticed the more obvious sexual attributes he or she possesses. Most of us don't end up in a long-term relationship with a partner because he has a large penis or she has large breasts. However, physical characteristics are an essential dimension of attraction, and they do draw us to one another.

While we may not be as overt in emphasizing body traits as we select partners, we need only turn on the television or pick up a magazine to see that our modern, "enlightened" time is astonishingly focused on physical appearance. Issues of emotional and spiritual compatibility come later.

The methods of the Kama Sutra are not without their limitations and shortcomings in helping people to find committed relationships, of course. The very fact that the Kama Sutra exists tells us that human partnerships have long been important to us. This ancient text presents a careful and surprisingly comprehensive analysis of what seems to matter in successful relationships. The Kama Sutra strives to identify and describe the ideal match of body size and passionate temperament. Its quest encompasses body, mind, and soul—the physical, emotional, and spiritual.

The Kama Sutra and the Physiology of Sex

The Kama Sutra, as is common in the Eastern view, puts a great deal of emphasis on the acts of loving that lead to sexual union. The Western view, by contrast, tends to emphasize the goal of union and the release of tension as the end itself. The Kama Sutra's teachings strive to show couples the most satisfying ways to enjoy sexual loving.

> **Sutra Sayings**
>
> At the start of sexual loving, the man's desire is so intense that he strives to reach completion. As love play continues, he receives greater enjoyment and then strives to delay completion. The woman is the opposite, striving for greater pleasure in the beginning and to reach completion near the end.

Preludes and preparation are very important. The Kama Sutra presents four levels of preliminary considerations for prospective lovers. These are the nine ways of union, the nine forces of passion, the three kinds of timing, and the four paths of loving. These different aspects of sexual loving are not directly connected to each other, but rather present a comprehensive perspective on all that goes into pleasurable sexual union.

The Nine Ways of Union

The sages of ancient India identified physical and temperament characteristics that they correlated with yoni and lingam size. According to this approach, the most pleasurable sexual unions are those between like bodies—the deer and the hare, the mare and the bull, the elephant and the stallion. (See Chapter 12 and Chapter 13 for descriptions of these body types.) The Kama Sutra calls these "equal" or "high" unions.

All other unions are unequal, and are considered low unions. Those between the next closest match, such as deer and bull or mare and stallion, are generally pleasing to both partners as long as they engage in the full range of preludes to heighten desire and receptiveness. Such unions are either superior (the lingam is larger than the yoni), or inferior (the yoni is larger than the lingam). Both superior and inferior unions are considered low unions, in reference to the level of desirability they represent.

Unions between extremes, such as deer and stallion or elephant and hare, are generally not as satisfying. Vatsyayana warns that the stallion-deer pairing could even damage the woman. The elephant-hare match-up is least likely to quell the passion of either man or woman, particularly if the elephant yoni is especially cavernous and the hare especially delicate.

The Kama Sutra recognizes that some people will find their attraction is strong, though their bodies are unequal. It offers adaptations and special instructions to overcome such differences for enjoyable sexual loving.

The Nine Ways of Union

High Union		Superior Low Union		Inferior Low Union	
Man	*Woman*	*Man*	*Woman*	*Man*	*Woman*
Hare	Deer	Bull	Deer	Hare	Mare
Bull	Mare	Stallion	Mare	Bull	Elephant
Stallion	Elephant	Stallion	Deer	Hare	Elephant

The Nine Forces of Passion

Despite ancient India's reverential perspective on sexual loving, the Kama Sutra recognizes that not everyone feels equally passionate about making love—even when attracted to one another. The sages classified passion in three categories according to its force or strength.

The man or woman with feeble passion has little enthusiasm for sexual loving. As a result, sexual union is fairly passive and, in the Eastern view, the flow of semen limited. The man or woman with intense passion, on the other hand, approaches sexual loving with great eagerness and gusto. Sexual union is ardent and exciting. Men and women who are in between these extremes have middling passion. They demonstrate affection for and interest in each other, and enjoy pleasant sexual unions.

Again, the most desirable and enjoyable unions are those between matching forces—feeble with feeble, middling with middling, and intense with intense. As with the ways of union, equal matches are called "high" unions. The least preferred are those between extremes—feeble with intense, intense with feeble. These are called "very low" unions. Pairings between middling and feeble or intense are generally satisfying, with proper attention to the needs of the other. These are "low" unions.

Vatsyayana notes that while certain temperaments are predisposed to particular intensities of passion, intensity can vary during sexual loving. This is more likely to be the case with the woman, who may begin with feeble or middling passion, then become aroused to intense passion. The Kama Sutra further explores these variations within types when discussing the kinds of timing, drawing a stronger correlation between passion and duration than exists between the other aspects of sexual union.

The Nine Forces of Passion

High Union		Low Union		Very Low Union	
Man	*Woman*	*Man*	*Woman*	*Man*	*Woman*
Feeble	Feeble	Feeble	Middling	Feeble	Intense
Middling	Middling	Middling	Feeble	Intense	Feeble
Intense	Intense	Middling	Intense		
		Intense	Middling		

The Nine Kinds of Timing

The Kama Sutra astutely observes that the highest union is less than perfect when the partners have different timing. Timing is important to completely and fully share the pleasures of sexual union. And in the Eastern view, timing was an important aspect of conception. A couple is most likely to conceive, notes the Kama Sutra, when they reach sexual ecstasy at the same time. The path to this achievement requires them to be synchronized in the pace of their lovemaking.

Timing is short, moderate, and long. The most ideal match is between those whose timing is the same—short with short, moderate with moderate, long with long. The least desirable union is between extremes—short with long, long with short. As with other aspects of sexual union, the most ideal match is considered a "high" union, while the others are considered "low" unions.

Kama Knowledge

Timing or pacing is a factor in compatibility both in and out of bed. The speedier-paced partner frequently feels unpleasantly slowed down, while the slower-paced partner feels like there is no resting place in the relationship. Both feel unmet in their natural rhythm. Pacing is like chemistry—when you are similarly paced, your connection is easy and comfortable. Interactions, whether erotic or not, move at a compatible pace. When you have disparate timing, you must make adjustments. Understanding that the problem is pacing can help you address it without making the other "wrong" for being different.

Vatsyayana observes that timing is often the most challenging aspect of sexual loving, because the man in general tends to need less time to become aroused than does the woman. Yet, he notes, the woman's arousal often continues after climax. Sexual unions that consider and address the different pacing of arousal as well as the length of time sexual loving continues are most likely to mutually satisfy the partners. The man and woman who take long in their sexual loving adventures please each other most completely when they also notice and respond to the ebbs and flows of their passions.

The Nine Kinds of Timing

High Union		Low Union		Very Low Union	
Man	*Woman*	*Man*	*Woman*	*Man*	*Woman*
Short	Short	Short	Moderate	Short	Long
Moderate	Moderate	Moderate	Short	Long	Short
Long	Long	Moderate	Long		
		Long	Moderate		

The Four Paths of Loving

However significant the physical attractions and matches between two people, the Kama Sutra observes, their pleasures and enjoyment of each other come from their minds and emotions. In this regard, love comes from four paths—imagination, habit, belief, and objects. The love between a couple often travels all four paths at different times in their relationship, which is most desired. Some couples may travel only one path, which gives them a less complete relationship. The paths are somewhat, though not exclusively, progressive.

According to the Kama Sutra, the love with which a relationship begins is generally the love of imagination. In this love, the mind rather than the body experiences the actions and sensations of sexual union. The love of imagination can also exist in an established relationship in which there are real experiences. In this context, it is the realm of sexual fantasy and encompasses those acts that would not be desirable for the couple to carry out, such as those that would inflict pain. Pain, Vatsyayana comments, is not an act of love because any satisfaction that might be derived from it is one-sided.

The Kama Sutra says that a couple that has been together for a long time forms a love of habit. In this love, the two acquire a taste for each other and for the acts of sexual union as their experience together grows. The experiences of imagination become reality (except for those that remain fantasy). There is a certain comfort and familiarity in their partnership. The love of habit is sometimes called the love of practice.

When two people share a love of belief, they share a mutual commitment to each other that makes them feel they belong to one another. This is a deep and abiding love that grows from, or includes, both imagination and habit.

The couple that binds together through their mutual love of material objects share the love of objects. Though Westerners tend to consider such a materialistic approach to love superficial, lovers in Vatsyayana's India held a more pragmatic view. If one partner desires possessions and wealth while the other cares little about them, their relationship will be one of continual tension. Within this context, the Kama Sutra considers the love of objects to be the highest and most desirable path of love.

> **Kama Knowledge**
>
> Despite the perception that these are times of sexual freedom, the average American adult spends only one hour a month engaged in sexual relations. About a third of them take 10 minutes or less for foreplay, while fewer than one in five continues foreplay for longer than 20 minutes. In one 1994 study that asked Americans what gave them the greatest satisfaction in their daily lives, making love tied with reading a good book for

Passion Play: The Essence of Sexual Loving

The Kama Sutra identifies 64 elements of sexual loving that precede sexual union. (Interestingly, there are about half as many postures of sexual union, not counting the endless variations ingenuity makes possible.) While there are various explanations for how there came to be the number of 64 preludes to lovemaking, the sages all agree there is only one point: sexual pleasure.

Though a man is capable of reaching climax in three minutes, the Kama Sutra sees little advantage to doing so beyond bodily release. The sole objective of sexual loving, Kama Sutra style, is for the partners to pleasure each other until the only possible outcome is climax—not to strive for orgasm. They achieve this objective by erotically exploring and enjoying each other's bodies, striving to please each other and in so doing, receive pleasure themselves.

Getting Started: Kisses, Petting, and Caresses

Kissing kindles love. It signals a partner's interest and intent, and awakens arousal. Kisses on the forehead, eyes, face, neck, and breasts or chest allow sexual excitement to grow in the body and in the mind. Kisses on the lips and moving into the mouth, using the lips and the tongue, increase stimulation and anticipation. Kisses on the arms, thighs, and belly get the sexual juices flowing.

Kisses increase stimulation and anticipation.

(Hrana Janto)

It is natural, the Kama Sutra says, to accompany kissing with petting and caressing. If the lips are on the face, the hands might be on the breasts or between the thighs as other body parts touch and rub. Gentle bites and pinches, when mutually pleasurable, also increase arousal.

Heating Up: Embraces

What the Kama Sutra considers embraces, Westerners might well mistake for sexual positions. An embrace Kama Sutra style is as close as you can get to sexual union without actually joining bodies. In a heated embrace such as the rice and sesame seed embrace, the lovers rub their bodies together as they lie entwined with one another.

Kama Sutra's embraces
bring lovers close.

(*Hrana Janto*)

Though there are circumstances in which the Kama Sutra views it acceptable for this to result in climax (which at times, of course, it will), the intent is for such embraces to heighten and intensify the state of sexual pleasure.

Joining Lingam and Yoni: The Acts of Sexual Union

When both partners are fully aroused and desire to join their bodies as closely as possible, they are ready to progress to sexual union. The Kama Sutra describes about 34 positions for uniting yoni and lingam. The chapters in Part 5 present a selection of these positions in detail.

Heightening the Pleasure of High Unions

The high union, from the Kama Sutra perspective, is that in which the man and woman are most perfectly matched—lingam, yoni, passion, and timing. For these fortunate couples, there are nearly endless choices for sexual union. Their drives and interests are similar, and they take pleasure in trying different unions just for the joy of it. They are able to enjoy a continual stage of arousal and excitement that culminates in simultaneous orgasm.

The challenge for such "perfect" couples is to continue exploring new experiences. They should, the Kama Sutra advises, observe the animals around them and attempt new unions to mimic animal behaviors. In this way they will always find excitement and pleasure with one another. Of course, this was in a different time, and animal life was abundant!

> **CAUTION**
>
> **Out of Touch**
>
> Attempting to hurry penetration, regardless of the "match" between organs, can cause pain and bruising, and even tear delicate tissues.

Making the Most of Low Unions

A number of the sexual positions the Kama Sutra describes are especially enjoyable for couples who don't quite match up physically or passionately. When a man who is a hare, of feeble desire, or short timing unites with a woman who is an elephant with intense desire and long timing, they often need to take extra measures to provide each other with sexual pleasure.

The Kama Sutra describes various positions to aid in any or even all of these potential mismatches. Some permit deeper penetration to give greater satisfaction for the man with a smaller lingam. Some keep penetration shallow, prolonging the man's arousal and increasing the woman's desire. Some allow a smaller yoni (deer) to enjoy a larger lingam (stallion).

Unique Circumstances and Special Interests

Sexual interests and tastes vary not just among cultures, as Vatsyayana notes, but also from person to person (and even time to time within the same person). Some people enjoy sexual union between lingam and anus. Others get pleasure from mouth union, or oral pleasuring.

Sexual loving between couples of the same gender was both common and accepted in ancient India. The Kama Sutra describes ways of lovemaking for same-sex partners, as well as for partnering that involves more than two people. The chapters in Part 5 provide detailed information about love play and lovemaking.

> **Sutra Sayings**
>
> The lingam soothes the fire in the yoni, and their union appeases both man and woman. But it is the kisses and embraces afterward that calm and comfort the mind and the spirit.

Climax: Uniting Body and Spirit

We might better understand the physiological dimensions of orgasm than did the couples of Vatsyayana's time, but all of our scientific knowledge doesn't mean we have any better ability to enjoy the climax of sexual union. In fact, what we think we know may well stand in the way of full and complete sexual pleasure.

In the Eastern view, sexual climax is the natural progression of sexual pleasure. In Vatsyayana's time, however, the climax was not of great pleasure unless the acts and events leading to it also created great enjoyment. The Kama Sutra notes that while most couples have a need to release the flow of their sexual pleasure through orgasm, it is also possible, and sometimes desired, to enjoy love play without coming to climax.

After the Loving

Though in the Western view orgasm marks the conclusion of lovemaking, the Kama Sutra observes that the desire for sexual loving and intimate connection continues beyond climax. Partners find pleasure in kissing, petting, caressing, and even embracing each other even though the fire of their passion no longer burns with intensity. This is the natural completion of the cycle of sexual loving—the return to the beginning.

Dr. Josie Suggests

Rather than abruptly ending lovemaking by turning over and going to sleep, hold each other and tenderly touch and talk to each other as you come down from the energy of lovemaking. Basking in the afterglow extends the pleasure and intimate connected feelings between partners.

Many couples may kiss and hug for a few minutes after making love, then roll apart and fall asleep. When they do, they miss the chance to extend the bond of their love. Between committed partners, sexual loving can be an ongoing affair. Holding each other, sharing a few words that acknowledge the joy and connection you feel, and spooning (lying snuggled together) before getting up or drifting off to sleep, continue to stoke the embers of passionate intimacy.

The Least You Need to Know

◆ The preliminaries of lovemaking are the most important part of sexual loving, yet many couples rush through them.

◆ Not all sexual unions are created equally. But no matter what your physical design, there are numerous ways to enjoy sexual loving.

◆ Climax should be the outcome, not the goal, of sexual loving.

◆ For a stronger sense of intimacy with your partner, take the time to snuggle and enjoy just being close to each other after the lovemaking ends.

Chapter 15

Kama Sutra Safe Sex 101

In This Chapter

◆ How the risks of sex have changed

◆ Assessing your behaviors and attitudes: a self-quiz

◆ Options for preventing pregnancy and STDs

◆ The importance of cleanliness and good hygiene

In Vatsyayana's India, about the worst that could happen as a result of sex were injuries from particularly acrobatic positions. And on occasion, Vatsyayana warns, there was the irate husband who didn't take kindly to another man lavishing affections on his wife.

Travel was considerably limited 2,000 years ago, and the various cultures that populated the earth existed without contact among them. The sexually transmitted diseases that plague our contemporary times hadn't yet surfaced, as best we know about a time from which there are few written records.

Ancient Indian lovers, we are told, desired rather than feared the other significant risk of sexual union, pregnancy. (When they didn't, it was usually because the liaison went against custom in some way.) It was important for a man to produce offspring to carry on his family line as well as to inherit his worldly possessions.

Risks of Our Modern World

Our modern world is a different place. Family lineage no longer determines a person's place in society. Infant death, rather than being the rule, is a clear exception. In October of 1999, the United Nations announced that the earth's population had climbed to six billion people! The majority of Westerners now view pregnancy as an option instead of a prerequisite, thanks to effective and widely available birth control methods, though unplanned pregnancies still happen when couples neglect to plan ahead.

Sutrology

Sexually transmitted diseases (STDs) refers collectively to about 25 infectious diseases spread primarily through sexual contact. Among the most commonly known are HIV/AIDS, gonorrhea, syphilis, chlamydia, and genital herpes.

Unprotected sexual encounters also carry the risk of diseases that are at best annoying and at worst fatal. Scientists estimate that one in five Americans will contract a *sexually transmitted disease* (STD) during his or her lifetime. And while the rate of infection with human immunodeficiency virus (HIV), which causes the incurable and fatal disease acquired immune deficiency syndrome (AIDS), is finally on the decline overall in the United States—though it continues to rise within particular population groups as well as worldwide—it remains a serious threat.

As a result of these risks, we've come to view sex as either safe or unsafe. Couples need to exchange sexual histories as a prelude to sex, and provide laboratory test results before they can feel comfortable about unprotected sex. In truth, there is no "safe" sex. When you open yourself sexually to another human being you become open, vulnerable, and able to receive great pleasure as well as pain. Hopefully, you will be conscious of the consequences of sex, and disease will not be part of the equation. There are safer sex practices, but no real guarantees.

A Self-Quiz: How Safe Are Your Sexual Practices?

Whether you've been together and faithful to each other for 10 years or are just beginning your journey of commitment, it doesn't hurt to take a look at the relative risks of your sexual practices. Choose the response that most closely depicts your behavior, attitude, or lifestyle.

1. When it comes to sexual partners …

    a. The more, the merrier.

    b. You're no novice, but you prefer a steady mate.

    c. There's only one for you.

2. You and your partner discuss previous sexual relationships …

   a. Only when you fight.

   b. When the topic comes up in the conversation.

   c. Openly and honestly.

3. The one lover you'd never tell your partner about is …

   a. The one you occasionally meet for a drink or whatever.

   b. The one you met at a party when you were in college and never saw again.

   c. Nonexistent, because you tell your partner everything.

4. A married co-worker had a one-night stand with another co-worker last week, then heard a rumor that the person has an STD. If you were the married co-worker, you'd …

   a. Do and say nothing.

   b. Get tested immediately and not have sex with your spouse until you knew you were disease-free.

   c. Get tested immediately, refrain from sexual contact, and tell your spouse what happened.

5. Things are getting hot and heavy, and suddenly you realize you're out of condoms. You …

   a. Try to get your partner to have unprotected sex.

   b. Ask your partner to hold that thought while you run to the drug store.

   c. Tell your partner you don't have a condom and that you'd like to shift to pleasuring other than intercourse.

6. What started as a relaxing shared shower has turned steamy, and you and your partner are not currently trying to become pregnant. You …

   a. Seize the moment and hope it's the right time of the month.

   b. Bring each other to orgasm without intercourse.

   c. Continue your lovemaking after confirming or acquiring contraception.

If your responses are mostly As, you're cruising in the danger zone. If your responses are mostly Bs, you could make some improvements but are generally responsible in your sexual practices. And if your responses are mostly Cs, your partner has a keeper!

If your responses were Cs for every question except #4, you might be thinking "Okay, honesty about STD exposure is one thing, but telling your partner *everything*—isn't that a bit extreme?" Many people think of safer sex as a mechanical function—avoid the contact, avoid the risk, avoid the STD. Yes, safer sex is about procedure. But the true cornerstone of safer sex, like intimacy, is total honesty. Keeping "little" secrets from each other compromises the entire premise. Safer sex, after all, is about being able to trust your partner.

Safer sex is as much about the relationship as it is about avoiding disease. Some of this ties into matters of sexual morality (see Chapter 2). Some of it is about trust and intimacy. And some of it relates to your definition of commitment. It may challenge you and your relationship to view safer sex this way, and you may choose to remain procedure-oriented. That's okay—the choice is yours to make. What matters is that you recognize there is more to safer sex than simply procedure, just as there is more to phenomenal lovemaking than simply technique.

How to Protect Against STDs

Knowledge is your best protection from sexually transmitted diseases. It's important for couples to be open and honest with each other about their sexual histories. If you've ever had an STD, you know how unpleasant it was and how betrayed you felt at receiving such an unwelcome "gift." Don't pass it on! If there's any possibility you could expose your partner to an STD, both of you should get tested through your doctor's office or a public health clinic.

CAUTION

Out of Touch

Though the birth control pill is highly effective in preventing pregnancy, it cannot protect you from STDs. Only barrier forms of contraception, such as condoms, offer any STD protection.

Many people believe using condoms during intercourse prevents STDs (including AIDS). While a condom is a good defense, to be sure, it's not a guarantee. Most STDs are transmitted through the exchange of body fluids during intercourse. The agents responsible (usually bacteria or viruses) like the warm, moist environment of your genital area. Condoms can break, and condoms made from animal tissues can block sperm but not some viruses. There is also the possibility of inadvertent contact with body tissues and fluids.

Common Sexually Transmitted Diseases

Disease	Main Symptoms	Treatment	Potential Consequences if Untreated
Syphilis	Painless sore where infection entered body; body rash 2 to 3 weeks later; symptoms will go away without treatment, but infection remains	Blood test to confirm; antibiotics (penicillin) in earlier stages; may not be treatable in later (tertiary) stage	In tertiary stage, can involve and damage any body system including heart and circulatory, brain and nervous; complications often lead to death
Gonorrhea	Burning or pain with urination; discharge from vagina or penis; symptoms may be mild enough to escape notice	Lab test to confirm; antibiotics	Infertility; blindness in newborns if eyes are infected during passage through birth canal
Chlamydia	Mild burning with urination; mild discharge; symptoms often not noticeable	Lab test to confirm; antibiotics	Infertility and pelvic inflammatory disease in women; urethral inflammation in men; can cause pneumonia in newborns who are infected during birth
Genital herpes	Painful sores and blisters in, on, and around the genitalia	Treatment to reduce symptoms; virus stays in the body and causes unpredictable recurrences	Can pass virus to partners or newborns any time sores are present
Genital warts (HPV)	Painless bumps (warts) in, on, and around the genitalia	Treatment to remove warts; virus stays in the body and warts often recur	Contact with warts can spread the virus
HIV/AIDS	No early symptoms; later symptoms include conditions and infections unique to AIDS	In HIV stage, drugs to delay activation of the virus; in AIDS stage, treatment targets symptoms and conditions that result; no cure	People can live symptom-free with HIV for 10 years or longer; life expectancy with full-blown AIDS varies greatly; AIDS is ultimately fatal

What You Need to Know About AIDS

AIDS burst onto the public health radar screen in the early 1980s. Because this deadly disease first emerged in the United States and Europe among gay men, intravenous drug users, and recipients of blood transfusions, it quickly became a social as well as a medical issue. By the mid-1990s, researchers had developed powerful drugs to combat the effects of AIDS that have extended the lives of those living with HIV, but there is still no cure.

Treatment typically includes powerful drug combinations, healthy nutrition, and diligent attention to health situations and needs. Many people who have AIDS find that complementary medicine such as homeopathy, herbs, and acupuncture helps sustain a good quality of life for 10 to 20 years and sometimes longer. Once AIDS develops, the disease so far is ultimately fatal.

Unlike STDs that generally make their presence known within days of infection, AIDS can take 10 to 15 years to show up. During that time, however, the person can infect others with HIV and not realize it. The Centers for Disease Control, a federal agency that studies and tracks disease patterns, estimates as many as a million Americans are living with HIV infections—and half of them don't know it. About 40,000 people who are HIV-positive (infected with HIV) develop AIDS each year.

> ### Kama Knowledge
>
> Despite its relative newness in the United States, AIDS has existed in Africa for decades. Researchers believe the deadly infection originated as a mutation of a similar virus that infects monkeys. AIDS is such an epidemic in some African countries that it threatens to wipe out entire populations. In Zimbabwe, for example, AIDS has reduced life expectancy from 65 years to just 39 years, a level not seen for nearly 40 years. The United Nations estimates that 35 million people in African countries have HIV, resulting in 16,000 AIDS cases every day.

Preventing HIV and AIDS

Researchers talk a lot about people with high-risk behaviors when they discuss AIDS. Generally these are people who use intravenous drugs (especially if they share needles) and who have multiple and numerous sex partners. Pregnant women can pass HIV to their unborn children, and there are other ways to contract the infection.

Anyone can get AIDS. Young, old, male, female, heterosexual, gay, married, single—no one is immune. The greatest challenge in preventing AIDS is the length of time it can take—a decade or two—to show any symptoms. By then, a person could infect scores of other people, directly or indirectly. This is the aspect of AIDS that scares health care providers the most.

An increasing number of couples entering into monogamous, committed relationships get tested for the presence of HIV, the virus that causes AIDS. Though it's not a guaranteed clean bill of health, a negative result is often reassuring. Depending on your personal sexual history and possible exposure to HIV, you may need to be retested over a period of years. If you are uncertain about your partner's or your own HIV status, barrier methods of protection can reduce your risks.

Out of Touch

STDs and AIDS can be transmitted through oral sex, too, though this occurs less frequently than through genital intercourse. Use a latex condom or dental dam (very thin sheet of latex rubber placed over body tissues) to avoid contact with your partner's fluids for the safest oral sex.

Using Birth Control

Pregnancy is beautiful … when you are ready to bring another life into the world. Unless you are, use a reliable birth control method. Holding your breath, withholding orgasm or ejaculation, and crossing your fingers are not, we repeat, *are not*, reliable ways to prevent pregnancy!

Contraception is a responsibility both partners share. While it might be easier for one partner or the other to take primary responsibility, it's still up to you both to be sure it happens. Some birth control methods are more effective than others. If you have questions or concerns about what methods of contraception are best for you, schedule an appointment with your regular health care provider or go to your local Planned Parenthood center.

Sutrology

Contraception is the attempt to prevent pregnancy from occurring. It's also called birth control.

The Abstinence Challenge

The only form of birth control that is absolutely, 100 percent guaranteed to prevent pregnancy is abstinence—no sex at all. This, understandably, is not a popular option for most couples. It can also be a misunderstood option, depending on how you define "sex."

Many people believe that as long as they don't "go all the way," they are practicing abstinence. In this view, no intercourse equals no sex, though everything else is okay. It's important to remember, however, that heavy petting which includes rubbing body parts together has on occasion resulted in—surprise!—pregnancy.

Sperm are, after all, microscopic cells. The semen that wets your clothing as you get sexually aroused is chock-full of sperm, even if you haven't ejaculated. Press wet spot to wet spot, and you've got contact. Those pesky sperm can also succeed in their biological mission by hitchhiking on the man's hand as it moves from his genitals to hers. Though you cannot get pregnant from oral sex by itself (thank heaven for small favors), any contact between genitals and hands during lovemaking can increase the odds of becoming pregnant.

To be practical, abstinence is not a viable method of birth control for most people who are reading this book. You're looking for ways to enhance and deepen sexual loving in your partnership. Intense and exciting sexual union is your goal, not something you're trying to avoid.

Methods for Him

Birth control methods for men are pretty much limited to two choices—condoms and sterilization. The latter, accomplished via vasectomy, is an option only for men who do not want to father children (who either already have families or have chosen to remain childless). We'll discuss sterilization and vasectomy in a moment.

The condom is one of the oldest forms of contraception known to humankind. There is evidence that ancient Romans, Greeks, and Egyptians fashioned condoms from animal intestines and other natural substances. By the Middle Ages condoms were made of such glorious materials as fish guts, neatly hemmed and often kept in special carrying pouches. How effective these early condoms were is uncertain, however, since it appears that a man held on to his until it wore out, simply reusing it (though not necessarily washing it first) when the need arose.

Out of Touch

Never use an oil-based lubricant (such as petroleum jelly) with a condom. The oil interacts with the latex rubber, causing it to break down. This weakens the condom, making it easier to rip or tear.

Because Eastern cultures view the male seed, or sperm, as divine, condoms were likely not used in Vatsyayana's India. To prevent undesired pregnancy, men were expected to withhold ejaculation. The Kama Sutra and other texts do provide a multitude of recipes for preventing pregnancy, however. These range from curses and spells to mystical potions and herbal concoctions.

Read the label before you buy condoms—there are many different kinds. Most people are satisfied with the "plain vanilla" variety, while others like to experiment with ribs and colors and other variations. These differences are primarily cosmetic. Some men complain that textured condoms reduce sensitivity for them, though some women find the texture increases their sensitivity.

Some condoms are lubricated, which means they have a thin layer of a water-soluble lubricant on the inside and on the outside. This helps the condom slide more easily over your erection, and may make penetration easier as well. Often the lubricant contains a spermicide, or chemical substance that kills sperm.

Most condoms on the market today are made of latex rubber, a synthetic material that can be stretched very thin without breaking. Latex condoms have the added advantage of blocking most STDs. Some condoms are made of lambskin, which are marketed as more natural and sensitive. Lambskin condoms do not provide protection against STDs and AIDS, however. As a natural substance, lambskin has pores—tiny holes you can only see with a microscope. While larger cells such as sperm can't fit through these pores, smaller cells like some bacteria and viruses can.

Put your condom on early in lovemaking, as soon as you have a firm, full erection. Doing so contains the fluid that seeps out as you become aroused, which does contain sperm and could impregnate your partner. Remove it as soon as you've ejaculated, before your erection begins to fade. Doing so keeps the semen from leaking out.

While properly used condoms are quite reliable, every now and then one breaks. Health experts recommend that couples who definitely do not want to become pregnant combine a condom with a spermicidal jelly or cream. Then if there is a sperm leak, it's less likely to have unintended consequences.

The permanent method of birth control is *sterilization*, usually achieved through the surgical procedure called *vasectomy*. Most vasectomies are done in the doctor's office under a local anesthetic. After numbing the area around the scrotum, the doctor makes a tiny incision to snare the vas deferens, the thin tube that transports sperm from the testes to the penis. The vas deferens is cut and the ends are tied off, closing the passage.

Dr. Josie Suggests

Instead of interrupting your lovemaking to put on a condom, make it part of your lovemaking. Have your partner unroll the condom onto your erect penis (taking care not to get any seminal fluid on the outside of the condom), using hands, lips, and even tongue to smooth it into place.

Sutrology

Sterilization is a permanent form of contraception. A vasectomy is surgery that cuts or ties off the vas deferens in the man to prevent sperm from leaving the testes.

A vasectomy takes about 20 minutes and usually requires no more than a few days' rest afterward. Many men have a vasectomy done on a Thursday or Friday and return to work on Monday or Tuesday. A vasectomy has no effect on a man's ability to achieve an erection or have an ejaculation—there's just no sperm in his semen.

Common Birth Control Methods

Method	Advantages	Disadvantages	Odds of Getting Pregnant if Using the Method Correctly
Birth control pills	Nothing to remember during the heat of the moment	Must remember to take your pill every day; requires doctor's prescription; no STD protection	Less than 1 percent
Cervical cap	Limited STD barrier; can insert up to 48 hours in advance	Requires fitting and doctor's prescription; must leave in eight hours after sex; must reapply spermicide for repeat sex; can't use during periods	5 percent combined with spermicide (15 to 25 percent used alone)
Condom (female)	More complete STD protection	Sometimes difficult to insert; may slip or irritate tissues	5 percent combined with spermicide (15 to 25 percent used alone)
Condom (male)	STD protection; easy to use; readily available	May reduce sensitivity; must use new one for repeat sex	5 percent combined with spermicide (15 to 25 percent used alone)
Diaphragm	Limited STD barrier; can insert up to six hours in advance	Requires fitting and doctor's prescription; must leave in six hours after sex; must reapply spermicide for repeat sex; can't use during periods	5 percent combined with spermicide (15 to 25 percent used alone)

Method	Advantages	Disadvantages	Odds of Getting Pregnant if Using the Method Correctly
Implantable hormones	Up to five years' protection; nothing to take or do	Must be surgically implanted by a doctor; can cause unpleasant side effects; no STD protection	2 percent
Injectable hormones	Three months' protection per shot; nothing else to take or do	Must see doctor for shot every three months; can cause unpleasant side effects; no STD protection	2 percent
IUD	Always protected; can stay in place for several years	Must be inserted by a doctor; can increase susceptibility to STDs and other infections	2 to 3 percent
Rhythm	No mechanical or chemical intervention	Requires close monitoring of woman's cycle; no STD protection	20 to 30 percent
Spermicides (alone)	Must apply within 30 minutes of intercourse	Messy; must reapply before repeat sex; no STD protection	40 percent
Sterilization (vasectomy or tubal ligation)	Nothing to do or take; permanent	Requires surgery; cannot be easily reversed; no STD protection	Nearly 0 percent (failures happen but are very rare)
Using no birth control	Maximum spontaneity	High chance of pregnancy; no STD protection	90 percent

Methods for Her

In less than 100 years, women have gone from no choices in contraception to half a dozen options (more if you count the various combinations). Through the ages, women have tried everything from willow bark tea to pessaries (vaginal suppositories) made of crocodile or elephant dung to prevent pregnancy. Fortunately, we have more palatable, and no doubt more effective, choices today.

Kama Knowledge

The fairy godmother of birth control in America was a soft-spoken but determined nurse named Margaret Sanger (1883–1966). She often cared for women in poverty-stricken families who had baby after baby. The babies, and often the women, faced serious health problems because of their poor living conditions. Sanger coined the phrase "birth control" and made it her life's mission to make education and contraception available to women of all social classes. Though she served time in jail for opening America's first birth control clinic, Sanger later became the first president of the International Planned Parenthood Federation when it was founded in 1953.

The most common and most effective method of contraception for women is the birth control pill. First marketed in the early 1960s, "The Pill" revolutionized sexuality in America. For the first time, sex could be free from worry about pregnancy without mechanical interference. Today's birth control pills use very much smaller doses of hormones than did their predecessors, resulting in fewer side effects and greater effectiveness. Taken correctly (every day at approximately the same time of day), birth control pills are nearly 100 percent effective.

Birth control pills work by supplying the body with hormones (estrogen and progesterone) that prevent ovulation. No egg, no conception. The so-called mini-pills contain only progesterone, and aren't quite as effective at preventing pregnancy. Progesterone turns the lining of the uterus into a hostile environment for sperm but does not stop the ovary from releasing an egg.

Out of Touch

Women who smoke and take birth control pills are at increased risk for blood clots and heart disease. Most doctors believe the risk is great enough that women smokers should not take birth control pills.

Some women have side effects from birth control pills, which can include flushing, nausea, weight gain, and spotting between periods. Often these side effects diminish or disappear after taking the pills for several months. Though there have been numerous worries through the years about whether the hormones in birth control pills increase a woman's risk of certain cancers, there doesn't seem to be any conclusive evidence to substantiate such concerns.

Barrier methods of birth control include cervical caps, diaphragms, and the female condom. These methods rely on placing an impermeable object between the vagina and the uterus to keep sperm from finding their way to a waiting egg. Cervical caps and diaphragms require a doctor or women's health specialist to fit and prescribe them. The larger diaphragm fits across the top of the vagina, deep inside, covering the entire cervix. The smaller cervical cap just fits over the cervix itself. Some women who can't use a diaphragm because of discomfort or difficulty inserting are able to use a cervical cap instead.

The female condom is fairly new on the American market, and is available without a prescription in most pharmacies or drug stores. It looks like a long plastic tube with a small ring on the closed end and a larger ring on the open end. The small ring goes inside the vagina and over the cervix, like a diaphragm. The larger ring stays outside the vagina. Because the female condom covers the labia and tissues outside the vagina, it offers good protection against STDs.

> **CAUTION**
>
> **Out of Touch**
>
> Don't use both a male condom and a female condom. There is no increase in protection against either pregnancy or STDs, and the two different kinds of material (latex rubber and poly-urethane plastic) will stick to each other.

Health experts recommend couples use a spermicide in addition to any barrier method of birth control. Spermicides are chemicals that are poisonous to the highly sensitive sperm cells, and come in a variety of jellies and creams.

Other birth control methods for women include intrauterine devices (IUDs), implantable hormones, and injectable hormones. An IUD is a small metal coil, usually copper, that the doctor inserts into the uterus through the cervix (this is usually done in the doctor's office). The IUD prevents a fertilized egg from implanting into the wall of the uterus. Some IUDs can stay in the uterus for as long as 10 years, while others need to be replaced every year. IUDs can cause cramping and spotting between periods, and also tend to increase susceptibility to STDs and other infections.

Implantable hormones are time-release sticks, about the size of matches, that a doctor inserts in the fatty tissue just under the skin of the upper arm. The hormone released prevents ovulation and also thickens the cervical mucous, essentially "closing the door" to sperm. They can last up to five years. Injectable hormones are shots that put a long-acting hormone in your system. Each shot lasts about three months. These methods combine the effectiveness of hormones with convenience.

The most effective form of contraception for women, as for men, is sterilization. The tubes tied in a woman are the fallopians, which pull the egg in after its release from the ovary and shuttle it up to the uterus. The surgery, called a *tubal ligation*, is done in a hospital because it involves cutting through the abdominal wall. It is a more risky procedure than a vasectomy. Tubals are often done on an outpatient basis, meaning you can go home the same day.

Observing Cleanliness and Good Hygiene

Cleanliness may be next to godliness, but it comes before good sex. Most mature adults have a pretty good handle on keeping their bodies clean. A daily bath or shower usually does the trick, though don't overlook oral hygiene (regular flossing and brushing, and twice annual dental visits). Many couples incorporate a shared shower or bath into their lovemaking. This is a pleasant way to relax and shift gears after a stressful day at work, as well as an arousing way to renew contact with one another. It's also a nice way to bring closure to your lovemaking.

The Least You Need to Know

♦ While sex can be the ultimate pleasure, it sometimes can have life-altering or life-threatening consequences. Partners share equal responsibility for safer sex.

♦ There is no "safe" time of the month during which pregnancy cannot occur. If you rely on birth control to prevent pregnancy, you must use it *every* time you have sex.

♦ STDs and AIDS can be transmitted through oral sex as well as through sexual intercourse.

♦ Safer sex depends on a foundation of trust within your relationship.

Part 5

The Art of Loving

When most people think of the Kama Sutra, they think of its famous 64 elements of sexual loving. Well, here they are. Not all of them, of course—but more than enough to indulge your fancy for longer than a single night. In fact, you'll discover as you read these chapters that the delicious pleasure these acts can give you rely on the trust and commitment you've built within your relationship.

Though flipping through the pictures might lead you to believe you have to be an athlete to manage these sexual unions, this is not performance sex. This is lovemaking at its most intimate, a communion of body, mind, and spirit made possible through sexual loving. Enjoy!

Chapter 16

The Language of Sexual Love

In This Chapter

◆ How words can arouse and touch

◆ What your body says about how you feel

◆ Self-explorations: What does and doesn't please you?

◆ How to ask your partner for what you want

The language of love is made up of the breath, movement, sounds, requests, and private pillow talk of lovers. They speak tenderly, or talk dirty, in the heights of passion when they've achieved a trusting intimacy that frees them to be open and unmasked with each other. Soft sighs, grunts, gentle murmurs, silly names, tears, laughter, roaring passion—the varied sounds of love express sides of ourselves that we hide from view in our daily lives.

Lovemaking has the capacity to take partners beyond the limits of their personalities. Your sense of separateness vanishes for a time as you become one with another. After making love, you bask in the glow somewhere between the borderless state of union and a sense of your separate self. What bridges these states of consciousness? Who of us has not wished for, or perhaps experienced a moment of, complete rapport where words seemed unnecessary, where you and your beloved were so synchronized there was no need to speak?

When this moment occurs, it is special and unique. Unfortunately, many partners believe that is the way it should be each and every time they make love. There is a myth in our culture that says, "If you love me, you should know what I want and need." Believing that lovers should know what the other wants sets the stage for disappointment. All lovers, even those who experience that rare and extraordinary connectedness in which words serve no purpose, need to communicate with each other about what they want and feel.

The Power of Words, the Power of Bodies

For some people, talking during sex is erotic and arousing, a turn-on. Words, like touch, can be erotic in themselves. Hearing your lover tell you what he or she is thinking and wants to do to you to give you pleasure builds anticipation and sexual tension. Some people find that talking during lovemaking frees them to fully surrender to their emotions and the pleasures of sexual loving. They may have certain words or a particular tone of voice that they only use in the throes of passion, helping to transport them from the ordinary to the ecstatic.

Other people find conversation awkward or distracting, a turnoff. They might be uncomfortable expressing their thoughts and desires by talking. Sometimes sounds—oohs, aahs, sighs—provide all the audible communication they need. Some couples feel they have a special language between them that needs no words.

> **Sutra Sayings**
>
> There is a language of the body that speaks without words. Through touches, gestures, and signals, couples express their desire for each other. Lovers understand and enjoy these unspoken messages.

Whatever its form, communication is essential. If words are not your cup of tea, it's especially important for you to tune in to other cues and messages. Listen to your partner's sounds and sighs. Feel and hear the deepening pace of the breath. See and feel the color changes and flushing of the skin, and the swelling of the lips. Read attentively as your partner's dilating pupils communicate growing arousal and desire. Your body also "speaks," sometimes taking your expressions of passion and love beyond what words can articulate.

What Your Body Says About How You're Feeling

For many of the sexual unions it describes, the Kama Sutra reminds couples (especially the man) that the woman needs to be fully aroused. Her body's signals of this are unmistakable to the partner who knows how to read them. Her vulva softens and swells, juices flow profusely from her yoni, and she arches and thrusts her genitalia to meet her partner's touches and body. The aware partner also notices that the woman's nipples are erect and enlarged, her skin is warm and perhaps flushed, her eyes are soft and inviting, and her mouth open.

Your bodies send the message of sexual arousal.

(Hrana Janto)

The man's body similarly sends messages describing its state of arousal. Most obvious is his lingam, which swells and flushes into an erection. Pre-ejaculatory fluid glistens on his glans, and his testicles draw up tight against his body. An aware partner also notices that as the man becomes more aroused, his nipples may also be erect. His body warms and relaxes, and he moves and thrusts to meet his partner's touches and body.

Signs and signals during the stages leading up to full arousal can be more subtle. Partners who are present and aware of each other's bodies as well as of their own can read and respond to these messages. Talking and making sounds expand the process of communication, affirming interpretation or redirecting touches and actions.

Mixed Signals: When Words and Body Differ

Sometimes confusion results when your body and your words give different messages. If you say "no" while your body strains to be closer to your partner's touch, your partner won't know which message to follow. There's a great myth that when a woman says "no" she's just being demure and really means "Yes! Yes!" This arises in large part from misplaced Victorian restrictions that taught women to refrain from expressing their sexual interests—good girls don't talk about such things. Men and women both may share this misbelief.

Always heed what your partner says, regardless of the signals you believe his or her body is sending. If your partner says "no," stop. Ask your partner to clarify mixed messages, so you know for certain what to do and how (or whether) to proceed. This is the only way to avoid hurting your partner, physically or emotionally, and to assure that you're giving your partner the sexual pleasure he or she wants.

If you are someone who says "no" when you know you mean "yes," you want "yes," and your body says "yes," pause for a moment to understand why you've said "no."

Out of Touch _____

When your partner's body sends one signal but he or she says something different, stop. Clarify what your partner wants.

Is your partner pleasuring you in a way you grew up believing was dirty or wrong? Understanding what's behind your mixed signals helps you to sort through your fears and desires so you can express yourself with honesty and consistency.

It's essential for both partners to say what they mean and honor what the other says during sexual loving.

What's Your Pleasure?

The Kama Sutra describes nearly 100 various acts of sexual loving, from preludes to positions. Not all of them are for every couple, and not all of them will appeal to you. What do you enjoy? To help you define and express your pleasures, here are two self-explorations, one for him and one for her. There are no right or wrong answers.

Dr. Josie Suggests _____

Learn to talk about sex easily and matter-of-factly. Tell each other something that you like to hear during lovemaking. Then say it when you make love.

Whether you answer your self-exploration by yourself and then share your responses with your partner or go through the self-explorations together, they're most useful when you share your likes and dislikes with each other. This process is especially helpful for people who aren't accustomed to thinking and talking about what pleases them sexually.

A Self-Exploration for Him

What pleases you? What is not pleasurable? Write your responses on the lines provided.

1. When we begin making love, I like it when my partner …

   _____

   _____

2. As my arousal increases, what I most enjoy my partner doing to me is …

   _____

   _____

3. The one thing my partner does that sends me into absolute ecstasy when we make love is …

_____

_____

4. The one thing my partner does that he or she thinks arouses me but really doesn't is …

_____

_____

5. When we're deep in the throes of passion and I know I'm on the edge of climax, I'd like my partner to …

_____

_____

6. The pressure my partner uses when stroking and rubbing my lingam is …

_____

_____

7. During oral sex, I'd like my partner to …

_____

_____

8. When I climax before my partner does, I like my partner to …

_____

_____

9. After the sexual loving ends, I like to …

_____

_____

10. The Kama Sutra interests me because …

_____

_____

A Self-Exploration for Her

What pleases you? What is not pleasurable? Write your responses on the lines provided.

1. When we begin making love, I like it when my partner …

   _____

   _____

2. As my arousal increases, what I most enjoy my partner doing to me is …

   _____

   _____

3. The one thing my partner does that sends me into absolute ecstasy when we make love is …

   _____

   _____

4. The one thing my partner does that he or she thinks arouses me but really doesn't is …

   _____

   _____

5. When we're deep in the throes of passion and I know I'm on the edge of climax, I'd like my partner to …

   _____

   _____

6. The pressure my partner uses when stroking and rubbing my clitoris is …

   _____

   _____

7. During oral sex, I'd like my partner to …

   _____

   _____

8. When my partner climaxes before I do, I like my partner to …

   _____

   _____

9. After the sexual loving ends, I like to …

_____

_____

10. The Kama Sutra interests me because …

_____

_____

Kama Knowledge

At the foundation of the Kama Sutra is the expectation that lovers thoroughly know their own and each other's bodies. Presumably this knowledge comes from studying the sciences as well as the erotic arts of the Kama Sutra. Carvings and paintings of couples engaged in the elements of sexual loving adorned many temples and public buildings. While such formal learning is important, Vatsyayana says, he consistently encourages lovers to follow each other's responses in choosing amorous activities. He instructs them to listen to the words the other speaks as well as observe the movements and reactions of the body.

What Draws You to Explore the Kama Sutra?

For all the books about sex and lovemaking that you can study, there is nothing quite like the Kama Sutra. This is partly because this love text comes from a time and place different from our own. The sexual _mores_ of that time in history were nothing like any we experience today. But the Kama Sutra appeals to modern couples for a more revealing reason: It puts us in touch with a dimension of sexual loving we've always suspected existed within us but we haven't quite known how to reach. The Kama Sutra presents sexual loving as an element of intimacy and connectedness that draws lovers together in a deeper, closer relationship.

Everyone will get something different from the Kama Sutra. Some partners will infuse their relationships with renewed eroticism and romance. Others will vastly increase their repertoire of sexual loving, enjoying each other in ways they've never considered. Some will find exotic and exciting ways to explore and indulge each other that take their relationships in a new direction. Still other couples will find a depth and strength of emotional and spiritual connectedness unlike anything they've experienced.

Sutrology

Mores (pronounced MOR-ays) is the sociological term for a culture's moral habits and customs.

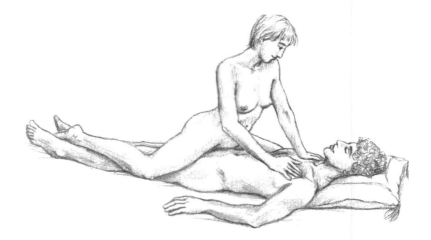

The ancient Kama Sutra evokes a new dimension of sexual loving for modern couples.

(Hrana Janto)

Giving and Receiving Sexual Pleasure

Many people think of giving and receiving as a process of give and take. This implies a process of taking turns, which is a common approach to sexual loving for many couples. If sexual loving is only about give and take, your lovemaking will be good enough. You give pleasure, and in return you take the pleasure your partner gives to you. Your reciprocity assures that each partner gets equal attention. But taking is a passive role. True communion—the melding of bodies and souls—happens when you forget about whose turn it is and lose yourself in the loving embrace. Giving and receiving become one and the same.

There is an exquisite joy in going beyond "doing" for each other to discover the bliss of letting lovemaking sweep you into forgetting where you end and the other person begins. In this discovery, you completely let go. Whose turn it is no longer matters as the loving embrace of rapturous union engulfs you both.

Asking for What You Want

Sometimes it's difficult for partners to ask each other for what they want sexually. Many couples just don't have much practice in doing this, so it feels awkward to ask for a certain stroke or kiss. When you can ask your partner to pleasure you in a particular way, however, it often clears confusion and misperceptions. Partners tend to expect each other to anticipate their needs and desires, which does often happen between those who have been with each other a long time.

But your partner can't read your mind, and sometimes won't read your body signals in the way you intend them, either. Gently and tenderly ask your partner to touch you as you want to be touched, and show your partner what you have in mind. Ask your partner to try a particular sexual union that appeals to you. He or she might be just as interested as you are.

To avoid any misunderstanding, be specific in your requests. "I'd like you to caress my breasts and nipples as I'm approaching climax" is going to get a more favorable result than, "Please touch me more." Ask "yes" and "no" questions. "Do you want this harder?" "Do you want this slower?" This allows your partner to stay focused on the pleasures of lovemaking while at the same time giving you directions to intensify that pleasure. When you ask for something, give your partner positive encouragement that lets him or her know that what they are doing feels good: "Oooh, yes, that's good."

> **Sutra Sayings**
>
> In the affairs of love, the man and the woman should do to each other what they both enjoy and desire. Those who act as the other likes will keep their love strong even for a hundred years.

When Partners Disagree

If you object strongly to something your partner wants to try, talk about your feelings, worries, fears, and concerns. Perhaps your relationship is still new. Or maybe your partner has had a bad experience in another relationship, and your request reminds him or her of that. And it could be that your partner just doesn't share your interest in a particular sexual union. But you won't know unless you talk about it.

Ending on a Positive Note

It's important for both partners to have positive feelings about the sexual experiences they try, even if one partner has less interest. Honor each other's feelings and preferences. The Kama Sutra frequently points out that different people have different likes and dislikes, often as a result of their cultural or social backgrounds.

What matters most in sexual union is that both partners enjoy what they're doing together. Otherwise one partner may feel angry or bitter toward the other, which is not good for sexual loving or for the relationship. And sexual loving should, after all, draw partners closer together, not drive them apart.

The Least You Need to Know

◆ Not every act of sexual loving is right for every couple. Do what pleasures you.

◆ Pay attention to your partner's words as well as body language. If you're getting mixed messages, stop and clarify.

◆ Each partner should find the sexual loving experience pleasurable.

◆ Learn how to ask your partner for what you want, and to tell your partner what feels good.

Chapter 17

The Power of Ritual in Lovemaking

In This Chapter

- ◆ Why ritual matters
- ◆ How to establish your own lovemaking ritual
- ◆ Using color, lighting, fragrance, and music to enhance the setting for your lovemaking
- ◆ Choosing sensuous locations for lovemaking, indoors and outdoors

Ritual lovemaking creates an atmosphere of specialness and celebration. It lifts what has become routine and unconscious out of the ordinary and, with awareness and attention, creates an intentional act of communion. It is a time to consciously put aside the issues and problems that accompany everyday life, and for a time enter into the open, generous arms of love.

The power of ritual lies in its deliberateness and repetition. We all experience ritual in our lives in some way. You might celebrate Christmas, Thanksgiving, the Super Bowl, Friday night Shabbat, weddings, funerals, or family night. During these times, we pay close attention to the setting, the food, and the accoutrements of our rituals. We anticipate eagerly and anxiously the event's arrival, which adds to the power of the ritual.

Establishing Your Lovemaking Ritual

At least once a week make the time for an extended lovemaking ritual. Arrange to be uninterrupted for several hours. There will be times when you are short on time and want to keep the sexual connection stoked. Lots of physical touch, holding, kisses, snuggling, and spooning do keep the pump of passion primed. A quick sexual experience when you are short on time, especially when you make a date for your weekly ritual, also stokes the connection. But nothing takes the place of the extended lovemaking ritual for its intention to be together in extended intimate communion.

Where you make love is as important as the attitude you bring to each lovemaking experience. The senses come alive stimulated by beautiful surroundings. If you choose your bedroom, begin by arranging the bed with clean and beautiful sheets and an array of different size pillows that you can use to support your body.

Making love in other parts of the house, such as in front of the fireplace, or outdoors in a secluded garden or other isolated and private places in nature, adds to the special-ness of your time together (see "Natural Wonders," a little later in this chapter). Bring a sound system and music, and also incense, aromatherapy oils, flowers, some-thing to sip on, and perhaps some strawberries or other light delicacies.

Begin your lovemaking ritual by bathing together. Lather and towel each other off, going slowly and sensuously. Sit together and meditate. Share appreciation and acknowledgements. Go slowly and make love without a goal.

Mood Music

Music has a profound ability to influence mood and feeling. Loud, fast music can wake you up and get you going. Soft, gentle music, on the other hand, can soothe and re-lax you. When you are selecting music for the extended lovemaking ritual, be aware that your choice of oboe music may do nothing for your partner. Choose something neutral and pleasant, make and ask for suggestions, and look at catalogs or online sources of music.

This is more than a matter of preference or taste. Music also appears capable of altering brain waves, which changes emotion and mood at a physiological level. The slower your brain waves, the more calm and relaxed you feel. Conversely, the faster your brain waves cycle, the more animated and excited you feel. Fast brain waves also exist when you're experiencing negative emotions, such as anger.

Yoga, meditation, and similar practices slow and unify various bodily functions such as breathing and heart rate. They also slow brain waves, helping to induce a sense of serenity. Music can accomplish the same result. In his book *The Mozart Effect* (see Appendix B), Don Campbell notes that music playing at a rate of about 60 beats a minute has the ability to lower heart rate, breathing rate, and brain waves to a level the same as that which occurs with meditation. This is a rate somewhat slower than the average resting heart rate of 72 to 80 beats a minute.

In such a state, you are more present, more calm, and more clear-headed. Your skin becomes more sensitive and responsive to touch and temperature. Certain classical music, such as many Mozart compositions, as well as romantic music (such as Tchaikovsky and Chopin), light jazz, and New Age music generally play at 60 beats a minute or slower. Classical compositions (such as those by Wagner) and rock are much faster, causing brain waves to cycle faster and making you want to rush through whatever you're doing. Music with a distinct rhythm but little discernible beat, as is typical of New Age compositions, tends to suspend your conscious perception of time and space. This can make your evening of lovemaking seem endless.

Seductive Scents

Fragrance guides us through far more of everyday life than we realize. Your nose leads you to delectable scents—a favorite coffee shop or bakery, perhaps, or to flowers and perfumes that you find pleasing. Foul odors warn that something is unpleasant or even dangerous. We also respond to smells without conscious thought. Mothers know the smells of their babies. Lovers intuitively breathe in the fragrance of each other's hair as they kiss and embrace. Because they are familiar, these smells give us a sense of comfort and confirm, on a very primal level, the existence of our loved ones.

People tend to associate certain odors with specific events. The smell of cinnamon rolls might instantly transport you to a sense of childhood in your grandmother's kitchen, for example, while a particular perfume or cologne immediately sets your heart racing and your loins stirring. You can use fragrances in various forms as an element of your lovemaking ritual. Incense, *essential oils*, and scented candles make this easy. Scented soaps and massage oils let you mingle the sensory stimulation of both touch and smell.

Aromatherapy formulas use certain mixes of essential oils to elicit specific responses. The somewhat earthy, pungent aroma of patchouli, for example, tends to relieve stress and increase sexual energy. Ginger, jasmine, and ylang ylang are other fragrances reputed to have aphrodisiac

Sutrology

An **essential oil** is the oil that gives a plant its characteristic fragrance or flavor. Aromatherapy is the use of essential oils to stimulate specific effects or results.

qualities. A recipe for romance might blend one or more of these essential oils with others to help set the mood for sexual loving.

The following table identifies some common fragrances and essential oils to help you establish an erotic aroma for your lovemaking ritual.

The Influence of Fragrance

Fragrance or Essential Oil	Effect
Cardamom	Warms and invigorates
Ginger	Stimulant, increases sexual interest and energy, relieves headaches
Jasmine	Instills a sense of romance, increases sexual interest and energy
Lavender	Calms and relaxes
Lemon	Improves alertness
Orange	Calms
Patchouli	Clears distracting thoughts, relieves stress, increases sexual interest and energy, stimulant
Rosewood	Calms and relaxes
Sandalwood	Restores balance
Ylang ylang	Increases sexual interest and energy, can instill euphoria

Evocative Lighting and Colors for Visual Appeal

Subdued lights, sensual shadows, and the flickering of candles can turn an ordinary room into an enticing environment. Soft lighting often feels exotic or romantic, and encourages tenderness. Color, too, subtly influences mood and atmosphere. A room containing shades of blue often feels calm and peaceful, while a room filled with vivid reds feels dynamic and exciting. Combining colors can help you create an atmosphere that evokes trust, playfulness, and passion, allowing you and your partner to enjoy being with each other and willing to explore new experiences in lovemaking.

Dr. Josie Suggests

Scented body oils combine fragrance with touch for an especially sensuous experience, such as using them to give your partner a sensual massage. Choose fragrances that smell good in combination with other scents in the room, such as candles or essential oils.

Color offers an easy way to set the mood for lovemaking. The following table identifies colors and their symbolic influences.

The Influence of Color

The Color ...	Stimulates ...
Blue	Peace, trust, calm
Brown	Stability, reliability, groundedness
Green	Growth, vitality, life, abundance
Lavender	Fantasy, romance, imagination
Pink	Commitment, compassion, companionship
Purple	Passion, inner vision, spirituality
Red	Pleasure, vigor, persistence
Teal	Creativity, energy, serenity
Yellow	Playfulness, eagerness, confidence

Food and Drink

Many an evening of romance starts with dinner out and concludes with lovemaking in. Eating and drinking are sensual activities that can let couples transition smoothly into love play. While a heavy meal can leave you feeling sluggish and drowsy, light foods can give you energy for the physical activity of sex. Fueling the body can also ignite passion. Feeding each other small slices of fruit and other light foods, or even just sharing food and drink that you both enjoy can be incredibly erotic.

In Vatsyayana's time, lovers typically ate fruits, sweets, and meats before, during, and after lovemaking. Mango fruit sweetened with honey or sugar was a popular treat. From a shared cup, couples also drank wines, fermented juices, and various brewed alcoholic beverages probably similar to today's heavy beers. The ancient Hindus attached aphrodisiac significance to foods that conveyed sexual imagery, such as cucumbers and eggplant. Potions combining milk, licorice, and the juices of certain plants and seeds were believed to have aphrodisiac or other magical properties.

> **CAUTION**
>
> **Out of Touch**
>
> Too much alcohol or other intoxicants can bring your love play to an unsatisfactory end by making you sleepy, unable to focus or concentrate, and sometimes unable to get an erection. If you drink wine and other alcoholic beverages, feel free to include them, in moderation, in your love play. But if you don't usually drink, don't feel compelled to start.

Many people enjoy wine or other alcoholic beverages as an aspect of lovemaking. Some do so because they find a small amount of alcohol relaxes and warms them. Others believe alcohol is an aphrodisiac, and find themselves more readily aroused after a glass of wine. Because alcohol has the effect of reducing inhibitions, this can appear to be the case.

Kama Knowledge

If you're planning to start your evening of lovemaking with a filet mignon or prime rib meal, you might want to reconsider your menu options. Despite the Western perception that real men eat meat, it appears that a diet high in saturated fat (the kind of fat found in red meat) can significantly lower a man's testosterone level, resulting in decreased sexual interest and energy. And if you're trying to conceive, add more fruits and vegetables to your diet—especially those containing vitamin C. Vitamin C boosts sex drive as well as invigorates sluggish but otherwise healthy sperm. Women trying to become pregnant should eat a diet rich in folic acid, a B vitamin, to greatly reduce their odds of having a baby with a neural tube defect (a potentially serious birth defect).

However, too much alcohol has the opposite effect—it can lessen sexual interest as well as your ability to focus and be present. Because alcohol affects the nerves and the circulatory system, having too much to drink can make it difficult for a man to get an erection. Reaching the point of being drunk also puts you in the situation of being unaware of what you're doing, which is not what sexual loving is all about.

Lovemaking as the Kama Sutra presents it always starts with food and drink. In Vatsyayana's view, this indulges and awakens the senses. The beverage of choice was generally some form of fermented brew, probably a substance somewhere between what we would identify as a beer and a wine today. But remember that in this time long before refrigeration and other forms of preservation, nearly all beverages quickly fermented (especially in the extreme heat of India's summers). Vatsyayana also encourages couples to share between them the water they use for drinking and rinsing their mouths.

Ambiance and Comfort

Many people keep their bedrooms cool to be comfortable while under the covers. But it's hard to feel much like making love when you're shivering. Be sure your room has adequate heat for you to be comfortable when you're unclothed and uncovered. And if, of course, it's hot, do what you can to cool the room. Candles, fragrances, and music also influence how comfortable a room feels.

Preserving the Mood and the Memory

In the times between your extended lovemaking rituals, display candles and play music that evoke memories of the time you and your lover spent together. Having sensuous surroundings keeps the passion pump primed.

> **Sutra Sayings**
>
> The man and his wife should live in a comfortable and spacious home, with different rooms for different purposes. One room should contain a soft and agreeable bed that is low in the center and has a canopy above. Flowers and garlands should adorn the canopy, and pillows should adorn the bed. Beside the bed should be a stool to hold scented oils and other substances to give the room a balmy, rich fragrance.

Interior Designs: Your Lovemaking Retreat

For most couples, the bedroom is the retreat of choice for sexual loving. This is usually a private place, so you can decorate as evocatively as you like without worries about what others will think. There's a bed, which makes for nice snuggling and sleeping after making love. There might be other furnishings such as chairs and stools that could come into creative use during lovemaking. This is a space to which you can comfortably retreat, leaving the concerns of real life behind you when you cross the threshold.

Create your own love nest.

(Hrana Janto)

Feng Shui for Lovers

Feng shui (pronounced *fung shway*) is the ancient Chinese art of placement to allow the most conducive flow of energy through a room (or an entire house). By strategically arranging furnishings and decorations, you can create an environment that suits the activities taking place within the room. While feng shui is far more comprehensive than we can cover here, there are a few simple concepts you can apply to get started. For a complete discussion on feng shui, *The Complete Idiot's Guide to Feng Shui* (Alpha Books, 1999) is an excellent resource.

Place your bed in a location where it is not in a direct path between the door and a window, or between two opposing windows. Energy flows most intensely between such openings, which will cause you to feel restless and unsettled if you are in its path. If you can't avoid such placement, use a room divider screen, draped curtain, or similar device to divert the flow of energy around your bed. Also place your bed so that while lying in it you can see the door.

> **CAUTION**
>
> **Out of Touch**
>
> Blow out those candles before you drift off to sleep! Never leave an open flame burning unattended. This includes candles you might be using with an aromatherapy diffuser. Place candles or incense in heat-resistant holders. It's a good idea to keep a fire extinguisher in the room, just in case.

Mirrors, fountains, and burning candles also influence the flow and circulation of energy. Fire and light bring more energy to an area or room. Fountains are especially helpful in drawing positive energy to a specific part of the room, and also make pleasant background noise. Mirrors can deflect and divert the flow of energy, altering its pathway to create a more harmonious environment. The color pink is the relationship color and can add enhancing energy.

Kama Sutra Bed Basics

In ancient India, beds were more like lounges. Their shape allowed lovers great flexibility in the postures of sexual union. Contemporary Western couples typically sleep on a traditional mattress and box spring combination, elevated from the floor on a frame. This presents a firm yet comfortable surface upon which you can lie, sit, or kneel. It also offers a means of support or bracing for some sexual unions in which one or the other partner stands.

Futons and waterbeds present other alternatives to the traditional bed. A futon on a frame generally sits closer to the floor than does a bed, which can be handy for trying kneeling unions. It's also easy to slide the futon onto the floor like a big cushion. Some people enjoy the movement and lack of resistance that making love on waterbeds affords.

No matter what kind of bed you have, clean, soft sheets are essential. Pillows and cushions can be both attractive and functional. Many couples like to have a thick quilt for adventures on the floor, and a bedside table to hold food, drink, and other items they might want access to during lovemaking, such as condoms or lubricant.

Special Places

The shower or bath can be a sensuous place to either start or end lovemaking. Lathering and shampooing each other can be a luxurious and erotic exchange. Warm water relaxes your muscles and helps wash away the tensions and stress of the day, transporting you to a mood and mindset that supports and encourages love play.

Kama Knowledge
The Kama Sutra considers the act of "shampooing" to be a form of caress bordering on an embrace, and encourages couples to shampoo each other as a preliminary to lovemaking. This activity had a different definition in Vatsyayana's time, however, most likely referring to a massage of the head. Soap as we know it today did not exist in ancient India, and debuted sometime between 500 and 1200 C.E. People instead cleansed their bodies with substances that created lather, such as berries and plant roots.

Many partners have a favorite room or location besides the bedroom where they enjoy making love. New locations can be exciting, giving you a chance to break with your usual habits to try something new or even enjoy something familiar in new ways. Or you might begin kissing and embracing in another location, perhaps a living room, and move into the bedroom as your arousal intensifies.

Natural Wonders

There is a natural sensuality in the great outdoors. The sun warms your skin, drawing more blood to your skin to intensify the sensations you feel. The wind blows through your hair, caressing and teasing those thousands of nerve endings surrounding the follicles. Fragrances and sounds fill the air. Emotionally and spiritually, there's a strong sense of being connected to all of existence as you stand in the midst of the earth's incredible abundance. It's only natural to want to share this connectedness with your partner through sexual loving.

Out of Touch

Use discretion if you and your partner decide to make love in a public place such as a beach or park. Not only could you end up in a close encounter of a less pleasant nature with local law enforcement officials, but you could create discomfort for others who might stumble across your liaison.

Mountain Peaks, Ocean Beaches, and Your Own Backyard

The sky's literally the limit when it comes to where you can make love outdoors. Locations with sensual appeal range from the exotic to your own backyard. Different sounds, smells, and sights make sexual loving in such places exciting and new. Just remember to seek reasonable privacy, and anticipate the unexpected—from bystanders who stumble across you to natural events such as rain.

Be Prepared

If you're on an outdoor adventure that you suspect could take a sexual turn, be sure you're prepared to take full advantage of it. Have a blanket or ground cover to shelter you from sticks, stones, sand, bugs, and other annoyances. Pack condoms or your diaphragm and spermicide if you use them. Tissues and trash bags come in handy, too. And if you might be gone after dark, take a flashlight. Have fun, and stay safe.

Kama Knowledge

Some couples enjoy love play in the water. There is a certain eroticism in having warm water caress every inch of your body while your lover focuses on particular areas. Vatsyayana discouraged sex in the water for lovers of his time, however. It was against the local customs in many locations. This likely had more to do with water quality than privacy. Water was sometimes in short supply, particularly during the arid summers.

Dressing for the Occasion

Clothing in ancient India was perfectly suited for erotic love play. Men and women both wore long, flowing garments secured with wraps and knots that were easily unfastened. Such clothing allowed partners to slowly undress each other, and to enjoy the anticipation of partially revealed bodies. Caftans and sarongs such as those worn in Polynesia are attractive unisex attire that both partners can wear.

The Least You Need to Know

- ◆ Ritual makes lovemaking special. Sensuous surroundings help set the tone for you and your partner to relax and enjoy the pleasures of each other.

- ◆ Use colors, soft lighting, and fragrance to create an environment that delights all of your senses.

- ◆ When you're not making love, display candles and play music that reminds you of your ritual lovemaking to keep your passion and interest high.

- ◆ Schedule an extended lovemaking ritual at least weekly. Even if you occasionally find yourself with less time than you'd like, setting aside time for each other builds anticipation and maintains a sense of closeness.

Chapter 18

Kiss Me, Hold Me, Touch Me

In This Chapter

◆ The pleasures of kissing

◆ How to give lingam kisses

◆ How to give yoni kisses

◆ Embraces that heighten passion

The Kama Sutra has endured through the centuries not just because it explicitly describes exotic sexual unions, but because it also emphasizes and describes extended love play leading to sexual union. Such love play, or what contemporary lovers might call foreplay, establishes passion and desire—the essential elements of sexual pleasure between loving partners.

Beginnings, even between married or committed partners, are a blend of invitation and exploration. Do you want me? Are you interested? Does desire stir within you as it does within me? These are the questions of initial contact—touches, kisses, caresses, embraces. Each response that says "yes" leads to another level of intensity and excitement, until the emphatic, impassioned answer becomes, *"Yes! Yes!"*

Beginnings: Lips and Mouth

Your lips and the tissues of your mouth are among your body's most sensitive places. Vatsyayana wisely suggests that all sexual loving begin with kisses. Kissing quickly arouses passion, progressing from lip-to-lip contact to body caresses as arousal intensifies. Vatsyayana identifies the face, lips, throat, breasts, and inside of the mouth as the places to start, moving on to the arms, legs, and "joints of the thighs" as passion builds.

The kiss is an intimate act, both subtle and passionate.

(Hrana Janto)

The Nominal Kiss

In this introductory kiss, the couple touches lips but nothing else. This is an exploration, seeking to determine the interest and response of each other.

The Throbbing Kiss

When one partner responds to a nominal kiss by pressing his or her lips against the other's, the other then moves his or her lower lip during the return kiss. Though there is still little physical contact between the two besides kissing, this throbbing kiss signals an interest in progressing to more erotic kissing.

The Touching Kiss

The tongue awakens and begins participating in love play, reaching out to touch the partner's lip during the kiss. At the same time, the partners reach out to touch each other with their hands, and move their bodies closer together.

The Straight Kiss

Like the nominal kiss, the straight kiss is gentle and affectionate (and refers to angle of entry—not sexual orientation!). The lips of the partners meet straight on, with only enough head tilt to make contact possible. The partners may be touching or caressing each other, though this kiss is fairly chaste.

The Bent Kiss

The bent kiss allows for full lip and mouth contact. The partners tip their heads to bend toward each other. The bent kiss also encourages tongue exploration and penetration. Partners often caress each other's faces, or pull each other closer with a hand around the back of the neck.

Sutra Sayings

What one lover does to the other, the other should do in return.

Dr. Josie Suggests

Remember to use and enjoy all your senses as you begin to sensually explore each other's bodies—touch, taste, smell, seeing, and hearing. Being fully present is the most arousing experience of all.

The Turned Kiss

The turned kiss is slow and erotic. One partner takes the other's chin or face in hand and turns his or her face upward. Like the bent kiss, the turned kiss exposes the lips and mouth for full contact by the other's lips and tongue.

The Pressed Kiss

In the pressed kiss, one partner presses firmly against the other's lower lip, either with his or her lips or a finger. This pressure, especially when done by the finger and accompanied by full lip contact, sends a clear message that this is now love play.

Kama Knowledge

Tantric teachings identify a nervelike connection between a woman's upper lip and her clitoris. When a man kisses and presses the woman's upper lip, she feels sensations along this connection from her lip and through her body to her clitoris. Likewise, a yoni kiss that caresses a woman's clitoris sends sensations through her body to her upper lip. Tantric teachings suggest a woman should visualize this nervelike channel to consciously open it to the flow of sexual energy.

The Kiss of the Upper Lip

The upper lip is especially sensual, particularly the place inside where the upper lip joins the gum. Kissing and sucking the upper lip is deeply arousing. When the kiss of the upper lip is done Kama Sutra style, the man kisses the woman's upper lip and the woman responds by kissing his lower lip.

The Clasping Kiss

One partner clasps or presses the other's lips between his or her own lips, creating erotic pressure.

Wrestling Tongues

From the clasping kiss, either partner touches the other's lips, teeth, inner mouth, palate, and tongue with his or her tongue.

Oral Pleasures

It's a natural progression to move from kissing the mouth and face to enjoying the oral pleasures of other parts of each other's body. The neck and throat are especially responsive to erotic touches from lips and tongue, as are the breasts and nipples (men and women both). Most couples find it as arousing to give as to receive kisses and strokes. As arousal intensifies, so does the eroticism of the touch. A tender kiss on the inside of the thigh or a tongue trailing across the belly can be incredibly evocative.

Dr. Josie Suggests

Cleanliness is crucial for both partners to enjoy oral pleasuring. Consider starting your love play with a shared shower or bath, or showering before bed if that is when you're most likely to make love.

Your Versatile Tongue

Your tongue has more different kinds of nerve endings than just about any other part of your body. It is highly sensitive to touching and being touched. And of course, the tongue is the organ of taste. Moving over various skin surfaces, it detects a mix of sweet and salt in flavors that defy description, yet are intensely arousing. And where the tongue goes, the nose follows, enhancing tastes with smells. Your tongue can give and receive great pleasure during sexual loving.

Erotic Explorations

Your partner's entire body is highly sensitive to the moist, warm contact and movements of your tongue. You can use your tongue to touch your partner anywhere you might use your hand. The texture of its surface delivers a variety of sensations, and its touch can be firm or soft. Your tongue's wetness adds a unique dimension to its contact, both warming and lubricating as it presses and strokes, then cooling as air follows its moist trail.

Because your tongue is also highly sensitive, kissing your partner's body is very arousing for you, too. It's a natural response for kissing to beget kissing. As kissing becomes a more intense exchange, what you do to your partner that feels good, your partner will want to do to you. Your love play can be a prelude to sexual union, or can result in orgasm without union.

Bites and Scratches

In ancient India, lovers left marks on each other from bites and scratches as a way to show possessiveness. Contemporary couples may find biting and scratching to be erotic during love play, though usually not to the extent of leaving marks. There are a number of ways to nibble and bite. One method is to suck your partner's flesh between your teeth, which usually keeps your teeth from piercing through the skin.

Scratches, too, can evoke intense sensations as fingernails rake across aroused surfaces. Try a pressing touch with the backs of your nails for a softer feeling. Whatever your preferences, don't force them on an unwilling partner. Eroticism requires desire in both partners. Without care in your methods and close attention to your partner's responses, bites and scratches can hurt rather than arouse.

Lingam Kisses

Lingam kisses (known in Western lingo as *fellatio*) are intensely arousing for a man. Many women also find the experience erotic and exciting. Some of the lingam kisses the Kama Sutra describes are tender and loving, while others are more intense and likely to bring the man to orgasm. In your lovemaking, explore the kisses and the different ways they arouse. Kissing and sucking on the lingam, like kissing and sucking the breasts of a woman, are highly reminiscent of being a nursing baby at the breast. These feelings of nurturance are highly pleasurable and reassuring for many people. Let yourself experience the feelings that arise during oral pleasuring.

> **Sutrology**
>
> **Fellatio** is the technical term for oral sex performed on a man. **Cunnilingus** is the technical term for oral sex performed on a woman.

Women: Use your hands to caress, stroke, squeeze, and kiss your partner's scrotum and inner thighs as you make love to his lingam with your mouth and tongue. If you don't want your partner to ejaculate while you're holding his lingam in your mouth, hold him in your hands or against your breasts as he climaxes. You can also move into a sexual union, taking him into your yoni.

Men: You can stand, sit, or lie down while your partner pleasures you with lingam kisses. Let your partner know the pressure, pace, and kinds of mouth touches that give you pleasure. Tell your partner if you feel you are near orgasm, and whether to continue or ease off to let you drop to a less intense level of arousal. If your partner does not want you to ejaculate while she has your lingam in her mouth, don't.

Nominal Lingam Kiss

Take your partner's lingam in your hand and place your lips around it. Move his lingam around in your mouth. Use your lips to press and release, then softly pull your mouth away.

Side Nibbling Lingam Kiss

Holding the lingam's head between your fingers as you might hold the bud of a plant. Kiss and gently nibble down and up the lingam's sides. Alternate firm and soft pressure as you pleasure your partner.

Outside Pressing Lingam Kiss

Press the lingam's head with your closed lips, then kiss it, using a gentle sucking motion, as if trying to draw it out.

Inside Pressing Lingam Kiss

Take your partner's lingam into your mouth, press it firmly with your lips, and suck it. Then withdraw the lingam from your mouth and repeat as your partner desires. This lingam kiss can be intensely arousing and bring your partner to orgasm.

Kissing the Lingam

Hold your partner's lingam in your hand, with your hand wrapped around it, and kiss it in the same manner you would kiss his lower lip. Gently press and move your lips.

Lingam Tongue Strokes

Hold your partner's lingam in your hand. Lick and stroke it all over with your tongue. Use your tongue to alternately flick and press his frenulum and other places that give your partner the most pleasure.

> **CAUTION**
>
> **Out of Touch**
>
> Men, thrusting into your partner's mouth can activate her gag reflex. Ejaculating while your lingam is in her mouth can have the same effect. Use care and control. Women, hold your partner's lingam with your hand to control how deeply it enters your mouth.

> **Dr. Josie Suggests**
>
> Some women may not like the taste of semen, or may notice that its taste changes. What a man eats influences how his semen tastes. Men, try eating less red meat and more fruits to sweeten your semen.

Sucking a Mango

Draw your partner's lingam halfway into your mouth and suck on it with pressure, as you might suck the sweet flesh of the mango fruit. This lingam kiss can bring your partner to orgasm.

Consuming the Lingam

Take your partner's lingam fully into your mouth, as deeply as you can, caressing it with your tongue and lips, and sucking it in as though you might swallow it. The intensity of this lingam kiss often brings the man to orgasm.

Yoni Kisses

Many women find yoni kisses (also known as *cunnilingus*) as intensely arousing as men find lingam kisses. Despite its relatively small size compared to its male counterpart the penis, the woman's clitoris is extraordinarily sensitive. While many women enjoy direct contact from a partner's moist finger or tongue early in love play, others find such touching too intense until they are fairly aroused. It is important for a woman and her partner to be closely attuned and communicate with each other.

In Eastern cultures, the yoni kiss symbolizes reverence and respect for womanhood and the role of the woman as the giver of life. The yoni is the flowering lotus, with the clitoris as its bud. Kissing and caressing this delicate blossom releases sexual energy. The juices that flow from the yoni during sexual loving carry this energy, which the woman shares with her partner in an exchange of deepening pleasure.

Women: You can stand, sit, or lie down while your partner pleasures your yoni with mouth kisses. Guide your partner in giving you the pressure, pace, and kinds of touches you want. Let your partner know how to continue if you climax.

Men: Sit, kneel, or lay to put your face between your partner's legs. Stroke your partner's thighs and caress her breasts as you make love to her yoni with your mouth and tongue. Use your moistened fingers to rub her labia and enter her yoni to give her extra stimulation. Many women enjoy multiple orgasms during such lovemaking.

The yoni blossom.

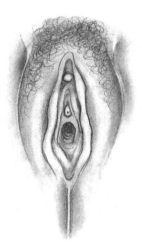

Pressing Yoni Kiss

Press your lips against your partner's labia, kissing but not parting them. Use your hands to caress her inner thighs, belly, and breasts.

Outer Yoni Tongue Strokes

Gently spread your partner's yoni lips with your fingers. Brush her outer labia with your lips and tongue.

Inner Yoni Tongue Strokes

Gently open your partner's outer labia. Brush her sensitive inner labia with your lips and tongue.

Kissing the Yoni Blossom

Tenderly spread your partner's labia to expose her clitoris. Gently stroke upward along the shaft and across the head of her clitoris with your tongue. Lick upward along each side.

Flutter of the Butterfly

While kissing the yoni blossom, softly flutter the tip of your tongue along the shaft of your partner's clitoris.

Sucking the Yoni Blossom

Take your partner's clitoris into your mouth in a tender sucking motion. Caress it gently with your tongue.

Kiss of the Penetrating Tongue

As your partner's arousal intensifies, penetrate her yoni with your tongue. Start with shallow, flicking entries and withdrawals. Proceed to deeper thrusts of your tongue as she desires.

Drinking from the Fountain of Life

Enjoy the subtle tastes and smells of the juices that flow from your partner's yoni. In the Eastern view, these juices carry sexual energy as well as the energy of life. To partake of them is to share in those energies.

Pleasure for Two: Kiss of the Crow

The kiss of the crow lets partners share intimate kisses with each other at the same time. For this kiss, the partners lie on their sides head-to-foot, facing each other. Each indulges the other with kisses of the lingam and yoni. An alternate posture is for the man to lie flat on his back and the woman to position herself over him, with her knees at the sides of his shoulders and her elbows at the sides of his hips.

Though the kiss of the crow is incredibly erotic, it can be difficult for partners to focus on both giving and receiving such exquisite pleasure. Many couples move in and out of the kiss of the crow during extended lovemaking.

While the names of many lovemaking postures the Kama Sutra describes reflect the Hindu reverence for animals, designating this posture as the kiss of the crow is especially significant. The crow was believed to have great mystical powers, including the ability to dissolve substances, transforming them from their original states into a blended form.

Dr. Josie Suggests

Yoni kisses during menstruation are a matter of personal preference. From a hygienic point of view, there is no reason to avoid them. However, some men find the smells and tastes of the yoni too intense during menstruation. Tantric teachings hold women's sexual juices in high esteem, believing they enhance a man's virility and vitality. A man who kisses his woman's yoni and is comfortable with her natural juices honors her fertility and sexual power.

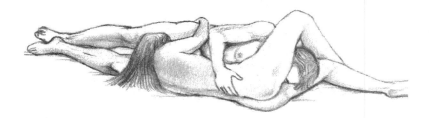

Kiss of the crow.

(Hrana Janto)

Getting Closer: Embracing

Many embraces can be either preludes to sexual union or acts of sexual union. Embraces bring bodies close together, enhancing their energies and intensifying passion.

Embrace of a Twining Creeper

The partners stand very close to each other, with their legs entwined and arms around each other. The woman raises one leg and wraps it around the man's thigh. The partners kiss and caress, and may be joined in sexual union.

Embrace Like Climbing a Tree

The partners stand close, with their arms around each other. The woman stands with one foot on her lover's foot and the other leg raised and wrapped around his thigh as though she were trying to climb him, as she might begin to climb a tree, trying to raise herself to kiss him.

Embrace like climbing a tree.

(Hrana Janto)

Embrace of Rice and Sesame Seed

The partners lie very close to each other. The man places his leg between the woman's thighs, and she wraps herself around him. Their bodies are intertwined and overlapped, making it difficult to distinguish one from the other.

Embrace of rice and sesame seed.

(Hrana Janto)

Embrace of Milk and Water

The man sits on the edge of the bed or on a cushion and the woman sits astride his lap, facing him. They embrace each other tightly, as though attempting to fuse their two bodies into one. This is an embrace of deep passion and intimacy.

Embrace of the Brow

The partners sit or stand close to each other. One touches the other's forehead, eyes, and mouth with caresses and kisses using his or her lips. They might also sit or stand with foreheads touching, looking into each other's eyes. This embrace is intimate and arousing for both partners.

Embrace of the Thighs

The partners use their thighs to grip the other partner's thighs. This embrace pulls their bodies close, and allows the man to press his lingam against the woman's front. Partners can stand, sit, or lie together for this embrace.

Embrace of the Middle Parts

The partners press the middle parts of their bodies, from belly buttons to thighs, tightly against each other. They may move and rub against each other to mimic the actions of sexual union. The embrace of the middle parts is very arousing because of the contact between lingam and yoni, even though there is no penetration.

Embrace of the Breasts

The man stands or sits close to the woman and presses his chest against her breasts as if to press himself between them. She presses back. Eye contact increases this embrace's intimacy.

The Least You Need to Know

- Your entire body is erogenous, responding to kisses, caresses, strokes, and embraces with increasing arousal.

- Lingam and yoni kisses can be intensely pleasurable, either as a prelude to sexual union or leading to orgasm themselves.

- Use all your senses to enjoy as well as pleasure your partner.

- The Kama Sutra tells lovers to enjoy the various kisses and embraces as they arise naturally during the course of lovemaking, and to improvise with them as suits the couple.

Chapter 19

Joyful Union

In This Chapter

- Sexual unions for intense passion
- Sexual unions when yoni and lingam are a less than ideal match
- Ways the man can move his lingam during sexual union
- How to develop control to intensify and prolong sexual excitement

In the West sexual union is the objective of lovemaking, while in the East it is the ecstatic closure that naturally evolves from increasingly intense passion and desire. Sexual union Kama Sutra style takes place when sexual pleasure reaches its peak, and honors the fulfillment of each partner. Both partners need to be fully aroused, physically and emotionally, and fully present as their bodies unite. When they are, they enjoy incredible sexual pleasure.

Most often, sexual union results in orgasm for both partners. But Vatsyayana reminds lovers that it is not the union itself that produces this result so much as the love play that precedes it. Men typically reach peak sexual intensity more quickly than women. Accordingly, the Kama Sutra counsels men to engage in as many of the 64 elements of sexual loving as it takes to bring the woman to full arousal before entering her.

Lying Down Together: Basic Unions

There are seven basic unions for uniting man and woman when they lie down together. The first three of these accommodate intense desire and arousal. The Kama Sutra recommends these three unions when the yoni is much smaller than the lingam, such as a deer yoni and a stallion lingam, or to increase sexual tension and pleasure for the woman.

Though the next four unions are less intense, their intimacy makes them every bit as erotic and exciting. The Kama Sutra recommends these unions when the yoni exceeds the lingam in size, such as an elephant yoni and a hare lingam, or to increase sexual tension and pleasure for the man.

The Wide Open Yoni

The three unions of the wide-open yoni present the woman's yoni to the man's lingam as an inviting blossom. All three unions begin with the woman lying on her back. The man lies, kneels, or crouches between her legs, facing the woman, and guides his lingam into her yoni.

Dr. Josie Suggests

As you practice these unions, it is important to remember the four keys to great intimate lovemaking. The first three you already know: breathe, look into each other's eyes, and let yourself make sound. The fourth key is movement. As arousal and sexual tension build, relax rather than tighten your muscles. Let your spine undulate like a snake and let lovemaking be a warm, playful, generous dance. Have fun. Laugh, cry, and share yourselves openly and freely.

It is important for the woman to be fully aroused before the man attempts to enter her. Arousal softens, expands, and lubricates the yoni so it can accommodate the erect lingam with pleasure and ease. The three basic lying down together unions feature deep penetration that exposes the woman's clitoris to contact and stimulation as both partners thrust their bodies together. The man can change pressure and contact by altering the angle of penetration.

Widely Open Union

The woman lies level on her back with her knees up, feet flat, and legs spread wide to allow the man between them. As the man approaches, the woman raises her hips and arches upward to welcome his lingam. This movement further widens and tilts her yoni to let the man penetrate deeply and intensely.

Women: Use the muscles of your thighs to push your pelvis upward, creating an imaginary line from your shoulders (which are still on the bed), through your hips, and to your upraised knees. This takes the strain away from your back and allows you to use the strength of your thigh muscles to arch and thrust against your partner. It's always a good idea to have various-size pillows nearby, and to use them to support your back and elevate your middle parts.

Men: Be sure your partner is fully aroused and well lubricated. This means her vulva should be wet, flushed, somewhat swollen, and her genitals should move toward you as you touch and lick her. Entry should be easy and smooth, with little resistance. Ask your partner if she feels ready for you to enter her. Use your hands and a supplemental lubricant to further stimulate her if she's not quite ready.

> **CAUTION**
>
> **Out of Touch**
>
> In many of the Kama Sutra's sexual unions, it is essential for the woman to be fully aroused to assure that her yoni is dilated, softened, and lubricated to allow her partner's lingam to pleasurably penetrate. If the woman is not sufficiently aroused, penetration can be painful and even bruise or otherwise hurt her.

Yawning Union

The woman lies flat on her back with her legs up and spread open in a "V" shape. The man kneels with his thighs spread and guides his lingam into her yoni. The back of the woman's thighs rest across the tops of the man's thighs. The man can support himself over the woman with his hands beside her, or the woman can hold his hands to help support him in a more upright position.

There is not as much direct contact with the clitoris during this union, and the man's body pressing her thighs apart limits the woman's movement. The man can watch his partner's excitement increase as he can see both her face and her yoni. The man can vary the depth and angle of penetration by changing how upright he remains while thrusting.

Yawning union.

(Hrana Janto)

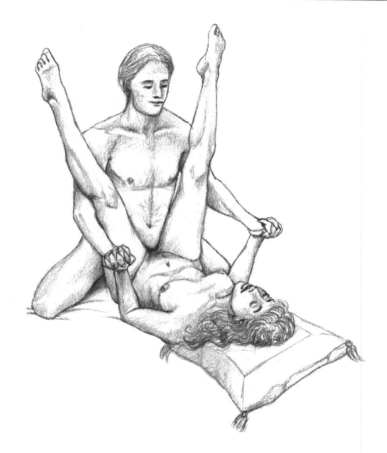

Women: Ask your partner to alter the angle of penetration or stimulate you with his hands if you're not receiving enough pleasure from the union. You can also modify the yawning union by putting your legs over your partner's arms and resting them against his shoulders. This pulls your legs against your body while keeping them spread and fairly straight, tilting your yoni upward to increase contact against your clitoris and vulva.

Men: Use your thighs to help you thrust so you don't put too much pressure against your partner's thighs with your upper body. In the modified yawning position, slide your knees back so you are pressed tightly against your partner (almost lying against her).

Union of Indrani

This union requires flexibility, endurance, and practice in addition to full arousal. The woman lies flat on her back and draws her legs against her body, calves touching thighs and knees touching her chest. The man kneels before her and she rests her feet against his sides, spreading her knees apart.

The union of Indrani pulls the muscles of the thighs and hips tight, which both tilts the woman's pelvis upward and opens wide her yoni. The man increases the tension of this movement by gently pulling the woman's thighs apart as he enters her. As the woman's yoni fully admits the man's lingam, the woman's buttocks rest against the man's thighs.

Though the union of Indrani offers less clitoral contact than the widely open union, it provides more contact to the perineal area. Depending on the angle of penetration, it can also stimulate the woman's G spot.

Women: Let your partner know if this union becomes uncomfortable. You might need to stretch your legs (shifting into a yawning or modified yawning position) or relax your back. Also let your partner know if you'd like more clitoral stimulation or extra lubrication.

Men: Again, be sure your partner is fully aroused before you attempt to enter her. Keep your thighs against her bottom to help you control the depth of your thrusts.

Full Body Intimacy

The remaining four basic unions for lying together in lovemaking feature the delight and intimacy of full body contact. The lingam's penetration is shallow, which increases friction. The clasping union is the basis for all four of these unions, which feature rhythmic and more gentle movements.

Clasping Union

The woman lies outstretched on her back with her legs slightly spread. The man lies on top of her with his legs on the outsides of hers and inserts his lingam into her yoni. Your bodies are in full-length contact, which creates a strong feeling of intimacy. Kiss and caress your partner's face, and look into each other's eyes to intensify this sensation.

> **Dr. Josie Suggests**
>
> Even a deeply aroused woman may need extra lubrication during extended lovemaking. Use a water-based product with condoms, and either a water-based or oil-based product if you're not using condoms. And if you're trying to become pregnant, use the white of an egg for lubrication—it most closely resembles the consistency of your cervical mucus.

The clasping union can also take place when you're lying on your sides facing each other. In ancient India, the man was always on his left side and the woman on her right side. In Hindu symbolism, Shakti (representing the feminine principle) sits to the right of Shiva (representing the masculine principle) in all circumstances except lovemaking. During lovemaking, Shakti moves to Shiva's left. Based in Tantra, this reflects the shift from ordinary to sexual energy.

Clasping union.

(Hrana Janto)

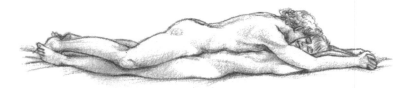

Pressing Union

Start in either variation of the clasping union. When the lingam is securely in the yoni, the woman presses her thighs together to increase pressure on her partner's lingam.

Twining Union

From the pressing union, the woman places her thigh across the top of her partner's thigh. This draws the man closer to her and pulls his lingam deeper into her yoni.

Union Like a Mare

From the twining union, the woman pulls her legs together and contracts the muscles around her yoni to hold the man's lingam tightly inside her.

Compact Unions

Unions in which the woman's legs are drawn up against her body in some fashion are more elaborate unions that open and widen her yoni. Though these unions give the man deep penetration and full contact against the woman's vulva, they severely restrict her ability to move. Many couples find this especially arousing, though it's important for the man to be sure his partner receives the stimulation and pleasure she desires to reach climax.

Women: Stroke and caress your partner's thighs as he thrusts, and push against his body as you are able to increase friction and pressure. Adjust the tilt of your pelvis for more clitoral contact or to control the depth of your partner's thrusts.

Men: Your partner's tucked position shortens and opens her yoni, and deep thrusting can hurt her. Alter the angle of your thighs to let her adjust the tilt of her pelvis and the depth of your penetration. Stroke and caress your partner's legs and buttocks, and her clitoris for additional stimulation.

> **Sutra Sayings**
>
> If the woman is not herself satisfied at the climax of sexual loving and shows she still wants enjoyment, her partner should rub her yoni with his hand and fingers as an elephant might rub with its trunk. He continues these actions until her body softens and relaxes, and she reaches fulfillment.

Full-Pressed Union

The woman lies on her back (either flat or slightly elevated against a cushion) and the man kneels before her. He raises her hips onto his thighs, aligning his lingam with her yoni. She bends her knees and draws her thighs to her chest, and places the soles of her feet against her partner's chest. The man enters her.

Full-pressed union.

(Hrana Janto)

Half-Pressed Union

From the full-pressed union, the woman stretches one leg out straight over her partner's thigh. This lets the woman increase the contact between her partner's body and her clitoris, and varies the angle and depth his lingam penetrates. She can move her leg up and down for even more variation in the sensations of their sexual union.

Half-pressed union.

(Hrana Janto)

Packed Union

The packed union is similar to the pressed union, except the woman crosses her legs one over the other at the ankles, keeping her thighs tightly together. Lingam and yoni join snugly for intensified friction as the man thrusts.

Packed union.

(Hrana Janto)

Unions Imitating Animals

In ancient India, there was much spiritual and religious symbolism attached to imitating the lovemaking positions and actions of animals. Two of the most revered animals were the cow and the elephant.

Union Like a Cow

The woman bends over from the waist and places her hands on the floor about shoulder-width apart. Her feet are spread about the same distance apart as her hands, and her knees are straight. The man stands behind her and enters her from the back.

Union like a cow.

(Hrana Janto)

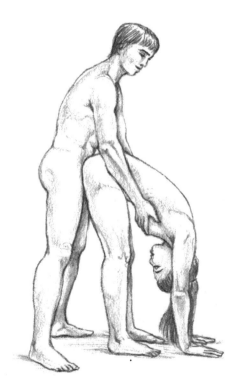

Women: Place your hands on a low table or bench if the stretch is too much. Tell your partner if you'd like him to stimulate your clitoris to increase your arousal.

Men: Caress your partner's back, buttocks, and breasts. Use your hand to stimulate her clitoris to give her added pleasure.

Union Like an Elephant

The woman lies face down with her hips somewhat flexed to raise her buttocks and her legs slightly spread. The man places himself over her, and draws in the small of his back to insert his lingam into her yoni. Once her yoni encloses his lingam, the woman can press her thighs together to hold it more tightly. The man supports himself with his arms so he can thrust and is not putting his weight on top of his partner.

Women: A cushion or pillow can help elevate your hips for easier penetration.

Men: You can draw yourself up somewhat onto your knees and tuck in your pelvis to more easily enter the woman.

"The Work of the Man"

The Kama Sutra specifies nine actions that are "the work of the man" during sexual union. These movements of the lingam stimulate and arouse the yoni, pleasuring both man and woman. The man can employ these actions in nearly any sexual union, and should vary them for the greatest enjoyment.

Moving Straight On

Move your lingam straight in and out of your partner's yoni, whether penetration is from the front or the back.

The Churn

Hold your lingam with your hand and move it around inside your partner's yoni, in a churning motion.

The Pierce

With your partner lying flat so her yoni is low, guide your lingam into your partner's yoni at such an angle that your thrusts gently strike against her clitoris.

The Rub

Raise your partner's hips so your lingam rubs against the bottom of her vulva and her perineum. You can achieve the angle necessary for this action by pulling her to the edge of the bed and standing as you enter her, or by placing a cushion or pillow beneath her hips to elevate her yoni.

The Press

Press your lingam against the inside of your partner's yoni for as long as it gives you both pleasure.

The Strike

Remove your lingam from your partner's yoni and gently strike, slap, or tap the outside of her yoni with it.

The Boar's Blow

Rub one side of your partner's yoni with your lingam.

The Bull's Blow

Use your lingam to rub both sides of your partner's yoni.

The Sporting Sparrow

With your lingam within your partner's yoni, move it up and down faster and faster. This action usually results in climax.

Flexing Your Pubococcygeal Muscle

At the base of your pelvis is a ring of muscle called the pubococcygeal muscle. You're most aware of this ring when it contracts and relaxes to start and stop urination. Both men and women have this muscle, though it gets far more attention in women. Childbirth can weaken a woman's pubococcygeal muscle, and most women's health care providers advise pregnant women to do *Kegel exercises* (named after the gynecologist who popularized them) to strengthen and tone this important muscle.

Sutrology

Kegel exercises are a series of "clench and release" exercises to strengthen the pubococcygeal muscle. They are beneficial for both men and women.

Kegel exercises are great for developing control and strength in this muscle during sexual union. The sensations a man feels when a woman contracts her pubococcygeal muscle while his lingam is within her yoni are often intensely arousing (sometimes even more so than thrusting). These exercises are easy to learn, and you can do them just about anywhere, anytime—no one else knows you're doing them.

Dr. Josie Suggests _____

Women: Once you're familiar with the feel and movement of your pubococcygeal muscle, lie down and insert a finger into your vagina. Contract and relax the muscle, and feel the movement of your vaginal walls. Do this again after you've been doing Kegel exercises for several weeks to feel how your muscles and control have strengthened. Men, you'll notice a strengthened pubococcygeal muscle gives you greater ejaculatory control.

Men benefit from toning and strengthening the pubococcygeal muscle, too. Being able to contract and relax this muscle aids a man in controlling ejaculation to enjoy multiple orgasms and prolonged lovemaking. For both men and women, pulsing the pubococcygeal muscle brings blood and energy to the pelvic area, and a pleasant glow of arousal to the rest of you.

Exercise: Pubococcygeal Control (Kegel Exercises)

1. First, learn to recognize this muscle's involvement when you urinate. Practice stopping and starting the flow of urine by consciously contracting and relaxing the muscle.

2. Practice holding and releasing your pubococcygeal muscle several times a day. You can do this fully clothed, whether you're sitting or standing. Contract and hold for three seconds, then relax for three seconds. Do this in sets of 10.

3. Within two weeks, you should experience a noticeable improvement in the amount of pressure you can generate when you contract this muscle.

4. Do your exercises faster and faster, until you reach a level of control where your pelvis (and in women, your vagina) feels as though it's vibrating or fluttering.

5. Extend your control over your pubococcygeal muscle by lengthening the contractions and relaxations. Contract slowly, as though you're trying to draw your pelvis up. Relax equally slowly, letting it back down again.

Prolonging Pleasure Through Ejaculation Control

Delaying or controlling ejaculation is a sensitive subject for men. Most men are at least a little attached to ejaculating. After all, that familiar explosive ejaculation feels good. If a man has not discovered the other kinds of orgasm, why would he want to give up what he knows and finds pleasurable?

Nearly every woman has had the sad experience of being with a man who climaxes quickly and without warning or apology and then recedes, becoming disinterested in her still-aroused state and interest in continuing love play. A man who ejaculates and rolls away into his own private reverie or slumber fosters frustration and a sense of separation in the woman he leaves unfulfilled.

> **CAUTION**
>
> **Out of Touch**
>
> Premature ejaculation—that is, orgasming and ejaculating sooner than desired—is a problem that many men experience at least occasionally. Strengthening the muscles in the pelvic floor with pubococcygeal toning (Kegel exercises) is helpful. If the situation persists, consult a physician for a thorough exam to rule out physical problems.

While there is plenty to be said for a man learning to delay his ejaculation to please his woman, there is still more to be found in his learning to delay or put off his ejaculation to experience multiple and full body orgasms. These orgasms occur separate from ejaculation and are at least as pleasurable. The difference is that rather than the intense release that happens with explosion, the orgasm happens independently from ejaculation.

Virility and Ejaculation

In the West, ejaculation defines a man's sexual power and virility. Porn movies always culminate with an ejaculation scene where the man "spurts" dramatically and with great bravado into or onto his partner. If he is a Real Man, he is able to ejaculate again and again. Some men resist the idea of nonejaculatory sex because they have been told that it is unhealthy.

In the East, the ability to control ejaculation defines a man's physical and spiritual maturity. Withholding ejaculation is believed to be a great physical and emotional benefit to men. A man should monitor his ejaculations with the seasons, his physical and emotional state, and his age. A young man should ejaculate more often than an older man. And those living in a warm climate more frequently than those in temperate or cold climates. The Taoists believe that when ejaculation is avoided for periods of time, his body will reabsorb vital elements and this will help to maintain vigor, clarity, and potency.

The Pleasures of Delay

The experience commonly known as male orgasm is made up of two stages. First there is an emission as the prostate gland pumps semen into the urethra, followed by the expulsion. The highly pleasurable involuntary contractions of the pelvic muscles pump the semen down the urethra and out the penis. A man can learn to experience and enjoy these stages separately, which enables him to have multiple orgasms.

Much can be said for learning to delay ejaculation. A woman's sexual response takes longer to arouse fully and her capacity to enjoy orgasmic pleasure is unlimited. She will appreciate and cherish a man who can delay ejaculation to satisfy her sexual appetite. The Kama Sutra expresses disdain for a man who does not last long enough to allow a woman full satisfaction in lovemaking.

Such extended sexual loving provides great enjoyment for the man as well as his partner. Controlling ejaculation allows him to let the first stage of ejaculation—"priming the pump"—and its pleasurable sensations take place. By interrupting the flow of semen through the urethra, he maintains sexual tension and erection.

Because there is no *refractory period* following each orgasm, the man can make love until both he and his partner are satisfied. This is a practice that requires time to master. Rather than replacing your usual way of making love, think of cultivating this way of orgasming as an addition and a way to expand into greater pleasure and connection.

> **Sutrology**
>
> The **refractory period** is the amount of time it takes for a man to be able to again develop an erection following ejaculation. This time varies among men and among sexual experiences.

Mastering Ejaculation Control

Learning to delay ejaculation takes time to feel confident and masterful. Allow that there will be times that you go over the edge and ejaculate, and there will be times when the desire to ejaculate is stronger than your desire to delay. Communicate with your partner what is happening and stay connected emotionally. You can continue to pleasure your partner with your hands, mouth, and when your energy builds again, with your lingam.

In the beginning of your learning, consciously choose that this time you will delay ejaculation. Pay attention to the difference in the sensations, feelings, and energy you experience in an orgasm in which you ejaculate and one in which you allow your semen to be reabsorbed.

Ejaculation control requires practice. The following exercise is for the man to practice by himself.

Ejaculation Control Exercise: Self-Pleasuring Ritual

1. Just as if you were creating a space for you and your partner to enjoy sexual loving, light a candle, put on soft music and spend a few minutes relaxing your body as you deepen your breath.

2. Use a good massage or coconut oil and begin to pleasure yourself.

3. When you feel yourself getting close to the edge of ejaculating, almost to the point of no return, stop stimulating yourself and become still.

4. Relax your anal and genital muscles (Kegel exercises will help you improve this control). Breath deeply and slowly.

5. Press your tongue against the top of your palate to ground your energy and delay ejaculation.

Practice the following ejaculation control exercise during lovemaking. Let your partner know in advance that you want to do this. Close communication is important so you and your partner are synchronized in your actions. Let your partner know when you want to ejaculate.

Ejaculation Control Exercise: Involving Your Partner

1. As you are coming close to the point of no return, have your partner put pressure on your frenulum (the area of your penis behind the glans).

2. Have your partner clasp your lingam with one hand or both, and gently but firmly squeeze until the urge to ejaculate subsides.

3. An alternative is to put pressure on the perineum point, the small indentation halfway between your scrotum and your anus. Before you reach the point of no return, have your partner press firmly on your perineum point. This will prevent semen from flowing into your urethra, letting you experience the pleasurable sensations that occur at the beginning of orgasm yet delaying ejaculation.

Sutra Sayings

Passion spawns amorous acts, which, like dreams, cannot be defined before they happen. Each enjoyment has its place and time, and not every pleasure is for every person.

Adaptations and Variations

The Kama Sutra tells lovers that the joys of sexual loving are limited only by their imaginations. Vatsyayana urges couples to watch the world around them, and learn from the habits of the birds and the tigers, the boar and the deer, the donkey and the cat. In these observations are endless variations to keep lovemaking fresh and exciting.

The Least You Need to Know

◆ In the Eastern view, sexual union culminates the pleasures of lovemaking. It is not a goal but an outcome.

◆ Most sexual unions require full arousal of the woman, both for her pleasure and for her physical safety.

◆ Not every form of lovemaking will interest or please every couple. Try what appeals to you, with whatever adaptations come naturally.

◆ Learning ejaculation control helps a man extend his own as well as his partner's sexual pleasure during lovemaking.

Chapter 20

Advanced Adventures

In This Chapter

◆ The symbolism behind the acrobatics

◆ Sexual unions for the strong and flexible

◆ Making adjustments and adaptations

◆ Symbolic representations in erotic art

Variety is the spice of life, as we're fond of saying in the West. This is one Western view with which Vatsyayana agrees. The Kama Sutra presents a number of sexual unions that challenge both the body and the mind. They require practice and concentration—efforts that are well rewarded once you master their physical and emotional levels. Chapter 24 describes additional advanced sexual unions from a later love text based on the Kama Sutra.

We present these unions as more advanced than those in Chapter 19 because they require strength, flexibility, or both. Many have symbolic significance as well. Lovers in ancient India often attempted to emulate the postures of animals, or to incorporate other elements of nature.

Balance, Strength, and Stamina

Sexual unions that require strength, balance, and stamina also require bodies that are physically capable of performing them. Though some of the sexual unions in this chapter may appear or sound simple, you can't just leap into them. These are unions that, in the time of Vatsyayana, were presented to young lovers as skills to acquire and look forward to over a long period of sexual loving with each other.

Yoga was a daily practice in ancient India, which many of the advanced Kama Sutra unions reflect. These unions require a degree of suppleness and focus that many Westerners don't typically associate with lovemaking. It's important to know both your own and your partner's capabilities and limitations before embarking on them.

A Willing (and Able) Body

In what shape is your body? Regular physical activity that keeps your muscles toned and your joints limber will improve your flexibility and stamina. If you're a bit of a couch potato but find these sexual unions intriguing, there's good incentive to get yourself moving and in shape!

Dr. Josie Suggests

Seeing the divine in your beloved helps to bring you and your beloved into a sacred space. You can do this by eye gazing. Look deeply into your partner's eyes while you relax and breathe. Allow your gaze to soften and become diffused while you see your partner with "new eyes."

Emotional and Spiritual Readiness

The advanced sexual unions aren't just acrobatic to challenge your physical flexibility and endurance. They are often symbolic—for example, the union of splitting a nail activates the energy of the third eye (the location of the sixth chakra, which governs perception and inner vision). In addition to the physical release that takes place with orgasm, these unions generate a release of emotional and sometimes spiritual energy as well.

Have Fun!

Making love shouldn't be a competition or a challenge. Have fun as you explore these unusual, and sometimes seemingly impossible, unions. It takes a lot of practice to achieve many of these unions, though usually your efforts are well worthwhile. Don't be afraid to laugh and enjoy yourself. If something doesn't work out quite right, or doesn't do much for you, try something else.

Erotic Acrobatics

Most of these advanced unions require agility and practice, practice, practice—as well as full arousal in the woman. Take them slowly, with modifications and adaptations to make them pleasurable for you as you're learning. The Kama Sutra advises that nearly all of these unions take considerable practice to master. Remember, the point isn't necessarily orgasm but also to bring each other to deep states of sexual fulfillment—emotionally as well as physically.

> **CAUTION**
>
> **Out of Touch**
>
> If it hurts, stop! It's possible for either the man or the woman to be injured if you ignore this most important signal from your bodies. You may need more lubrication or to stretch a cramped muscle. Stretch and breathe. Keep a sense of humor, and laugh and have fun with each other. You can try again or stop until next time.

Union Like a Pair of Tongs

The man lies on his back and the woman sits astride him, facing him. He may leave his legs outstretched or bend his knees somewhat to spread his legs apart. She draws his lingam into her yoni and holds it tightly. She contracts and relaxes her vaginal muscles to press and stroke his lingam. In this way, she stimulates the man and herself.

This union is considered advanced because it takes great control of the vaginal muscles to press the lingam with enough strength and rhythm to create the intense pleasure that will lead to orgasm. The woman may also move her hips slightly to vary the lingam's placement within her yoni. Though movements are subtle, this union is one of deep penetration, allowing the woman to guide her own pleasure as well.

Union like a pair of tongs.

(Hrana Janto)

Turning Union

The turning union begins with the woman on her back and the man between her legs. With his lingam in her yoni, he turns his body (taking care not to hit the woman with his feet) until his head is between her feet and his feet on the sides of her shoulders. The objective is to remain within her yoni throughout the movements. This union gives the woman an unusual and erotic view of her partner's buttocks.

Thrusting is difficult once turned, however. Pleasure is more likely to result from pressing the yoni around the lingam and gentle movements. In the turned stage of this union, the man's lingam is pressing down against the back of the woman's yoni, which may be uncomfortable for her.

Women: Lie still while the man is turning, to help contain his lingam within your yoni.

Men: Move slowly and in stages. If you feel yourself slipping out of your partner's yoni, move back to a position in which you can re-enter her. The turning union requires smooth movements and lots and lots of practice.

Turning union.

(Hrana Janto)

Union of Fixing a Nail

The woman lies back, either flat or against a cushion, with one leg outstretched. She raises the other leg and places her foot against her partner's forehead. Her partner kneels between her thighs, and presses against her raised leg as he thrusts. The angle of the woman's yoni changes with each thrust, as her partner's chest against her thigh moves her up and down. These movements arouse intense sexual passion, though require much practice to perfect.

The union of fixing a nail stimulates the energy of the third eye, which is symbolically located in the center of the forehead. By pressing her foot against her partner's third eye, the woman releases energies that provide clarity, vision, and perception. This intensifies the experience of sexual loving for both partners by keeping them fully present with each other.

Union of fixing a nail.

(Hrana Janto)

Union of Splitting Bamboo

The woman lies back, either flat or against a cushion, with one leg outstretched and the other raised. Her partner kneels before her and rests her raised leg on his shoulder as he penetrates her. She alternates the outstretched and raised legs as her partner's lingam remains within her yoni. Though these movements are intensely arousing, they require much concentration and practice. The man can caress the woman's breasts, inner thighs, and clitoris while she exchanges leg positions.

Union of splitting bamboo.

(Hrana Janto)

Lotuslike Union

The woman lies on her back and crosses her legs across her midsection, lotus style, with her thighs touching her breasts. This pulls the yoni wide and upward. Her partner kneels over her, supporting himself with his arms, and enters her, with his thighs pressing against hers. Penetration is deep, and there is good contact between the man's body and the woman's G-spot for stimulation during movement.

Lotuslike union.

(Hrana Janto)

Women: This is a difficult union to achieve or hold for very long, though it can give you intense pleasure. Tell your partner when you've had enough, and slip into a more comfortable union.

Men: Like other unions that open wide the yoni, the lotuslike union is pleasurable for the woman only when she is fully aroused. Use your thighs pressing against hers to help you regulate the depth and force of your thrusts.

Union Like a Crab

As in the lotuslike union, the woman lies on her back with her legs crossed and drawn to her midsection. Her knees point out and stay below her chest, and her feet are tucked under her partner's belly. Her partner kneels over her and enters her. Penetration is deep, and the angle of the yoni pleasurably pressures the lingam.

Out of Touch

Unions that require the man to lift the woman in some way can cause injury to either or both partners. Consider your physical capabilities before attempting these. If in doubt, first try a modified variation. If anything you do hurts, stop immediately.

Union Like a Spinning Top

The man lies on his back with his legs outstretched. His partner straddles him, her feet flat at his sides and her knees up, and takes his lingam into her yoni. She slowly and smoothly pivots around until her back is to her partner.

Women: Move slowly and smoothly to keep your partner's lingam within you and to avoid hurting your partner. Once you've completed your movements and your back is to your partner, lean forward or backward to alter the angle of his penetration.

Men: Guide and support your partner as she goes through the movements of this union. Caress her back, buttocks, and thighs as she moves up and down on your lingam.

Union like a spinning top.

(Hrana Janto)

Union Like a Swing

From the union like a spinning top, the man lifts his middle parts after the woman has turned her back to him. He then sways from side to side and moves up and down, and his partner rides him like a swing. This requires a strong back and a light woman, and is definitely not something you should try if you have any kind of back problem.

A less straining variation is for the man to lean against a cushion or support himself in a semi-sitting position by leaning against his arms. He can then thrust his pelvis in the described motions without pressuring his back. The woman can lift herself slightly using her thighs and join in her partner's movements.

Union like a swing.

(Hrana Janto)

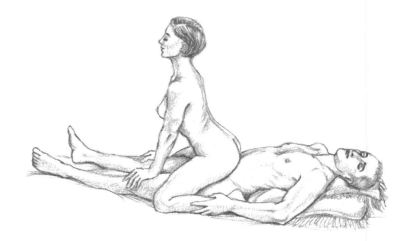

Supported Union

In this standing union, the woman faces her partner and raises herself to take his lingam into her yoni. The man might need to stand with his legs further apart to lower himself to enter her. The man holds and supports the woman as he thrusts. This union requires good balance. If either partner becomes uncomfortable, just switch to another union.

Women: Wrap one leg around your partner's thigh for deeper penetration. If you're on your toes with the other leg in order to reach your partner for union, it will be hard to stay this way. Stand on a low stool to equalize your height difference and allow you to stand with your foot flat.

Men: This union is difficult to maintain for very long. You can extend your ability to sustain it by leaning against a wall.

Suspended Union

The man stands bracing his back against a wall for support. The woman wraps her legs around the man's waist and her arms around his neck. As his lingam enters her yoni, she hangs suspended from him, pressing her feet against the wall at her partner's back. The man holds the woman's buttocks or thighs and moves her against him.

Like the supported union, the suspended union can be intensely exciting though difficult to maintain.

Suspended union.

(Hrana Janto)

Erotic Symbolism

Much erotic art depicting the time of ancient India shows various multiple unions as symbolic representations of the many facets of sexual loving. As sculptures, carvings, and paintings, these works of art can still be seen on temples and other sacred sites in India today. One of the most common images is that of a man either lying on his back or standing. Using his lingam, mouth, fingers, and toes, he pleasures six or seven women simultaneously.

Kama Knowledge

Sculptures, carvings, and paintings from ancient India to as late as the fifteenth century present erotic and explicit images of ancient Indian lovers engaged in elaborate sexual unions. Though the Western world tends to view these works of art as inappropriate and even obscene, in the Eastern view they honor the spiritual and religious dimensions of sexual loving. Eastern art displayed sensuous pleasure as a normal aspect of joy and love in adult relationships. No doubt these wonderfully detailed depictions also served as models for young couples learning the joys of love and the 64 elements of sexual loving.

One of the differences between Eastern and Western thinking is that the West is more literal. When we approach the Eastern teachings around sacred sexuality, we interpret the image of a man and several women as an orgiastic sexual experience when in actuality the erotic representation may be symbolic of the many-faceted experience of life.

Give Yourself Time

Sutra Sayings

Not every pleasure of sexual loving is for every person or every time. Each should be enjoyed in its place. Those who know well the science of love know how to balance strength and tenderness in sexual loving.

Learning to make love in new ways takes time. Remember to bring a sense of humor to your endeavors in pleasure. There will be times when you begin uncertainly and half-heartedly, only to discover each other and an amazing ecstasy that you never imagined existed. And there will be times when the energy goes flat for any number of reasons. The best medicine is acceptance and wonder. Give yourself and your love-making plenty of time and space to grow and evolve.

The Least You Need to Know

- The sexual unions of the Kama Sutra give both physical and emotional connection and satisfaction.

- Be mindful of your physical capabilities and limitations.

- If it hurts, stop immediately. Stretch and relax, if you need to, then carefully resume or try something else.

- Have fun with your experimentations! If you can't quite get into the correct alignments, try something else.

Chapter 21

After the Loving

In This Chapter

◆ The different kinds of orgasms

◆ What happens in a man's body during sexual climax

◆ What happens in a woman's body during sexual climax

◆ How to prolong the intimacy of lovemaking

How often do you linger in the afterglow of lovemaking with your beloved? Are you one of those people whose mind turns to the next thing on your agenda as the last shudder of pleasure has barely passed? We invite you to reconsider your approach to departing the loving embrace too quickly.

First, couples usually have different timing, at least some of the time. One is more complete and ready to move into the day's activities or night's rest before the other, or one simply wants more contact—touching, holding, stimulation, or intimate conversation about what has been shared in the lovemaking. Second, when partners continue to touch and delight in each other in afterplay, the warm glow of their sexual energy continues to nourish the connection they have established through lovemaking as they fall asleep or begin the day's activities. Lovemaking does not have to be an isolated or time-limited event. When you are conscious of how small, shared gestures—lingering together after sex, sharing a passing affectionate pat, kiss, or reminder of the closeness you feel for each other—can extend sexual intimacy, your closeness continues to be a part of the other aspects of your life.

In the West most couples consider that sex is good enough when there has been a reasonable amount of foreplay and both partners achieve orgasm. It is then that men most often retreat to sleep or their own worlds while women often still have more energy to connect emotionally and physically. The discrepancy between the masculine and feminine response to orgasm can be a problem and a source of distrust for couples. Fortunately, partners can find greater intimacy in sex by paying attention to what occurs in orgasm and after.

The Cycle of Ecstasy

Many people believe that there is still only one kind of orgasm—the clitoral or vaginal for women and the penile orgasm for men. In reality, men and women can experience a number of different kinds of orgasms, some that are limited to the genital area and others that encompass the whole body. Some are powerful throbbing releases that build to a peak and are over, some build to peak after peak of release, and some ride a slow wave across a high plateau and leave the body vibrating for hours.

While both men and women can ejaculate, when a man ejaculates his energy drops off and he requires a period of time to reawaken his erection. This is not the case for a woman. Her appetite is not necessarily diminished by her ejaculation or orgasm. A man can also orgasm without ejaculation, and when he does he can experience a series of multiple orgasms and full body releases that are exquisitely pleasurable. A man who does not experience ejaculation with orgasm usually has continued energy to connect with his partner. Of course, there are exceptions to this.

Kama Knowledge

Physician William Masters and psychologist Virginia Johnson began collaborating in research studies of human sexual response and behavior in the 1950s. Masters and Johnson worked together for 30 years (and were married to each other for many of them), conducting landmark research into the physiological responses of the body during sex. They were the first researchers to use sophisticated monitoring equipment to directly measure and record numerous physical responses in men and women during the act of sexual intercourse. Holistic sexology includes the study of sexual researchers such as Masters and Johnson, and adds the teachings from the schools of esoteric sexuality, Tantra, the Kama Sutra, body-oriented psychotherapy, and relationship therapy.

To understand what happens after climax with ejaculation, it's important to remember what leads up to it. The research of the Western world's best-known sex researchers, physician William Masters and psychologist Virginia Johnson, has identified four distinct stages in the cycle of sexual intercourse.

The Four Stages of Sexual Loving

In the first stage of lovemaking, the stage of excitement or arousal, the body responds to physical stimulation. In both men and women, the heartbeat and rate of breathing both quicken, the skin begins to warm and flush, and nipples become erect. The man's penis swells into an erection. The woman's vulva and vagina swell, soften, and exude fluid. Her clitoris also swells and hardens. This stage can last up to several hours.

As sexual arousal progresses, the man's testicles enlarge and move tight against his body. The woman's breasts and uterus become enlarged, and her pubococcygeal muscle pulses. All sexual sensations intensify as man and woman approach the brink of orgasm. This is the second, or plateau, stage. Lovers can extend this stage by playing the edge or building toward the orgasmic peak, slowing down for a moment or two, and then building again toward the peak a second time, a third time, or as many times as they wish.

The third stage of the sexual cycle is climax, or orgasm. This is an explosive physical release of accumulated sexual energy, marked by intense, rhythmic contractions of the muscles in the pelvic area of both man and woman. Climax is an experience that engulfs the partners, sweeping them into an exquisite pleasure that envelopes them. People experience the full range from mild to ecstatic states of release and union in orgasm. If you are relaxed at the moment of orgasm and breathing deeply and fully, the contractions that begin in your pelvis can spread throughout your entire body into a full body orgasm.

As orgasm concludes, the changes you experienced in the previous stages begin to reverse. Heart rate and breathing slow. Skin flushing fades. Body parts return to normal size and condition. Man and woman both may feel a sense of euphoria and intimacy. This is the fourth, or resolution, stage.

> **Dr. Josie Suggests**
>
> In Dr. Josie's work with women, she teaches that the keys to orgasmic pleasure are breathing in a deep full way, allowing the body to move in a fluid undulatory (snakelike) way, opening the throat so you can allow sounds to happen, and opening your eyes to connect with your partner.

Orgasm can be elusive for women. Frequently, women learn to have orgasms through masturbation in a particular fashion, then have difficulty becoming orgasmic during the transition to sexual loving with a partner. In the effort to be orgasmic, many partners become frustrated and try harder and harder to please and be pleased to the point of orgasmic release. Contrary to their efforts, being orgasmic is less a matter of will and more stimulation than it is of relaxing, breathing, focusing on pleasure, and being able to let go of striving for the orgasm. Though orgasm is a physically felt event that can barely tremble or deeply rock a woman to her core, orgasm is an emotional and spiritual event as well. The fear of not orgasming, abusive past experiences, the inability to let go of thinking about the rest of life and focus on pleasure, and the reluctance to give up control are ways that a woman prevents the open, receptive, responsive, and allowing state that leads to orgasm.

What Happens After Climax: His Body

Men who have mastered ejaculation control (see Chapter 19) are able to have several orgasms without ejaculation, prolonging pleasure for themselves and their partners. But once a man ejaculates, his ability to have another orgasm ends until his body recycles and he returns to a state of readiness. This refractory period can take 20 minutes to several hours or longer. It is possible for a man to maintain a partial or even full erection for a time following ejaculation, though often the erection fades.

What Happens After Climax: Her Body

A woman can immediately have a second as well as subsequent orgasms, and often enjoys the pleasures of doing so. Her body does not require a refractory period, and she can maintain a high level of sexual arousal for as long as her interest and her partner's participation continue. Women who have multiple orgasms may experience them in different ways. One may crash through her body in waves of ecstasy, while another primarily throbs through her pelvis. Not every woman has multiple orgasms, or ejaculates as she orgasms, or has them with every sexual union.

Dr. Josie Suggests

You may end lovemaking with orgasm and ejaculation, or you may end it without ejaculatory orgasm because you feel complete in the moment. Either way, what's important is that you tell your partner where you are. "I'm ready to stop now, how about you? Is there anything more you'd like to do? Or like me to do? How would you like to bring the energy to a close?"

Savor the Experience ... and Each Other

It is easy to see why Western men tend to consider sexual loving "done" after they ejaculate. A man might feel very relaxed, warm, and "spent," and want to drift pleasantly off to sleep. This is partly physiological—his body won't let him reach a state of full arousal again for a variable period of time. And it's partly emotional or psychological—he feels contented, tranquil, and safe.

Most women, on the other hand, are fully capable, when encouraged, to continue love-making after one or many orgasms. They desire intimacy and contact after orgasm to complete the experience of sexual loving. Yet many women find it difficult to ask for more attention once their partners have ejaculated.

If both partners approach this difference between men and women with tenderness and joy, it gives the man the opportunity to continue pleasuring the woman or simply to be attentive. Sometimes a woman may want to extend the intimacy of sexual union by just lying close and gently sharing strokes and caresses with her partner. Sometimes she may want continued sexual pleasure. Talking about what you are each feeling and desiring is important in creating an outcome in which each feels loved and cared for.

The Kama Sutra repeatedly counsels the man to assure the woman's satisfaction after he has reached his pleasure, warning that a woman left wanting for sexual climax will be frustrated and even angry. There is some physiological basis for this frustration, particularly if the woman doesn't reach orgasm.

Both male and female genitalia engorge with blood during sexual arousal. Orgasm releases the muscle tension that makes this possible. When orgasm does not occur, engorgement persists and then slowly dissipates. Either the man or the woman can feel an uncomfortable heaviness and even aching in the pelvic area until the swelling subsides.

> **Sutra Sayings**
>
> If the woman continues moving against the man after he has had his satisfaction, and does not let him get up, she still desires excitement and release. The man should lie on his back and pull the woman on top of him, so she may reach her satisfaction.

Staying in Touch

Because a woman's body remains in a heightened state of arousal for longer than a man's, a woman often enjoys continued physical contact and gentle stimulation even if she doesn't desire additional orgasms. A man, too, often finds it enjoyable to stay in touch with his partner's body to extend the shared intimacy between them.

Kissing

Kisses after lovemaking are often tender and gentle. They are kisses to express appreciation and gratitude for the wonderful experience both partners have just shared. They are kisses to express warmth and love for each other. They are kisses that show respect and honor for the relationship and for the union that draws its partners together in body, mind, and spirit. Such soft kisses are calming and soothing.

Caressing and Embracing

Like kisses after lovemaking, caresses and embraces show affection and tenderness. Lovers lie together and stroke each other's bodies, enjoying the wonder of the ecstasy those bodies have just provided. These touches are gentle and caring, conveying fulfillment and serenity.

Sharing Nourishment

Food and drink can be an erotic and enjoyable part of early love play. You might also be hungry and thirsty now, after extended lovemaking. Feed each other pieces of fruit, cheese, chocolate, or whatever other foods you like. You might enjoy a glass of wine or chilled water. Because you're sexually satisfied, you're more relaxed and at ease. There is no sense of urgency or sexual tension, just the pleasure of sharing.

Sutra Sayings

The lovers should go modestly to the washing room after lovemaking is completed, and cleanse themselves. When they return, they should apply fragrances and oils to each other, embrace, and speak pleasant words. They should drink from a shared cup, and feed each other sweetmeats, fruit, and other delicacies. This is the true conclusion of sexual union.

Bathing and Refreshing

Some partners enjoy bathing or showering together after making love, to refresh and relax. It can be very sensuous to lather, enjoying the heightened sensations that follow orgasm. Bathing together before lovemaking, which tends to be quite erotic and arousing, helps to establish intimacy. Showering together after sexual loving prolongs the familiarity and intimacy of your union. You feel tender and gentle toward one another. If you return to bed and fall asleep, you feel comfortable awakening to another lovemaking session.

Others prefer to clean up more privately, retreating for a quick shower and then returning to their partners. And some people just want to lie together, joined as long as possible, until they fall into the deep and restful sleep of satiated lovers. If they awaken to make love again, they enjoy the feel, tastes, and smells of bodies still warm and moist from the previous session.

Out of Touch

Don't let that warm tub of water lull you to sleep! You're especially relaxed after intense lovemaking, and may find the comfort of warm water too much to resist. If you feel sleepy, get out of the tub and snuggle together in bed. It's much safer.

Togetherness is the true culmination of sexual loving.

(Hrana Janto)

What you do is more a matter of personal preference than anything else. Some people find the remnants of earlier lovemaking somewhat messy, while others find them arousing. The Kama Sutra counsels couples to discreetly retreat to separate chambers to cleanse themselves, then return to the chamber of their togetherness and enjoy food, drink, and music together. The key point is to extend your sense of connectedness and intimacy through whatever actions you prefer, rather than separating and falling asleep or leaving.

Intimate Discourse

The warmth and closeness that follow lovemaking as you lay together touching and caressing often frees you to talk about the joys of your sexual loving. Many couples feel an especially emotional or spiritual bond to each other at this time, and a desire to extend the pleasure of their lovemaking with tender conversation. They find it easy to suspend many of the inhibitions that might otherwise keep them from sharing so openly and intimately.

Tender Talk

Conversation following lovemaking can take just about any course you let it. You can talk about the softness of your partner's skin, the joy you felt when your partner touched you in a certain way, the pleasure it gave you to feel and see your partner in sexual ecstasy. You can talk about the unexpected excitement you felt with a particular movement, or how much you enjoyed trying something different. You can talk about your feelings for each other.

Don't talk about the kids, the bills, your job, your parents, and other such potential "hot button" topics. Honor and cherish this time of closeness between you. Real life will intrude soon enough—there's no need to hasten its return.

The Joy of Laughter

Laughing together is a great way to share with each other after the loving. Laughing implies shared fun as well as shared values. It is a way to express your joy and happiness. Lovers who can laugh together can enjoy the humor that naturally arises from human situations. Laughter diffuses discomfort and awkwardness, and can turn a potentially devastating moment into an experience of understanding and pleasure.

Reawakening

Sometimes your continuing love play will lead to another sexual union as you stroke, kiss, and embrace each other. Subsequent sexual loving can be quite tender, as erotic tension often rebuilds more slowly and luxuriously after it's once been released. Enjoy and explore different sensations as your passion rekindles. This might be a good time to try unions that are more leisurely and relaxed, or perhaps sexual loving that doesn't necessarily lead to union.

The Least You Need to Know

- Both men and women can experience orgasm in many different ways.

- While men tend to feel "finished" with lovemaking following ejaculation and orgasm, women may want lovemaking to continue.

- Touching, talking, and staying close help extend your sense of intimate connection following sexual union.

- Afterplay is just as important as foreplay for sexual loving to be fulfilling for both partners.

Part 6

Beyond the Kama Sutra

After all this, could there be more? Indeed! The Kama Sutra is just the beginning for couples who want to more fully explore the joys of sexual loving and the pleasures of truly intimate sexual union.

The first chapters in this section deal with two of life's most significant transitions—pregnancy and aging. Other chapters explore different experiences in sexual loving. The Ananga Ranga, a love text based on the Kama Sutra but written a mere 500 years ago, presents enjoyable variations on postures that are sure to intrigue you. Tantric sex offers a spiritual journey with sexuality as your guide. Wrap it all up with a look at how to use what you've learned in this book to carry forward into the future of your relationship.

Chapter 22

Pregnancy and the Kama Sutra

In This Chapter

- Sexual loving, fulfillment, and conception
- Kama Sutra unions that might help when you're trying to conceive
- What happens to a woman's body during pregnancy
- How to use the Kama Sutra to maintain intimacy during and after pregnancy

In the realm of life's great mysteries, love, sex, death, and birth have the most potent force upon us. The circumstances surrounding the moment of our birth and the conditions that lead up to that moment impact us for life. In so-called more primitive cultures and in the Western folk medicine of earlier centuries, people recognized that the emotional, mental, physical, and spiritual climate surrounding conception, gestation, and birth influenced the well-being of a child. Special positions, potions, and prayers assured that conception led to the desired gender and good life circumstances that the family hoped for. When we as a culture took birthing out of the hands of women, intuition, and midwives and turned it over to physicians and science, what we gained—more sterile surgical and technological developments—was offset by a lack of sensitivity to the needs of the unborn child.

It has taken centuries to again seriously consider the influences upon a child from the time of conception to the time of birth. Forty years ago physicians "humored" a woman who played music or spoke to her unborn child. The adverse influences of cigarette smoke, alcohol, and caffeine were not an issue during pregnancy, nor was exercise. Natural childbirth—the way women gave birth prior to the use of anesthetics—was a thing of the past, and modern women bought formula in cans rather than nurse their babies at their breast. Our consciousness of the life of unborn children and our treatment of children once they are born are finally returning to an emphasis on the natural.

Sutra Sayings

As a man and a woman require food to survive, so do they also need sexual loving. They must feed their desires to create sons and daughters, so they may continue the existence of humankind.

We now recognize that what a woman eats, drinks, smokes, thinks, and feels, and the sounds a baby listens to while inside the womb all influence the baby's well-being. This awakening to the sensitivities and needs of unborn, newborn, and young children is vital if we are to raise people who cherish life and hold the future of the earth in high regard.

What Does the Kama Sutra Say About Getting Pregnant?

In the time of Vatsyayana, there was great reverence and respect for sexual loving for several reasons. Sex is the intimate glue between couples. Our most powerful pleasure, sex is a way we enjoy being in a body, connecting to another. And it is creation, the means by which we bring in new life. In the Eastern view during Vatsyayana's time, a man's seed should not be wasted. Every ejaculation carried the potential of pregnancy and was considered a sacred act.

Tantric teachings revere the woman's yoni as the divine doorway of fertility and physical existence. The lingam enters the yoni to transport its cargo of life-giving semen. Every person enters life through this sacred passageway, leaving the womb to begin his or her separate journey on Earth.

When Pregnancy Is Your Desire

In Vatsyayana's time, people believed the joy and intensity of sexual union determined the nature and destiny of the child conceived through it. The Kama Sutra emphasizes mutual satisfaction not only because it deepens the bonds of sexual loving between partners, but also because it influences the life path of the as yet unconceived child.

The Right Time for Sex: Maximizing Your Opportunity

There are only about five days each month when conditions are ideal for a woman to become pregnant. They are the four days immediately before, plus the day of, ovulation. A woman whose menstrual cycles are normal menstruates consistently every so many days—between 21 and 35 days is the norm. This is roughly once a month for most women, though women whose cycles are shorter have more periods and women whose cycles are longer have fewer periods.

However, pregnancy can and does result during other times of a woman's cycle. Many variables factor into the pregnancy equation, and every woman who has ovaries, fallopian tubes, and a uterus should consider herself fertile even if pregnancy seems to elude her. This includes women *going through menopause*—you are not considered beyond fertility until you've gone 12 consecutive months without a period. There are blood tests that measure hormone levels that your doctor can use to confirm whether you are post-menopausal, too. Unless you are certain you cannot become pregnant (because you've had your uterus removed, had a tubal ligation, or have gone through menopause), use a contraceptive to prevent pregnancy unless you want to conceive.

Ovulation—the time during which the egg travels up the fallopian tube on its way from the ovary to the uterus—takes place 14 days *before* the first day of menstruation. If your periods are regular, you can predict when you are likely to ovulate each month. Women whose periods are irregular have difficulty determining ovulation, and may in fact not ovulate with any consistency.

You are most likely to conceive the day you ovulate, and least likely to conceive longer than 12 to 24 hours after ovulation—the life span of the egg following its release from the ovary. Even in women whose cycles are very regular, it's nearly impossible to predict the precise time of ovulation. This is one reason you can become pregnant during a time you thought was "safe." While 90 percent of the sperm in a man's ejaculate die within hours, among the remaining 10 percent are those that could survive up to 48 hours. This makes pregnancy possible, though less likely, during the three or four days before ovulation.

CAUTION

Out of Touch

Women whose menstrual cycles are irregular, unusually short or long, or extremely painful may have difficulty getting pregnant. Irregular, long, or short cycles may indicate you're not ovulating. Very painful periods suggest endometriosis, one of the leading causes of infertility. If you have these signs, consult your health care professional.

Many fertility specialists now recommend that couples trying to conceive have sex once a day during the five days before and on the day of the woman's predicted ovulation. New information surfaces regularly as research provides more answers to the mysteries of fertility and pregnancy, however, so it's a good idea to work closely with a fertility specialist if you're trying to become pregnant though are having difficulty. There are so many variables involved with fertility and pregnancy that each couple's situation is unique.

Predicting ovulation and avoiding sex during your most fertile days is not an effective way to prevent pregnancy. No time of the month is impossible for conception. On rare occasions, women have been known to conceive even during menstruation. Women who have irregular menstrual cycles have more difficulty determining when, and often if, they are ovulating. Generally speaking, 85 to 90 percent of couples who are trying to conceive succeed within a year. When you're eager to become pregnant, this can seem like an eternity. If you have concerns about whether you can conceive, a visit to your gynecologist or women's health care provider can help you determine whether your fears are grounded in anxiety or reality.

Kama Sutra Unions for Enhancing Fertility

Postures of sexual union that best support efforts to conceive (see the following table) are generally those in which the woman is on her back, especially if her pelvis is elevated with a cushion or pillow. These unions encourage deep penetration, which deposits semen against or close to the cervix. They also encourage the semen to flow inward through the cervix and into the uterus. Unions in which the woman is on top, or in which partners lie on their sides or stand, generally involve shallow penetration and allow semen to drain quickly to the outside.

> **Sutra Sayings**
>
> When the duration of sexual loving is long, the woman receives pleasure and fulfillment. A child born of such a union will enjoy much happiness and success in life.

Beyond the physiological functions of sexual union, the Kama Sutra stresses the correlation between a couple's ecstasy during sexual loving and the likelihood that they will conceive. According to the beliefs of Vatsyayana's time, a woman who is fully satisfied during sexual loving will become pregnant, while one who does not reach fulfillment will not. Ancient Hindu couples believed that conception was a spiritual event. The woman's emotional state was considered far more important for procreation than posture or position during sexual union.

Though we now know far more about conception and the conditions that are most likely to support it, Vatsyayana wasn't so far off on one point. The depth of the woman's pleasure can influence the likelihood that she will become pregnant. Modern science has shown that a woman is more likely to conceive if she orgasms while the semen is in contact with her cervix. The muscular contractions that occur during orgasm help propel the semen through the cervix.

Kama Sutra Unions to Enhance Conception

Sexual Union	Described in Chapter ...
Widely open union	19
Yawning union	19
Full-pressed union	19
Half-pressed union	19
Union of fixing a nail	20
Union of splitting bamboo	20
Lotuslike union	20
Union of the enfolding embrace	24
Union like a bow	24

The Stages and Changes of Pregnancy

During pregnancy, a woman's body undergoes an amazing and wondrous series of changes that begin even before she knows another life is growing within her. Pregnancy is divided into three parts, called trimesters. The first trimester runs from conception to 12 weeks. The second trimester covers weeks 13 through 28. The third and final trimester goes from week 29 to delivery, usually at 40 weeks or so.

By the end of this nearly 10 months (even though common perception pegs pregnancy as a nine-month adventure), what started as the passionate union of two bodies culminates in the birth of a new human being. Between conception and delivery, lovemaking can take on a new and exciting dimension.

Changing Sexual Desire and Response

Hormones flood a woman's body during pregnancy. While their primary purpose is to sustain the pregnancy and prepare for delivery, these hormones also affect a woman's sexual desire. During the first trimester, many women find their interest in making love takes a nosedive. More than half of pregnant women experience morning sickness, fatigue, and tender or painful breast swelling.

By the second trimester, these symptoms disappear. Hormones begin softening the tissues in the pelvic floor as a preparation for delivery. This results in increased blood flow to the vulva, making the area extraordinarily sensitive. Many, though not all, women find sexual loving especially intense during this time as touching and stroking the labia, clitoris, and outer parts of the vagina trigger powerful sexual responses. However, this engorgement leaves some women feeling full and uncomfortable after making love, even if they experience otherwise satisfying orgasms.

> **Out of Touch**
>
> If your pregnancy is at higher than normal risk for premature labor, your doctor may tell you not to have orgasms, since this causes the uterus to contract. If you have any concerns or questions about sex during your pregnancy, discuss them with your health care provider.

In the third trimester, and particularly near its end, many women don't feel much like making love. Their enormous bellies make movement of any kind a challenge. Swollen breasts and genitalia may feel engorged and tender. The contractions that result from orgasm can be quite intense, even uncomfortable, and can continue as long as 30 minutes. If the contractions last longer, are painful, or become more intense, or there are other indications present that suggest labor could be starting, contact your health care provider.

Her Changing Body

The most obvious change, of course, is the pregnant woman's enlarging belly. It may seem to expand slowly at first. Some women don't "show" until well into their fourth or fifth month of pregnancy—the middle of the second trimester. Others display a small bulge that's not quite enough for casual acquaintances to know whether it's pregnancy or weight gain. Then during the second and third trimesters, their bellies grow rapidly as their babies do the same.

Breasts, too, enlarge as they prepare for the task of nourishing the child following birth. In the third trimester (and occasionally earlier), a pregnant woman's breasts may ooze a clear or pale fluid especially during love play. Breasts often again become tender and even sore near the end of pregnancy, as hormonal changes complete their transformation to the source of sustenance for the soon-to-be-born baby.

A woman's enlarging body parts aren't the only changes taking place during pregnancy. Vaginal secretions change as well, becoming thicker and more profuse. This can be beneficial during lovemaking by providing extra lubrication, or can become a hindrance by reducing friction. Pregnancy is the beginning of transition that will transform couples physically, emotionally, and spiritually. From changing bodies to fluctuating hormones, fears about parenting and its effects on partnering, couples are entering unknown territory, and the only certainty is that big changes are in store.

Kama Knowledge
There is no time when a woman's body experiences more rapid and more extensive change than during pregnancy. Her body produces hormones that are present only during pregnancy, which affect literally every cell in her body. These changes make the woman's body a hospitable environment for the developing fetus. Sometimes the hormones produce less-than-pleasant effects for the woman, such as morning sickness. No one really knows what causes morning sickness, though many doctors believe it has something to do with the flood of hormones that surge through the woman's body as pregnancy begins. Morning sickness affects about half of all pregnant women, usually during the first trimester of pregnancy. Most morning sickness, though unpleasant, causes no problems for either mother or baby, and goes away as the second trimester gets underway.

The more a couple can turn to and confide in each other, the deeper their bond and intimate connection becomes. All of these changes and hormonal fluctuations affect a pregnant woman's emotions. Wide swings are not uncommon. She might go from the heights of pregnant bliss, contented and fulfilled, to the depths of despair at her changing body, loss of freedom, or fears of not being able to rise to the task of motherhood. Her temperament may at times be volatile.

Changing emotions can be confusing and disconcerting for partners who haven't been through pregnancy before. The wild roller coaster of changing emotions does eventually calm down. In the meantime, talk to each other about what you are each experiencing. Keep in mind that in the face of all these confusing changes, a little kindness and tenderness can soothe anxiety and connect you on this journey.

Overcoming Worries and Fears

Many couples worry that making love, especially when their responses are intense, will hurt the baby in some way. Unless you have a complicated pregnancy or are at high risk for miscarriage or premature labor, sexual loving will have no effect on your baby. A plug of mucous forms in the opening of your cervix early in pregnancy, serving as a barrier that prevents just about anything from gaining access to your uterus. As well, amniotic fluid surrounds and cushions the baby, protecting it from bumps and jolts.

Because orgasm produces a series of contractions, you may be especially aware of contractions in your uterus during and following orgasm during pregnancy. Your uterus ordinarily contracts when you climax, though you aren't aware of it because your uterus isn't large enough for you to feel it. Though these can be quite strong in some women, they are not the kind of contractions that produce labor and won't harm either you or your baby.

Some couples feel it just isn't "right" to continue making love once the woman becomes pregnant. Sexual loving, whether or not it leads to sexual union, remains an essential dimension of your relationship. Through kissing and caressing and lying close, you reinforce the intimacy and connectedness you share as loving and committed partners. This is at least as important now, as you stand together at the cusp of one of life's most significant events—parenthood.

Using the Kama Sutra During Pregnancy

During pregnancy can be a good time to explore new dimensions of sexual loving, particularly if contraception previously kept you from trying activities and unions that otherwise interested you. Since a woman's sexual desire is often intensified during pregnancy, she may want more prolonged and varied lovemaking. Men often find their partners' pregnant bodies surprisingly arousing, and may feel a renewed sense of tenderness and loving.

Kama Sutra Positions During Pregnancy

Many couples find their lovemaking becomes quite tender and intimate during pregnancy. Hormonal changes make the woman's body more sensitive to touch, and there is a certain eroticism to the woman's burgeoning belly. Some women experience multiple orgasms for the first time during pregnancy, a surprising and enjoyable consequence of swelling in the vulva and perineum. Kama Sutra unions that particularly stimulate this area, or allow your partner to touch and stroke you, can be incredibly pleasurable.

CAUTION

Out of Touch

Not every pregnant woman responds with increased sexual desire to the hormonal changes affecting her body. Some women find the heightened sensations to be uncomfortable or irritating.

Unless your doctor has restricted your sexual activity, let comfort and enjoyment be your guides in choosing from the many pleasures of the Kama Sutra during your pregnancy. Generally your enlarging belly doesn't become an obstacle until the third trimester. In fact, it can lead to some fun and exciting modifications in activities and postures that were your favorites before pregnancy. Just keep a good sense of humor, and be willing to move on to more manageable activities if what you're attempting doesn't work out.

Sexual union during pregnancy can hold special intimacy.

(Hrana Janto)

Woman-on-top unions are especially enjoyable during pregnancy. The woman's belly can rest against the man's, and he can support it as needed. These postures also give the woman control over the depth of penetration and let her set the pace. Unions in which the man enters his partner from behind, though potentially less intimate because they prevent eye contact, can also be quite pleasurable. If you like these positions, try using a small mirror placed in front of you for intimate eye contact.

Kissing and caressing are good ways for partners to enjoy love play when one or the other doesn't desire sexual union. You can keep things sensual if the woman isn't feeling particularly sexual, which maintains a sense of intimacy between you. If the woman plans to breastfeed, having her partner play with and suck on her nipples on a regular basis (if she likes this) can both toughen her nipples in readiness for the baby and be quite erotic for both partners.

Sexual loving during the third trimester can be awkward, especially as the time for delivery approaches. As her belly grows, a woman's sense of balance changes. She may also experience low back and pelvic discomfort. This is a good opportunity to shift to sensuous massage and other forms of loving touch. If lovemaking and sexual union happen, great. But if not, that's fine, too. If the woman doesn't feel like making love but her partner does, she might pleasure him in other ways instead.

Dr. Josie Suggests

Shared intimacy is important during pregnancy, especially as delivery nears and you begin focusing your attention on your impending role as parents. Talk to each other about your hopes and fears. Connect with each other, holding, touching, and making love with the awareness that you are now loving and nurturing a family.

Kama Sutra Positions to Avoid During Pregnancy

Unless your midwife or doctor restricts your sexual activity, you can usually enjoy whatever gives you pleasure through most of your pregnancy. Because of heightened sensitivity a woman may find deep penetration postures uncomfortable or painful, especially as pregnancy progresses. Most couples prefer to avoid such postures in the latter part of the third trimester, as the cervix becomes more tender.

Sexual unions in which the woman sits astride the man, facing him, are likely to become awkward as the woman's belly expands to the point where it keeps them from satisfactorily uniting lingam and yoni. Her protruding belly can affect her balance, too. Unions that require the woman to draw her legs across her abdomen or chest are also difficult or uncomfortable during pregnancy. Late in pregnancy, woman-on-top postures can become uncomfortable for the woman if it becomes difficult for her to control the depth of penetration.

Your doctor may entirely prohibit lovemaking and orgasm if …

◆ You experience unexplained vaginal bleeding.

◆ You have a history of miscarriage (usually prohibited only during the first trimester).

◆ You have a history of premature labor (usually prohibited only during the third trimester).

◆ The placenta is abnormally close to your cervix.

◆ Yours is a high-risk pregnancy (you're carrying multiple babies or you have health problems).

Using the Kama Sutra After Pregnancy

It often takes several weeks at the least, and sometimes several months, for a woman to feel she's ready to return to lovemaking following the birth of a child. There might be physical concerns, such as a healing *episiotomy* or recovering from major surgery if the delivery was by *C-section*. Postpartum bleeding generally continues for up to six weeks. Women who are breastfeeding sometimes find it takes a few weeks to adjust to the tenderness and engorgement of their breasts. A number of women report low or reduced sexual desire during nursing, while other women find that pregnancy and giving birth awakens new and erotic aspects within them, including increased sexual desire.

Sutrology

An **episiotomy** is an incision made into the perineum and vagina to widen the woman's vaginal opening during childbirth, to allow the baby to pass through without tearing these tissues. A **C-section,** or Caesarian section, is a surgical delivery in which the baby is delivered through an incision in the woman's belly.

Postpartum Pleasure

Your health care provider can tell you when it's okay for you to resume sexual activity. When there are no complications following delivery, many midwives and doctors follow a "whenever you feel ready" guideline. Others suggest you abstain for a certain period of time. Your own body and energy will be your best guides. Do not push yourself to have sex until you are truly ready. When you do feel ready to resume lovemaking, take it slow and easy.

Communicate with each other about all the changes that are taking place in your body. The added responsibility of a child to your lives, loss of sleep, fluctuating hormones, body image, hopes, fears, and frustrations all need attention. Make time on a regular basis to share what you are feeling with your partner.

Even if your desire for sex has not returned, stay connected by communicating what you are feeling and by being tenderly physical. Touch, kiss, and hold each other, and enjoy eye-to-eye contact combined with breathing in unison to keep your connection alive. This is particularly important when the new family member seems to require every waking moment of your time and attention. Affection, acknowledgement, playful teasing, and humor go a long way in terms of expressing your feelings for one another, even if you are too tired or busy to act on them any further.

How to Be a Mom or Dad and Still Love the Kama Sutra

You may wonder if your little bundle of joy ever sleeps—or will ever let you sleep or have time for much needed time alone with your beloved! Exhaustion is the main complaint of most new parents. You may feel there's not enough of you to go around, especially if you have other children. All the physical and emotional changes you are going through throw you into a transition that can be stressful and confusing.

It is tempting to fall into a pattern of expectation, of the woman wanting her partner to recognize how much she is giving to the baby and to put his own needs and desires for intimacy aside so she doesn't have to deal with them. When you are focused on a new baby's needs, the idea of a partner's wanting something more from you can be the final straw. But most couples long to return to the intimacy they felt in their relationship before the baby. Doing so requires you to make time for yourself as well as for each other. Some ways to get started with your return to intimacy might include …

- ◆ Making a time each day for 10 minutes of talking as friends.

- ◆ Asking for help when you need it so you can take a nap, go for a walk, get a massage.

- ◆ Making a weekly date to return to your lovemaking ritual. You may have to shorten the time and your expectations to fit the baby's schedule in the beginning.

- ◆ When you feel comfortable doing so, having a trusted family member, friend, or babysitter stay with the baby for a few hours so you can truly get away with—and to—each other.

Change is a constant in our busy lives, and major transitions like having a baby add stress and can push our emotional buttons. Victim, martyr, abandonment, a sense of feeling overwhelmed or rejected—these are some of the old emotional responses we fall into when we are in stressful life situations. Pregnancy is a life-transforming experience that is asking more of you and your partner. It is an opportunity to share your hopes and fears with each other. In this way you and your family connect through the transition of birth and deepen your commitment.

The Least You Need to Know

- ◆ Many couples enjoy lovemaking particularly during pregnancy, when there are no longer worries about contraception.

- ◆ Usually the only limitations to sexual loving during pregnancy are a woman's own interest and her comfort level.

- ◆ You can still enjoy being intimate with each other when the woman isn't feeling particularly sexual. Kissing and stroking each other can be very pleasurable and loving, even when this doesn't lead to sexual union.

- ◆ It's important to make time for the two of you as a couple after the baby arrives, to support and maintain an intimate relationship.

23

You're Never Too Old for the Kama Sutra

In This Chapter

◆ How bodies and relationships change through time

◆ What changes take place in a woman's body as she ages

◆ What changes take place in a man's body as he ages

◆ How to restore intimacy to your lovemaking

Does sex get better with age? It does, if you don't equate sex with athletic positions and multiple ejaculations. Sex as we age is less driven by hormones and more by the desire to connect body and soul with someone who loves and cares for us.

Our youth-oriented culture suggests that older couples don't enjoy the same desires and pleasures as younger couples. Nothing could be further from the truth! Many older couples find they finally have time to indulge themselves with long weekend mornings in bed or extended loveplay in the middle of the day. The changes that your bodies undergo can affect your lovemaking in very positive ways.

The Transformations of Sexual Loving

For a couple that has been together a long time, sex can go through several transformations during their relationship. In the beginning, hot, frequent sex is typical. Then come the babies and the careers—one or the other for some couples, both for other couples. Sex takes a back seat while tired and busy partners juggle responsibilities. By the time the kids are grown and careers are established, bodies, psyches, and hormones are changing.

While hormones do play a significant role in these changes, the main cause of low sexual desire that couples may experience is emotional. Keeping the fires ignited in a long-term relationship requires real intimacy, which happens when you reveal yourself and let yourself be seen. Many couples slip into a comfortable though distant and separate existence out of fear of rocking the boat and shaking up the agreements, routines, the secure life they have created together. Other couples get caught in power struggles in which sex becomes yet another battleground.

Couples whose sex lives get better over time are those that are able to reinvent their relationships as time and circumstances change. Couples who remember they are individuals with paths of their own to travel maintain an identity that is energetically alive. Couples who are folded in on each other in a comfortable pile of mush don't have the kind of "spaces in their togetherness" that keeps the erotic charge kindled.

The myth of youth would have us believe that aging bodies are no longer beautiful, sexy, or capable of intense exquisite pleasure. Who can deny the fresh bloom of youth's beauty? But have you ever studied the character in the face and body of an aging person? As we grow older, we bring with us all the ages we have ever been. You might look at your 50-year-old lover in the light of a candle and be surprised to see the eyes and smile and luminous skin of a teenager looking innocently out at you. Yet on a bad day a 30-year-old can look haggard and spent. Real age and beauty are determined to a great extent by how we feel and think.

Your Changing Body

Many of your body's changes as you approach middle life and beyond are obvious when you look in the mirror. You may find gray hair or a balding head staring back at you, and laugh lines around your eyes. Some of the most significant changes, however, aren't immediately visible. Both men and women experience hormonal shifts that affect various bodily functions, including those related to sexual activity.

A Woman's Body Changes: Menopause

Menopause can be a time of paying attention to health and your changing body, mind, and spirit. On a physical level, menopause officially marks a woman's transition to nonfertility. Her body dramatically slows down the production of estrogen, which ends ovulation. While on average women enter menopause around age 50, it can occur any time between the early 40s and late 50s. A hysterectomy (surgical removal of the uterus) can hasten the onset of menopause. A hysterectomy that includes removal of the ovaries as well brings on immediate menopause as your body's estrogen supply suddenly ends.

Many doctors typically prescribe *hormone replacement therapy (HRT)* to maintain estrogen levels in women who are menopausal, especially women in whom menopause is early. In addition to its role in fertility, estrogen has a number of other effects that are important to a woman's overall health (see Chapter 12). HRT is not for every woman, though. Some women have adverse reactions to HRT, or cannot take it because they've had, or have a family history of, certain cancers.

Many women choose not to use synthetic sources of hormone replacement and opt to ease menopausal symptoms with diet, exercise, nutritional and herbal supplementation, meditation, yoga, and bodywork including massage, deep tissue therapy, and polarity therapy. While once considered by only the most health-conscious women, these approaches have become a viable option for most women who want to make the journey through menopause naturally.

With the drop in estrogen levels come a number of physical changes. While both HRT and a natural approach offset these to a great extent, almost every woman experiences these changes to some degree. In some women vaginal tissue becomes thinner, loses elasticity, and produces less lubrication. This is often most apparent during lovemaking, when friction can become irritating (from reduced natural lubrication) and deep penetration painful (as diminished elasticity keeps the vagina from expanding as widely as it once did).

Sutrology

Menopause is the period in a woman's life when menstruation ceases and she can no longer become pregnant. **Hormone replacement therapy,** or **HRT,** is the medical approach to replacing the body's natural estrogen supply with pills containing estrogen.

Many women can offset vaginal dryness during lovemaking by using additional lubrication (something you can easily adapt into love play). And to guard against painful penetration, women can try sexual positions that give them greater control over the depth. There are various medical treatments and natural remedies for vaginal dryness and other manifestations of menopause, so see your health care provider before resigning yourself to these as unpleasant "facts" of aging.

One thing that *doesn't* change is the sensitivity of the clitoris. As a bundle of nerve endings, it is not subject to the hormone fluctuations that affect other tissues. It never loses its ability to feel pleasure!

A Man's Body Changes: Erections

Most men in their 20s and 30s can get erect at the mere hint of anything sexual. Because this happens without conscious thought or effort, men tend to take their immediate response for granted. As they make their way through their 40s and 50s, this happens less frequently. It might take more effort, and more physical stimulation, to get an erection. Older men often notice that their erections are not as hard as when they were younger. And a man in his 50s, 60s, or beyond also may find it takes longer for him to reach orgasm than it once did.

These changes are the result of a slow but steady decline in testosterone levels (which begins when a man is in his mid-20s) as well as other physical changes. Blood vessels become more rigid with age, reducing the amount of blood that can flow through them. Changes in the tiniest blood vessels—capillaries—affect the functioning of nerves as well. Chronic health problems, such as diabetes and heart disease, can further affect this delicate system.

Though it's less firm than it once was, an older man's erection can give his partner considerable pleasure. The extended time and cooperation it takes to achieve an erection and orgasm can make lovemaking a relaxed, intimate, and caring experience unlike the heat and urgent lust of earlier years. The man can bring his partner to repeated orgasms while maintaining strong sexual pleasure himself.

Some men do experience physical problems that affect their ability to get erections, such as prostate surgery and blood vessel disease that hardens and narrows arteries throughout the body, including those that serve the penis. The medical term for this is erectile dysfunction (see Chapter 13). Most men who experience this can benefit from a variety of medical treatments that can restore erectile function.

> **CAUTION**
>
> **Out of Touch**
>
> Quite a few medications can cause erectile difficulties in men. Check with your doctor or pharmacist to see if your prescription or over-the-counter drugs could be causing problems for you.

Alcohol, tobacco, and drug use can inhibit erections. So, too, can a number of prescription medications. Drugs for which erectile dysfunction (sometimes called impotence) is a common side effect include those used to treat high blood pressure (called antihypertensives), depression (antidepressants), and gastrointestinal reflux disorder and ulcers. Over-the-counter cold preparations that contain a decongestant (such as pseudoephedrine) relieve nasal congestion by constricting blood vessels—an effect you'll notice in your penis as well as your nose.

There are so many kinds of prescription drugs available today that it's often possible for a man to work with his doctor to find one that treats his medical condition without causing erectile dysfunction.

Desire Issues

Desire is the fire that gets us off the sofa and away from the computer, and onto the telephone to locate a cozy bed and breakfast or an overnight play date for the kids. Many couples complain that their desire for sexual loving has slipped. In the beginning sex was easy and frequent, but now it seems to be an effort. They may avoid sex entirely and slip into a comfortable platonic marriage. Desire is a problem, but not because of the diminishing hormone levels which are only part of the picture.

The hormone testosterone regulates sexual interest in *both* men and women. While a woman's body greatly decreases its estrogen production after menopause, it continues to produce the same tiny amount of testosterone that it always has. As the amount of testosterone a man's body produces begins to slowly diminish as he grows older, his sexual responses tend to slow a bit as well. This usually doesn't affect desire, however, and often instead has the pleasurable result of making extended lovemaking the norm rather than the exception.

Sexual desire is the feeling of wanting to merge, to become one with another through the physical act of love. This desire is most intense in the beginning of a relationship, when there is an obstacle such as distance keeping partners' anticipation high, and when there has been a fight or issue that has come to resolution.

The enemy of desire is the merged and fused state of mushy togetherness in which couples cling to one another for safety and security. Desire depends on differentiation and thrives on variety and excitement. When two people meet and are attracted to each other, there is chemistry.

> **Sutra Sayings**
>
> The mixture of ghee (clarified butter made from the milk of cows or buffaloes), sugar, milk, licorice, honey, and juice from the fennel plant in equal parts produces a drink that increases a man's sexual vigor, preserves life, and tastes sweet to the tongue.

The beginning of the relationship is filled with excitement and discovery as each learns about the other. Desire in this "honeymoon" phase runs high. It feels so good that the partners want to make the relationship permanent and embark upon a life together. Inevitably, however, desire falls into a comfortable slumber. The chemistry between the partners shifts, and the chemicals now coursing through each of them are more sedating than exciting.

Sometimes issues surface once a couple has fewer distractions competing for attention. Sometimes the changes of aging, such as vaginal dryness, cause sexual activity to be painful. Additional lubrication is often all it takes to end this problem. Pain that persists needs medical evaluation. Sometimes the man is uncomfortable with the changes taking place in his body, and is reluctant to talk with his partner about them. It's important to communicate with your partner, however, to restore intimacy to your relationship.

The Kama Sutra offers an attitude of conscious lovemaking that complements a couple's evolving sexual relationship. Its emphasis on ritual lovemaking, including mutual pleasuring and extended love play before sexual union, is the ideal prescription for bringing both partners to full arousal.

Accepting Your Body

While you can influence your body's shape and condition through diet and exercise, you can't control everything you might like to as you grow older. Just as it was important for you to accept your body for what it was when you were younger, it's important for you to accept the changes it goes through as you get older.

Dr. Josie Suggests

Take pleasure in looking at each other's bodies, no matter how old you are. Watching your partner become aroused can be arousing for you, too. When you make love with your eyes open, you are more aware of your partner's responses and lovemaking becomes more intimate and connected.

If you're in a long-term, committed relationship or marriage, you're probably just as attractive to your partner as you were when your relationship was young. Mysteriously and delightfully, our tastes seem to change along with our bodies. When attraction seems to fade, there are usually other relationship issues responsible. Remember, your sex life usually reflects the overall condition of your relationship. If you and your partner enjoy and respect each other, this carries through to your sexual loving no matter what your age.

Kama Sutra Possibilities

The Kama Sutra encourages couples (and especially men) to take time to fully enjoy the many nuances and subtleties of lovemaking. While this is good advice for all partners, it can mean the difference between frustration and fulfillment for older lovers.

Loving Experience

One advantage older lovers have is experience. Whether you've been partners for a long time or have had several partners through your life, you've learned a lot through experience. You know how to arouse and be aroused. You know your body and how it responds. If yours is a long-term relationship, you know your partner's body and how it responds, too. This is all knowledge that allows you to enjoy exciting and varied lovemaking.

Modify and Adapt

So you're not quite as flexible and strong as you used to be? Not a problem, as far as the Kama Sutra is concerned. Vatsyayana says the most important aspects of lovemaking are imagination and innovation—and the flexibility that lovemaking requires resides between your ears. Sexual union, from the Kama Sutra's perspective, is just part of the process, not the goal, of lovemaking.

Much of the pleasure in sexual loving comes through the process of exploring each other in varied and different ways. Whether you put your foot on your partner's forehead or adapt by draping your leg over his shoulder isn't nearly as important as the intimacy you and your partner share through the experience of joining your bodies and your minds.

Liberating Love Beyond "The Change"

Many women find that contrary to what they expect, their interest in sex actually increases after menopause. There are numerous reasons for this, from no more concerns about becoming pregnant to other factors in your life that change at the same time, such as children leaving home. Without the many pressures of raising children and running a household, some women find themselves more relaxed and more receptive to exploring new ways of making love. Partners who retire or cut back their work hours also find they have more time for each other, which can rekindle and renew sexual loving.

> **Out of Touch**
>
> Though a woman can no longer become pregnant after menopause, she remains fertile during the years before menopause is complete. Continue using contraception until you are certain your periods have stopped—unless, of course, you and your partner desire becoming pregnant, an increasingly common choice for many couples at midlife! And remember—a man produces sperm well into his senior years.

The Virility of Experience

Men often enjoy their ability to maintain prolonged or repeated erections as they get older. Though arousal takes longer, the sensations that result can be more complete and fulfilling. Kissing, caressing, and stroking can stimulate the entire body. Being present and aware during lovemaking intensifies both the tenderness and the eroticism of this contact. Many men awaken to, or rediscover, the joys of oral lovemaking, and find it very arousing to pleasure their partners with yoni kisses.

Embracing Sexual Loving After Illness or Injury

It's a sad reality that serious illness and injury become more common as we grow older. Health conditions such as heart disease, diabetes, high blood pressure, prostate problems, and cancer are more likely to affect you if you're over 50. When facing such potentially life-threatening matters, it's difficult to reorient yourself to the pleasures you enjoyed before disaster struck.

Many people fear that resuming sexual loving following a heart attack, stroke, or major surgery can be harmful to their health. Unless your doctor specifically tells you this is the case for you, however, making love is more likely to speed your return to health than it is to hinder your progress.

There are many studies that look at the connections between physical health and emotional and spiritual happiness. Being in a close, loving relationship greatly reduces stress. Someone else cares about you and for you, which is comforting and affirming. It also takes your mind off your health and problems when there is someone in your life whom you can care about and for, too.

Lovemaking After a Heart Attack

People who have had a heart attack or heart surgery often worry that sex will strain or further damage their hearts—or, even worse, that they will die while making love. Yes, someone will occasionally die during lovemaking, just as every now and then someone has a heart attack and dies while driving a car or taking a shower. But most people—about 80 percent—who recover from heart attacks or heart surgery are fully capable of returning to a rich and satisfying sexual relationship.

Sexual excitement and orgasm do raise blood pressure, quicken heart rate, and speed breathing. But generally, if you can walk two or three flights of stairs without becoming winded or experiencing chest pain, you are physically able to have sex as far as your heart is concerned. Of course, if you have heart problems or have had heart surgery, ask your doctor what activities are okay for you to do, and follow your doctor's advice.

Kama Knowledge

Studies show that less than 0.5 percent (one-half of 1 percent) of people who die suddenly from heart trouble die during or immediately after sex. Of the half-percent who do, most are married but having sexual relations with a partner other than a spouse when they die. Most have also been drinking large quantities of alcohol. Researchers believe that stress caused by fear of getting caught, coupled with raised blood pressure from drinking alcohol, are the factors that strain the heart, not the sex itself.

If your partner has had open-heart surgery, such as a coronary artery bypass, the scar on his or her chest may remain tender for several months. The incision through the skin, muscle, and other tissues disrupts the nerve endings, and it takes time for the body to repair them. Pain in the area of the scar after the scar has healed is seldom related to heart or other health problems.

If you're returning to sexual loving following heart surgery, start slowly and gently. Enjoy kissing and caressing and being in close contact with each other. If you get an erection (or your partner does), fine. If not, that's fine, too. Try postures that don't put any pressure on your chest. Some people are more comfortable lying on their backs with their partners on top (sitting or kneeling, without putting pressure on the chest). Others are more comfortable when they are in the on-top position. Experiment to find what works for you.

Accommodating Arthritis and Back Problems

Arthritis and back problems can severely restrict your flexibility and even your ability to move. These conditions are often painful as well, which can certainly put a damper on your desire. However, you don't have to let them keep you from enjoying lovemaking. In most cases, gentle activity actually helps with arthritis and back pain. Movement helps loosen stiff muscles and joints. Tender lovemaking, using positions such as side-facing or rear entry while lying on your sides, can be a pleasurable way to get your muscles moving.

Dr. Josie Suggests

Try starting your love play with a warm bath or shower, followed by a tender massage to relax your body and gently stretch your muscles. Use a good massage oil.

Some people with arthritis feel better at certain times of the day than at others. Plan your lovemaking for when you're feeling your best. If you take medication, pay attention to when it helps the most and try to make love during those times. Other sexual unions that are often more pleasurable for people with pain or limited movement are those in which the man enters from the rear while standing. His partner can lean over a piece of furniture such as a bed for support.

When Disability Strikes

Health problems such as stroke can leave you with a permanent disability. This doesn't mean your interest in sexual loving disappears, however. Be creative in adapting Kama Sutra activities and unions to accommodate your unique circumstances. With attentiveness and care, nearly every couple can find ways to continue lovemaking in spite of moderate disability.

Keeping the Joy Alive

Partners who have been together for 20 or 30 years or longer have a lot of history between them. They often have a sense of comfort and security between them as well. While for the most part this is a good thing, it can cause them to drift away from looking at each other as lovers. This can result in feeling that their sexual relationship is boring. With a little attention and imagination, however, couples can enjoy a lifetime of pleasurable lovemaking.

The Least You Need to Know

- With attentiveness and caring, sexual loving can indeed get better with age.

- Hormonal changes don't influence sexual desire nearly as much as intimacy does.

- Take pleasure in looking at each other's bodies as you make love. Lovers find each other's bodies sensuous and arousing, no matter their age.

- Most couples can return to active sexual relationships after recovering from heart attacks and other health problems.

Chapter 24

More Stages of Love: The Ananga Ranga

In This Chapter

◆ Erotic caresses involving your hair

◆ Sexual unions that challenge and excite

◆ Woman-on-top sexual unions

◆ Enhancing your sense of connectedness through sexual union

Sometime in the late fifteenth or possibly early sixteenth century, Kalyana Malla, another Indian writer, used the Kama Sutra as the basis for his own love text, the Ananga Ranga. Scholars know little about Kalyana Malla beyond that his intention was to craft a book about sexual loving for married couples.

Richard Burton, who first translated the Kama Sutra into English, also published an English translation of the Ananga Ranga. In 1885, two years after publication of the English version of the Kama Sutra, the Ananga Ranga debuted for selected Western readers through Burton's secretive Kama Shasta Society. Burton translated the title of this love text as the "Stage of the Bodiless One," though the work is also known as the "Stage of Love" and by its Arabic translation, "Pleasures of Woman." Though it's every bit as exotic and detailed as the Kama Sutra, the Ananga Ranga has not achieved similar widespread recognition.

This probably has more to do with writing styles than content. While Vatsyayana wrote in an open, direct manner to his readers, Kalyana Malla took a rather unemotional, instructional tone. Beneath its somewhat cumbersome presentation, however, the Ananga Ranga presents variations on love play and sexual unions that are erotic, exciting, and often challenging.

Fourteen Hundred Years of Practice

At the time Vatsyayana compiled the Kama Sutra, sexual expression was quite free and open. Though Vatsyayana encourages husbands and wives to remain faithful to each other, he readily acknowledges that men and women have other sexual attractions. The Kama Sutra addresses sexuality broadly and without judgment, as a dimension of life's learnings.

Fourteen centuries later, society was quite different and quite regimented. Extensive rules structured and regulated every aspect of life, even down to saying what could and could not be done at specific times of the day. By this time, the only socially accepted form of sexual relationship was that which took place within marriage. But sexual drives, desires, and interests certainly had not changed.

However dry his writing style, Kalyana Malla recognized the power of sexual intimacy in strengthening and supporting the bonds between couples. He wrote a book especially for married couples that bypassed the philosophical foundation of the Kama Sutra, jumping right to an enticing and varied menu of sexual activities.

Kama Knowledge

To emphasize his point that couples could find all the sexual pleasure they could ever desire within their marriage, Kalyana Malla presents an elaborate formula calculating a grand total of 243 different ways of sexual union. In his zeal, he conveniently overlooked the fact that his mathematical exercise factored in all of the possible combinations of yoni and lingam types, though each couple would of course have between them just one of the nine possible. His formula also included the four "unusual" unions he chose to omit (what these were isn't entirely clear, though they likely included the extreme mismatches—such as elephant and hare—between yoni and lingam in terms of size). Even disallowing these exaggerations, however, the Ananga Ranga does present an astonishing variety of lovemaking activities.

Like the Kama Sutra, the Ananga Ranga emphasizes pleasure and enjoyment for both partners. Many of the preliminaries—kissing, caressing, embracing—remain essential and enjoyable elements of sexual loving. Because we've covered these in earlier chapters, in this chapter we present only the unions that are different from those in the Kama Sutra.

Erotic Hair Play

The hair on your head is an erotic element often overlooked in love play. Many couples enjoy running their fingers through each other's hair, both for the silky feel of the hair as it slips through their hands and for the stimulating touch of the fingertips on the scalp. The smell of your lover's hair can also be quite evocative, as can the feel of hair brushing across your body during sexual loving.

The Ananga Ranga adds another dimension to foreplay by encouraging couples to explore the eroticism of hair. Partners run their fingers through each other's hair, and softly grip the other's hair to pull closer in passionate embrace. These acts are most arousing when done at "the rising of hot desire," and are done with loving tenderness.

Two Hands in the Hair

At the onset of love play, the couple is sitting or standing. One partner entwines his or her fingers in the hair at the sides of the head of the other, palms against the face, and pulls the two of them together in a passionate kiss. The initiating partner presses the lower lip of the other partner, who then responds with the same action.

Drawing and Kissing

The couple is standing or sitting. As lovemaking becomes more intense, one partner slides his or her fingers into the hair at the back of the other's head and draws the two of them together in a pressing kiss. With the other hand, the partner strokes the other's face and neck. The other reciprocates.

Pull of the Dragon

With passion hot and anticipation high, the partners stand with their bodies pressing together and their legs intertwined. One partner grasps the other's hair at the back of the head and presses their mouths together in a deep, full-contact kiss. Though sexual union has not yet taken place, the two appear connected from head to foot.

> **Sutra Sayings**
>
> Each act of sexual loving has two meanings, the meaning of the loving body and the meaning of the loving spirit.

Embracing Hair Union

As the partners join in sexual union, they press their fingers through the hair above the ears and hold their faces close. They look deep into each other's eyes, and give fleeting, frequent kisses all over the face and mouth.

Exotic Delights

These are among the more exotic sexual unions the Ananga Ranga describes. As with the Kama Sutra's unions, these are the culmination of lovemaking. It's both enjoyable and essential to become completely aroused before attempting them.

Union of the Enfolding Embrace

The woman lies on her back and crosses her legs over her midsection with her knees spread wide to open and lift her yoni. The man kneels or sits so her buttocks press between his thighs, and he enters her. He leans forward with his chest against the backs of her thighs as he thrusts. This union exposes the woman's vulva and clitoris to full contact with the man's body. This gives the woman intense stimulation with each thrust, even though her position limits her ability to move.

Union of the enfolding embrace.

(Hrana Janto)

Union of Balance

The partners lie on their sides facing each other, legs straight and bodies touching from head to feet. The man enters her. Movements are gentle and rhythmic as the couple breathes in unison. This union can be immensely arousing as the man adjusts to stroke his lingam against the woman's clitoris and labia.

Look into each other's eyes and stroke each other's bodies to give added intimacy to this tender union. This is called the union of balance because it emphasizes equilibrium in physical movement as well as emotional and spiritual connection.

Women: Squeeze your thighs together for added pressure on the man's lingam.

Men: Move your body up (toward your partner's head) to extend contact between your lingam and her clitoris.

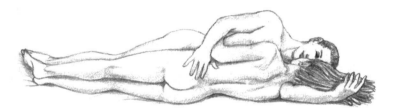

Union of balance.

(Hrana Janto)

Union of Pressed Thighs

The man sits with his legs outstretched in front of him. The woman sits between his thighs, facing him, and he inserts his lingam into her yoni. The man presses the woman's thighs together. Though this union limits movement for both partners, they can generate intense sensations by contracting and relaxing their pubococcygeal muscles.

Increase the intimacy of this union by looking into each other's eyes and caressing each other's bodies.

Women: Vary the angle of penetration by leaning back, using your arms for support.

Men: Caress the tops and sides of your partner's thighs.

Union of pressed thighs.

(Hrana Janto)

Union Like a Bow

The woman lies on her back with a pillow or cushion beneath her head and under her middle parts. This curves her like a bow. She raises and spreads her knees, and the man kneels between them and enters her. This union exposes the woman's vulva for contact with the man's body as he thrusts, and also enables the man to stroke her clitoris with his hands.

Elevating the woman's head as well as pelvis gives a different angle of penetration than does raising just her hips. The Ananga Ranga identifies this as one of the most enjoyable unions for both man and woman.

Dr. Josie Suggests

Cushions and pillows can give you additional support in a number of sexual unions. If the described posture doesn't quite work for you, try altering the angle between you by elevating one partner or the other.

Raised Leg Union

The man sits in the lotus position with the woman sitting on his lap facing him. She raises one leg by putting her hand under her foot. She moves her leg rhythmically back and forth to create great pleasurable sensations.

Raised leg union.

(Hrana Janto)

Lotus Union

The man sits cross-legged. The woman sits on his lap, facing him, and wraps her legs around him. He puts his hands on her shoulders. The woman gently guides the man's lingam into her yoni, and both partners experience deep pleasure. The tight and extended contact between the genitals makes external movement unnecessary.

Kiss and caress each other's faces and upper bodies, and look into each other's eyes. You can sustain this union and enjoy its pleasures for a very long time. The lotus union is very intimate, joining your physical bodies as well as your energies (chakras).

Lotus union.

(Hrana Janto)

Wheel of Kama Union

The man sits with his legs in front of him like a "V." The woman seats herself facing him, taking his lingam into her yoni as she lowers herself onto him. Her legs extend behind the man like a "V." The man places his hands under her arms at her back, and lays her back as far as his arms can reach. She holds his arms, and they look into each other's eyes.

Though movement is slight in the wheel of Kama union, the sensations can be intense. Partners often feel a strong emotional connection as they enjoy the pleasure of their union while kissing and gazing deeply into the eyes that are the windows of their souls. The Ananga Ranga identifies this union as one that is "very much enjoyed by the voluptuary."

Wheel of Kama union.

(Hrana Janto)

Woman as Initiator

It's often exciting, and a pleasurable variation, for the woman to take the role of initiator. The Ananga Ranga suggests these positions when the man is tired, or when he has reached full satisfaction but the woman has not.

Inverted Union

The man lies on his back and the woman lies on top of him, taking the role of the initiator. Her breasts press against his chest, and her legs stretch along the outsides of his. She guides his lingam into her yoni, and controls the depth, rhythm, and intensity of penetration as she moves her pelvis up and down and from side to side.

Union Like a Buzzing Bee

The man lies on his back and the woman crouches over him, with her knees bent and her feet flat. She lowers her yoni over his lingam. The woman then moves her pelvis in circular motions, alternately churning and milking the man's lingam. This union gives intense pleasure to both man and woman.

Union like a buzzing bee.

(Hrana Janto)

Union of Resurrection

The man lies on his back. The woman sits astride him cross-legged, facing him, and inserts his lingam into her yoni. Bracing her hands on her partner's thighs or against her partner's hands for support, she moves her pelvis up and down, rising nearly off of him and then plunging back down. The Ananga Ranga presents this as a union to bring the woman to climax after the man has achieved his through a union less satisfying to her. However, the union of resurrection can be very enjoyable for both partners.

Extraordinary Indulgences

These unions offer a degree of challenge as well as intense pleasure as partners experience deep physical and emotional connection. Many of them require much practice. Like their Kama Sutra counterparts, they also require the partners to be fully aroused.

Entwined Lotus Union

The partners start in the lotus position, then wrap their arms around each other's neck in a close embrace. Using their arms, they coordinate their external movements to generate exquisite pleasure. This, like the lotus position, is easy to sustain and enjoy for a long period of time. Intensify your enjoyment by looking deeply into each other's eyes, and by kissing and caressing each other.

Lovemaking lotus-style stimulates the chakra energy centers and increases the spiritual union of partners, as energy is released and exchanged between them.

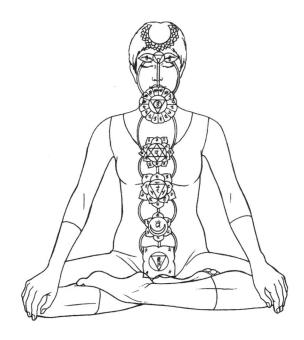

Union of Hands and Feet

The man sits with his knees apart and his feet nearly touching. The woman sits astride him, facing him, with her knees bent and her feet at the sides of his buttocks, and guides his lingam with her yoni. When the two are deeply united, the man holds the woman's feet with his hands. The woman reaches behind her to hold the man's feet. This creates a circuit of energy that intensifies their pleasure.

Acquiring Union

The man sits with his legs slightly spread. The woman slides his lingam into her yoni as she sits on his lap facing him. She lifts her knees to the level of his elbows and hugs the man with her legs. The man presses her legs closer to him using his arms, and holds her shoulders or neck with his hands. He rocks her back and forth, pleasuring them both to ecstatic release.

Acquiring union.

(Hrana Janto)

Union Like a Tortoise

The man sits in the lotus position with the woman seated on his lap facing him. As yoni and lingam unite in closeness, so, too, do the man and woman join hands to hands, arms to arms, breasts to chest, and mouth to mouth. They are completely paired, generating electrifying sexual energy that circulates between them.

Union of Full Enclosure

The man and woman enter into the tortoise union. The man puts the woman's knees over his bent elbows, opening and widening her yoni for deep penetration and full contact between his body and her clitoris and labia. This union is intensely pleasurable for both partners.

Union of full enclosure.

(Hrana Janto)

Union of Ecstatic Delight

This union requires strength and balance in the man. The man sits back on his heels with his knees bent and somewhat spread. The woman seats herself on his lap, facing him, and guides his lingam into her yoni. Once they are securely united, the man passes his arms under her legs, holding the woman suspended from him. Using his arms, he sways her back and forth and from side to side until she erupts in climax.

Union of ecstatic delight.

(Hrana Janto)

Union Like a Monkey

As in the union of ecstatic delight, the man holds the woman suspended from him as he sits back on his heels. He moves the woman only straight away from and toward his body until she reaches climax.

Standing Pleasures

These standing unions require great strength and balance, and take much practice to master.

Three-Legged Union

The man and woman stand facing each other. The woman raises one leg and rests her thigh against the top of his thigh. She stands closer to or further from him to position her yoni to receive his lingam. The man holds her raised thigh to support her as he thrusts. The shorter of you may need to stand on a stable, secure object, such as a stool or low bench, to adjust the height of your body.

Union of Elbows and Knees

The man and woman stand facing each other. The man places his hands between the woman's knees and lifts her up so her knees bend across the inside of his elbows. Her legs are spread widely. He interlocks his fingers at the small of her back to support her. She guides his lingam into her yoni, then wraps her arms around his neck. The man swings and bounces the woman, and they wildly enjoy each other.

Like the union of ecstatic delight, the union of elbows and knees requires strength and balance in the man and is easiest when the woman is slight. The man can't really lean against anything for support, since this would restrict his movements.

> **Out of Touch**
>
> Occasionally women can experience "honeymoon cystitis," in which repeated and intense sexual activity irritates the bladder and urinary tract. The symptoms are similar to those of a urinary tract infection—burning with urination, frequency, and lower abdominal discomfort. If you have these signs, see your health care provider.

Union Like a Hanging Basket

The man and woman stand facing each other. The woman puts her hands on the back of the man's neck and hops up to wrap her legs around his middle. After his lingam enters her yoni, she squeezes his waist with her thighs. The man holds her with his hands under her buttocks to support her as they sway and rock in sexual ecstasy.

The Least You Need to Know

- The Ananga Ranga expands on the elements of lovemaking and the sexual unions of the Kama Sutra to keep sex fresh and exciting for the long term.

- Begin your Ananga Ranga adventures with the essential preliminaries from the Kama Sutra—kissing, caressing, and embracing.

- Consider your physical capabilities and limitations before undertaking sexual unions that require strength and balance.

- Feel free to modify and adapt the sexual unions of the Ananga Ranga to create new and exciting explorations in lovemaking for you and your partner.

Tantra and Tantric Sex

In This Chapter

- ◆ Understanding Tantra and Tantric sex
- ◆ Using sexual loving for deeper spiritual connection
- ◆ The importance of ritual lovemaking
- ◆ How to enjoy total body orgasm

Tantra is an esoteric blend of psychology and philosophy that has its origins in ancient India, dating back to some time between 7000 and 5000 B.C.E. Tantra seeks to unite the polarities, or apparent opposites, at all levels of existence—physically, intellectually, emotionally, and spiritually. Tantra cultivates a way of being that embraces every aspect of experience as an opportunity for growth. Joy and sadness, pleasure and pain, love and hate, the sacred and profane—these are pairings that simply exist side by side like flip sides of the same coin.

You may have experienced fully feeling anger or grief or so-called negative emotions all the way through to resolution without judging or intellectualizing them away, to discover that the feeling transformed and you were filled with an inexplicable joy or energy of peace or sexual openness and desire. An example of this is the surge of sexual passion many couples experience after they've had a fight that concluded when each of them has spoken honestly and the air between them has cleared.

When you get in touch with the physical aspect of your emotions—for example, focusing on feeling sadness as a pain in your heart or fear as a tight stomach—you begin to experience them with awareness and without judgment. This begins to transform the energy. When held without judgement, anger's intensity and aliveness softens to become passionate and creative. This is most likely what accounts for why many couples find themselves making love after a fight. Sadness experienced without judgment or self-pity carves a space to feel greater joy.

Emotions add texture, color, and vividness to our experience of life. When we can feel our feelings without pushing them away or clinging to them, we cultivate an allowing and generous way of holding life's conflicting situations. This process of transformation opens us to feeling vulnerable and tender as we develop acceptance toward ourselves and life. The capacity to transform experience into something whole and unified is the essence of Tantric philosophy and teaching.

The Origins of Tantra and Tantric Sex

According to Hindu mythology, the sexual and spiritual union of Shiva with Shakti gave birth to the universe. In *Tantra,* the god Shiva (the embodiment of pure consciousness) and his consort, the goddess Shakti (the embodiment of pure energy), represent human existence as an erotic act of love that combines their two essences. The ecstatic dance of Shiva and Shakti is the *archetype* of passionate communion that touches our spiritual longing to be one with another. This image of balanced union and of opposites joining forces in creative union is the essence of Tantric sex.

> **Sutrology**
>
> From the Sanskrit word meaning "weave" or "web," **Tantra** is a system of philosophy and psychology that seeks to embrace and unify life experiences beyond their apparent oppositions. An archetype is a representation of a universal concept or behavior. A tantrika is a person, often a woman, who has mastered and can teach the Tantric learnings.

Tantra, unlike the Kama Sutra, was never a mainstream teaching. On the contrary, it was always practiced secretly in an underground fashion by *tantrikas,* frequently women, who passed the teachings on experientially rather than intellectually. In translation, the word "Tantra" means "weaving."

The Evolution of the Tantric Movement

Tantra developed as a rebellious response to the strict codes and religions of the time. Pre-Tantra Hindu priests and leaders believed and taught that abstinence—voluntarily foregoing sex—was the only path to enlightenment. Tantra evolved as the opposing belief that an illuminated, harmonious way of living existed when all the aspects of life, including sex and all the feelings connected with passion, could be included and woven together.

This inclusive philosophy reached its peak between the eighth and twelfth centuries. Spreading from India through Buddhist and Taoist traditions, Tantra touched Western civilization as early as 2000 B.C.E. through the cults of ecstasy that arose to worship the Greek god Dionysus. There is renewed interest in Tantra today. Some who seek to explore Tantra are searching for a more spiritual, integrated existence. Others are intrigued by the sexual teachings that are inherent to Tantric teaching.

A Secretive Tradition

The mystic traditions of Tantra have always existed in secret, no doubt a reflection of Tantra's origins as a rebellion against established beliefs and practices. To find a true teacher of Tantra, the interested student had to travel an arduous and often convoluted path. Tantric practitioners and teachers typically revealed themselves only after the seeker proved his or her sincerity. The search for a true teacher and gaining their acceptance as a student might take considerable time and effort on the part of the seeker.

Because there is no formalized structure to or practice of Tantra, learning is frequently an informal affair with the teacher tailoring the teaching to a student's particular temperament and *karma*. The teachers of the Tibetan Tantric tradition, for example, used stories, questions, and startling behavior to jar students from their beliefs and attitudes.

Sex was (and remains) a powerful component of some Tantric schools, though Tantric sexual teachings weren't given until the student was ready. Readiness is determined by the teacher, who guides the student to cultivate an open and spacious state of mind that is not attached to any beliefs or philosophies, yet is anchored firmly in moment-to-moment awareness and a flexible way of being.

Sutrology

Translated from the Sanskrit, **karma** means "fate." In the Hindu and Buddhist traditions, karma is the energy that results as a consequence of a person's actions and inactions.

Westernizing Tantra

A Westernized version of Tantra has emerged as people have explored more open and experimental attitudes toward sexuality and discovered that sexual variety alone is not fulfilling. Tantra appeals to the soul's longing to find greater meaning in sexual loving. While the current popularity of Tantra in the West draws those who are committed to the personal and spiritual growth Tantra offers, many are interested primarily in sprucing up their love lives through the sexual aspects of Tantra. Since Tantra is a spiritual path and art form that makes sexuality a vehicle for self-awareness, taking only the sexuality of the teachings out of the larger context of Tantra makes them little more than techniques for better sex.

The West thrives on an "instant gratification" approach to life, which is contrary to the Eastern approach that emphasizes long and rigorous practice. Traditionally, Tantra views the sexual teachings as a way to expand and integrate the whole being; the Western version of mainstream Tantra interprets them as a means to regain passion in a relationship. We agree wholeheartedly that sexual loving is an integral and essential aspect of a relationship. What makes Tantra unique is that it views sex as not only an act of pleasure but also a vehicle of transformation and enlightenment.

Kama Knowledge

Because they evolved in the same time period and in the same place, the Tantric teachings of India and Tibet, as well as China, all have their version of the 64 arts that the Kama Sutra presents. (The number 64 has mystic though unexplained meaning in many contexts.) Though the Kama Sutra doesn't explicitly mention Tantra or Tantric practices, there are many overlaps between them. The Kama Sutra is distinctly ethical, moral, and technical. It presents actions and behaviors within the framework of what was culturally acceptable in its time. Tantra is a mystical philosophy, an art form, and a science. While the Kama Sutra focuses on pleasure and protocol to create harmonious sexual union, Tantric sex is an experience of energy, spirituality, and transformation.

Tantric Philosophy and Modern Lovers

In the West, we tend to embrace aspects of a spiritual system that appeal to us without considering the whole. With Tantra, these aspects are its sexual teachings. The West is still in a state of transformation regarding sexuality. Our tradition in sexual matters has been one of reticence and suppression. Sex has long been shrouded in innuendo and hidden behind closed doors. People had sex and enjoyed sex, but they did neither openly.

As sex in the West began to come into the open over time, greater permissiveness led to experimentation and new forms of relationships. People started exploring sexual loving as a dynamic and natural dimension of life that could deepen and intensify partnerships. This newfound joy has led us to desire and expect fulfillment from relationships.

Recognizing the soul's desire to find oneness through an intimate sexual relationship makes Tantra appealing. Just as the Tantric teachings and practices cultivate in us a capacity to live in the unknown without the need to have a fixed goal or know the outcome of every situation, Tantra shows us the possibility of melding body and soul with our beloved through sex without losing our centered connection to our individual sense of identity. This capacity gives the freedom to fully experience and enjoy life, and to completely surrender to sexual bliss as a dimension of that freedom.

The Path of "Yes"

The Indian mystic Osho identifies Tantra as the path of "yes." While yogic practices require abstinence, fasting, and rigorous discipline as the way to achieve self-realization, Tantra has no rules. It asks only that you are present, aware, and capable of great flexibility in the face of intense contradiction. Yes, you can simultaneously feel turned-on and afraid of losing yourself, be overcome by joy one moment and sadness in another. Rather than giving in to the no's and letting them run you, the Tantric path suggests that you say yes to both sides.

When you say yes to both sides of a contradiction, a middle path appears. In the West we call this compromise, but the Eastern approach includes the contradictory feelings and does not seek to eliminate one for the sake of the other. This requires nonattachment, openness, and flexibility. It is not a path for those who are attached to knowing, to being right, or to having fixed and certain outcomes on life's unpredictable journey. Rather, Tantra asks that you be open to the mysterious nature of love and life and not be attached to the outcomes of your efforts.

Gender as Polarity

Tantra is a philosophy of wholeness. It views the concepts of male and female not as opposites but rather as complementary—two polarities that come together in every individual and in every union. In Tantra, as in the Kama Sutra, a man and a woman each has masculine and feminine qualities. Rather than being divided by gender, in Tantra the masculine and feminine unite in a balanced dance that celebrates the coming together of opposites.

When we honor the other polarity within ourselves we expand our sense of sexual identity to include the other so-called opposite gender. This helps heal the sense of separation that men and women experience as a limitation of their connection to the other.

> **Sutra Sayings**
>
> Once passion ignites between lovers, there are no limits to the pleasures of sexual loving. Enjoyment comes from the total giving of one's self to the other.

A man finds great freedom when he allows himself to explore his receptive, vulnerable qualities. He can stop performing and relax. He can take time to enjoy sexual loving in new ways, without having a goal. He can explore and enjoy being receptive while his partner initiates. A woman who is exploring the polarity of her masculine energy becomes more of an initiator. She can be bold and creative, becoming a teacher and guide to her more receptive partner as she embraces this aspect of herself.

Tantra as a Doorway to Sacred Desire

The desire to join with another sexually reveals our fundamental spiritual desire to experience oneness, to fulfill the longing to become one with another and alleviate the pain of feeling separate. Sex can be procreative, pleasurable, playful, or simply a way to satisfy needs. But the satisfaction is short-lived and soon desire returns, and we are once again seeking to be fulfilled. Recognizing the sacred in sex opens another dimension in a relationship. We step into a realm of experiencing the divine pulse of existence, where sex transcends the physical and becomes an archetypal theater in which the gods dance through us. The satisfaction that lovers experience when they invite the sacred into their loving embrace transcends the physical and emotional. Lovemaking becomes a soul-fulfilling experience that lasts beyond the act of sex and has the capacity to bond lovers to each other and to an awareness that they are one with existence.

The Desire for Deeper Intimate Connections

Tantra offers us a transcendent view of love and relationship that views the other as an embodiment of the divine. There is a great appeal to such an idealized vision. Our twenty-first-century lives are full, busy, and stressful, often leaving little time and energy for relationships. Many people believe heart-centered, passionate relating is possible only in the "honeymoon" stage of a relationship, when we adore and delight in every aspect of each other. Then it's back to "real" life and the drudgery of its routine. Taking care of business often takes over the relationship, and romance and passionate intimacy lose out.

Kama Knowledge

In the Eastern view, orgasm is energy and carries a frequency or vibration. Esoterically speaking, the vibratory state of orgasm is akin to the energy of the life force of all living things. Once we have fully explored the heights and depths of orgasm sexually, it is possible to tap into the erotic pulse of existence beyond the act of lovemaking. You can begin to practice this by being aware of the afterglow you feel after extended lovemaking and by practicing activities that involve breathing, dancing with abandon, and meditating.

When you bring a Tantric perspective to a relationship, you see your partner as an embodiment of the beloved—the idealized or spiritual lover. This lifts relationships out of the mundane—the relationship is no longer about who empties the garbage or picks up the kids. A Tantric relationship elevates love to an art form. It promises balanced, harmonious integration and the union of seeming opposites—body and spirit, Eros and transcendence, passion and bliss. One of the challenges of a relationship is to not shrink your partner into a small and limited package of judgments, but to see and accept all the facets of her or him. A Tantric perspective gives partners a way to practice greater presence, sensitivity, awareness, compassion, and reverence.

Ecstasy and Communion Through Sexual Love

The desire for ecstasy through sexual loving and relationships is as ancient as human consciousness. Sex can be a purely physical release that ranges from modest to earth-rocking. Sex can be emotionally bonding or a friendly, playful joining of bodies. Sex can be a place to act out fantasies and try out roles, to experiment with dominance and submissiveness, and sex can be a vehicle for transcendence through ecstatic states.

The physical act of sex releases great stores of energy. This is not only physically pleasurable but also takes people into states of deep emotional release. Lovers spontaneously hear themselves and their partners laugh, cry, curse, and cry out in ecstasy. At this level, couples begin to transcend the purely physical and enter into a bonding communion with one another. As two separate people open physically and emotionally, they move beyond the boundaries of the personality and enter into a merged and unbounded state. It is here that bodies and souls unite in an ecstatic dance that transcends our separate existences and unites us with all the love in the universe.

In Tantric sex, what is different from ordinary sex is an awareness and conscious cultivation of energy. The idea is to be able to cultivate a lot of energy, to contain and channel energy, and to be able to discharge energy only when you wish. Tantric sex makes orgasm not merely a discharge of tension and release prior to rest, but a state of energetic existence. In this way we cultivate a capacity to vibrate with the hum of existence, which is what we experience in orgasm.

Lovers who connect deeply and enjoy extended states of lovemaking that include full-body, multiple orgasms with or without ejaculation can maintain a relaxed and energized orgasmic state for hours or days. This pleasant hum that lasts beyond the physical release energizes and vitalizes your full being. This is Tantric sex taken to its conclusion, to a connectedness that becomes a transcendent experience. Your lover becomes both a gateway to and an embodiment of the divine and orgasmic energy that is life. With time and dedicated practice, people can cultivate the ability to duplicate the experience of orgasm outside of the sexual experience.

Ritual Lovemaking

Ritual lovemaking is an important element of Tantric sex. Through ritual, we establish beliefs, acts, and events as special and worthy of honor and celebration. Ritual provides a "trigger" that puts us in a particular frame of mind. It activates emotions and initiates anticipation, both of which are essential in lovemaking. (Chapter 17 discusses ritual in lovemaking in detail.)

Ritual requires awareness and presence. When you are fully present in any activity, the ordinary becomes unique. Experiences that might otherwise be routine or rote (a common complaint about sex from couples who've been together for a long time) are instead precious and memorable. The elements of ritual often have the ability to evoke a desire to engage in the ritual. Walking into your bedroom and smelling the lingering fragrances of the candles you always burn during sexual loving is likely, at the very least, to trigger a pleasant memory—and many times to send a flash of desire sparking through you as a lovemaking scene replays in your mind.

Kama Knowledge
Some ritual lovemaking in the Tantric teachings is formalized and structured to visualize union with deities and raise energy for healing, creation, and spiritual awakening. This is called maithuana sadhana, which means "sexual rite." This form of ritual lovemaking is highly symbolic and deeply spiritual. One such maithuana sadhana, for example, involves preparing and eating small amounts of certain foods that represent the essential ingredients of the universe. Partners make love in front of a fire or burning candles, with symbolic colors and fragrances present to evoke the desired emotions and stimulate sexual desire. Meditation is a significant element of maithuana sadhanas, serving to heighten awareness and spiritual connection.

Preparing for Tantric Sex

The Kama Sutra emphasizes proper preparation for lovemaking that follows a continuum of physical and emotional pleasures. Setting, mood, intimate connection, and sexual arousal are essential elements of this preparation. These elements are important in Tantric sex, too. But preparing for Tantric sex also involves readying your mind for an open and complete sharing of energy.

Learn to Meditate

Meditation helps you to settle your mind and directly experience your body, emotions, and thoughts. It helps you cultivate an open, spacious, and generous way of being with yourself that translates to others. Meditation helps you to understand the way your mind works and puts you in touch with your deepest longings and basic goodness.

Meditation cultivates awareness of the mind and how we are distracted by thoughts, feelings, sensations, and the recurring stories that the mind generates. Meditation is not about doing—it is about being. This is an odd concept for Westerners who sometimes even want meditation to produce results.

When couples meditate together, they take time to be together and put aside the business and responsibilities of their lives to simply *be* together. The following couple's meditation practice is designed to cultivate open-hearted presence.

Dr. Josie Suggests

A shared partner meditation requires more presence and focus than many couples are used to bringing to each other. You may find that 15 minutes seems like a lifetime and you may wonder what the point is. It is to share heart space together without an agenda. If this feels too intense for you at first, start with five or 10 minutes and gradually extend the time as you become more experienced and familiar with meditation.

Exercise: Meditation with Your Partner

This is a meditation practice to bring partners into a shared heart space and connects them in a nonverbal way. Make sure you are sitting in a comfortable, straight-back posture that allows you to breathe deeply and make eye contact.

1. Sit facing each other with your eyes softly open. Visualize your heart growing soft and receptive.

2. Breathe deeply and imagine the breath being drawn up from the soles of your feet and resting in your soft heart.

3. As you exhale, breathe the breath out of your heart and visualize it resting in your partner's heart.

4. Continue for 15 minutes or more.

Feel the energy flow between you.

(Hrana Janto)

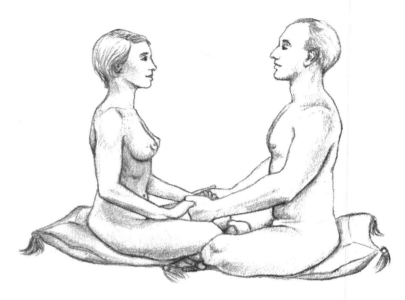

Learn to Allow Yourself Pleasure

Our culture teaches that too much of a good thing is not good and that it is better to give than to receive. It is not surprising that many people are afraid of what will happen if they indulge in pleasure. We feel we ought not to be sitting about doing nothing (and enjoying it), but should be doing something productive. And fun is not something to be having—it's somehow better to *not* be having a good time or feeling too good.

Instead of having to earn your pleasure—making pleasure the payoff for hard work or restrictions—let yourself receive more pleasure when you are eating, breathing, making love. Let yourself feel the pleasure of touching and of being touched, of tasting and of being tasted, of taking a long time to build the energy as you make love, and of being there, of being present and feeling all along the way.

Become Unconditionally Present

We may not even be aware of how often our thoughts, hopes, fears, and judgments distract us. Like a radio playing in the background, our stories keep us distracted from being present in the moment. Meditation cultivates the ability to allow these distractions to simply exist without getting stuck on them or blaming ourselves for having them. Simply holding ourselves in the same regard as a caring, generous mother would her child, accepting ourselves and the mind's busy-ness with an attitude of acceptance and warmth, is the heart of unconditional presence. It is this attitude of generosity that allows us to be in deep communion with another and with life.

Forget About the Destination and Enjoy the Ride

In the West, people are always looking for a technique to make their sexual connection stronger and more spiritual. There is no technique for sexual communion or the kind of deep, full-bodied release that comes when two people lose themselves together in the moment. The best thing you can do is to be present, give up your goals, and enjoy the ride!

Practice Compassion with Yourself and Your Partner

Learn to be kind to, and forgive, yourself and your partner. Learn to talk, laugh, cry, and share as friends. And learn to limit your psychological processing to a minimum—don't analyze every little detail of your relationship and your lives. Keep judgment and criticism out of the bedroom, and be aware of each other's vulnerabilities when talking about sex.

Exercise: Cultivating Compassion with Your Partner

This practice comes from the Buddhist tradition and is a way to soften and open your heart to another. Couples who are disconnected emotionally can benefit from this meditation.

1. Sit facing each other.

2. Gaze into your partner's eyes and see your partner's pain, anger, hurt. See your partner's vulnerable and wounded soul.

3. Continuing eye contact, breathe in your partner's pain as you inhale. Take his or her pain into your heart, and on the exhale breathe out forgiveness and compassion.

4. Continue for 10 minutes.

Tantric Ecstasy: Full Body Orgasm

Typical lovemaking is a relatively short affair that is highly energetic, with vigorous movement and hard breathing. The outcome of all this energy is a sexual charge that builds to a crescendo and discharges in an explosive outward release. Climax (accompanied by ejaculation for a man) is a kind of reflex action in a cycle of sexual tension—build-up, peak, climax, and release.

Extended lovemaking can carry you beyond this external release when you learn to relax your body, breathe deeply and slowly, allow your body to undulate with the orgasmic pulsation, and open your throat chakra to allow sounds to come through you. Relaxing right as you go into the orgasmic phase, delaying ejaculation while going with the energy, you enter into the full-body orgasm and an energetic union where bodies merge and melt and the act of love becomes an experience of deep communion.

In such full-body orgasm, release becomes an extended and conscious energetic experience. Undulating or wavelike pulsations, ranging from subtle and barely perceptible to strong tremors, spread throughout the body in a prolonged series of ecstatic shocks and aftershocks. Many people describe the experience as a feeling of melting into yourself and into your partner. With practice, it's possible to achieve this state of release independent of any genital contact.

Dr. Josie Suggests

Create a ritual space for lovemaking that cultivates and enlivens the senses. Use fresh, clean linens and beautiful fabrics that appeal to the eyes as well as to the touch. Arrange oils for lubrication and massage beautifully and conveniently by the bed. Wear silk robes. Play soft, sensual music. Place fruit, juices, champagne, or chocolates in the room. Use fresh flowers, incense, aromatherapy fragrances, or perfume oils of your preference.

When you are fully engaged in lovemaking, rather than building to a peak of arousal and climaxing or alternating between arousal and retreat, try the following exercise.

Exercise: Cultivating Full Body Orgasm

1. Allow your sexual energy to rise higher and higher while you simultaneously and consciously relax into the pleasure and excitement. Notice how the sensations spread throughout your body.

2. At the point of orgasm, let your mind become still and quiet. Don't think about the orgasm. Simply relax throughout your body. Let your muscles relax, breathe deeply and slowly, open your eyes, and look into your partner's eyes.

3. Let the orgasm have its way with you. Remember to keep breathing deeply and slowly, and to relax rather than tense your muscles. Your body may vibrate or shake and you may feel out of control. This is the beginning of what is known as the full-body orgasm.

Enjoying Tantric Sexual Union

Sexual union in Tantric sex is more about connectedness and energy than the physical act itself. Unions that allow you to feel connected to your partner's body and energy, and to look deeply into your partner's eyes as you make love, encourage and support a transcendent experience.

As always, enter into these unions following unhurried, pleasurable love play that fully arouses both partners.

Shakti Expressing Her Energy with Shiva

In this union the woman is the initiator, bestowing her wisdom and energy to her partner. The man lies on his back with his legs outstretched. The woman sits or crouches over him, and takes his lingam into her yoni. Lovingly caress and touch each other, and gaze into each other's eyes. Feel the union of your bodies as well as the union of your minds and spirits. Prolong your lovemaking to enjoy full-body orgasm.

Shakti expressing her energy with Shiva.

(Hrana Janto)

Ecstatic Union

The man sits on a low chair or low bed, with his knees spread. The woman puts her legs over his thighs and guides his lingam into her yoni as she slides forward to sit against him. This union spreads her widely, and the union is close. Press your bodies together and enjoy the pleasures of your closeness. Feel your bodies merge and your souls connect. Allow orgasm to arise from within you and encompass all of your being.

Ecstatic union.

(Hrana Janto)

Alternate Thrusting Union

The woman lies on her back, either flat or with a pillow behind her head and shoulders. She spreads her thighs and draws her bent knees back. Her partner kneels or sits between her thighs. She can lay her legs over his thighs or rest her feet against his shoulders.

Out of Touch

Deep penetration and deep thrusting can be painful to the woman even if she is fully aroused. Avoid discomfort by adjusting the angle of contact and using additional lubrication.

As he enters her, the man looks into his partner's eyes and the partners focus their thoughts and attention on the union of their two bodies and two souls. Keeping this focus, he makes seven shallow thrusts and then one deep thrust. Alternate slow and rapid thrusting in this pattern, pausing after each deep thrust. This union generates intense pleasure and often full-body orgasm for both partners.

Yab Yum Union

The man sits in a cross-legged position, and woman sits astride him with her legs partially around his back. This posture emphasizes emotional and spiritual connection by looking into each other's eyes and breathing in harmony. It can be equally pleasurable with or without sexual union.

Yab yum union.

(Hrana Janto)

The Tantric Way: Embrace Life's Experiences

Instead of presenting rules, Tantra's method is one of being fully and unconditionally present in all that you do and to all that you are. It asks only that you go beyond your mind and your beliefs to experience life directly, without preconceived notions.

The Tantric way embraces everything, because every situation is an opportunity to become aware of who you truly are. This attitude of saying "yes" to all of yourself, both the parts you normally love and the parts you have learned to hide out of shame or fear, allows you to reclaim your true nature and your basic goodness. This puts you in touch with a joyful, tender innocence and capacity for delight.

The Least You Need to Know

◆ In Tantra the beloved is a revered teacher and consort in life's course on loving.

◆ Tantra brings consciousness to every aspect of daily life, uplifting sex to the sacred.

◆ Tantra is an awareness that the erotic is an aspect of the divine.

◆ Breath, energy, sound, and movement facilitate the full-body orgasmic release.

Chapter 26

The Future of Sexual Loving

In This Chapter

◆ The future of relationships

◆ Why it's important to maintain your sense of self within a relationship

◆ Why sex for the sake of sex can leave you feeling empty and unfulfilled

◆ How attentiveness to sexual loving can strengthen and nurture a committed relationship

Where are our relationships headed as we move into the twenty-first century? Relationships as our grandparents and parents knew them no longer exist. The world is changing rapidly and so are our relationships. Gone is the close-knit, extended family involved with each other on a daily basis. The staple of a community life along with the continuity it provides to people is mostly gone as well. Except for pockets of small-town living or consciously structured support systems of people in similar circumstances helping each other to make life easier and less isolated, people are pretty much on their own. Even though the standard of a committed relationship, the marriage model, has changed radically in the last 100 years, it is to marriage and our most intimate one-on-one relationships that we primarily turn for friendship, companionship, family, sex, and emotional support.

Committed relationships offer us a promise of continuity in a sea of change. Even though the forms of our families and our relationships are changing, we still long for the promise of security and intimate connection in our lives. Today people want more than the "safe and secure" relationship forms of the past. In addition to continuity and companionship, equal partnership and good sex, we want a passionate intimacy that nurtures personal and spiritual growth. The longing to experience the divine through love and sex is not new. The Kama Sutra stands as a testimony that loving well, honoring the feminine and masculine differences, and seeing sex as a vehicle for pleasure and consciousness have long been vital and valued parts of life. Rather than honoring the sacredness of love and sex in relationships as being new, it is a direction that we are reclaiming after a period of time when the sacred in sex and life was lost and neglected.

The Eastern teachings on the erotic sentiment remind us that it is in the sexual embrace, with its potential of erotically charging and nourishing the masculine and feminine, or yin and yang, energies that we can achieve a balance of opposites. The teachings of the Kama Sutra, the Ananga Ranga, and the esoteric erotic practices of Tantra all emphasize the importance of presence and awareness in love and sex. When we bring consciousness to the loving embrace, we invite the sacred and divine into our relationships. And it is this element of the sacred and spiritual that many people are longing for today.

The Lessons of Relationships

As we grow older we look to relationships for different things than we do when we are young. Now that we live longer lives, have multiple careers in a lifetime, and frequently have more than one marriage or marriage-like relationship, we want our relationships to change and grow along with us. It is not unusual to find that the person we fell in love with at age 20 does not share our interests and values at age 50. With less stigma attached to divorce, many couples choose to leave relationships that are no longer growing and alive to pursue fulfillment on their own or perhaps with another. Still, most of us desire the continuity and companionship that a committed, intimate relationship promises. While it can be tempting to move on from a troubling relationship, it is always a difficult decision to reach.

People leave relationships because they can no longer live with who *they* have become in the relationship. If you have been married or in a marriage-like relationship more than once and look inside yourself to gain understanding of your relationship patterns, you may discover that you are repeating a variation of the same relationship issues with each partner. You might find that your last partner was distant and unavailable, then find yourself in a relationship with another partner who after a while displays another version of distant and unavailable behavior. Some people remain convinced that the problem is that they choose the wrong partners, and keep trying to find someone who will fit their picture of the ideal partner. Unfortunately, as long as we are looking outside ourselves to solve the problems in our relationships, we are looking in the wrong place. In reality, if we are seeking greater intimacy, passion, and spiritual connection in a relationship, we are going to be asked to look at ourselves and grow. When we follow this path, the relationship becomes our teacher.

Living in daily contact with another who sees us at our best and worst can make us feel vulnerable and exposed in uncomfortable ways. When the vulnerability is too great and we are afraid or anxious in a relationship, we erect defenses to protect ourselves from too much exposure. But the protection only closes us off from the intimacy we desire. Hopefully, the protection we put up is temporary. We can let down our walls and let our partners into our hearts by honestly and vulnerably sharing our hopes and fears with each other. This paves the way back to connection.

> **Sutra Sayings**
>
> When lovers share mutual pleasure, they create between them a bond that is a connection in the truest way.

Kama Knowledge

According to some estimates, as many as 40 million American women are dissatisfied with the sexual aspects of their relationships. Experts say that when sexual loving is good, it accounts for about 15 percent of the relationship. Sex is integral to the relationship's foundation and health, though it doesn't consume the relationship. When sexual loving is bad, it accounts for 85 percent of the relationship. Sex becomes the only aspect of the relationship the couple focuses on, creating barriers and power struggles that infiltrate all other dimensions of their partnership.

We need to recognize and honor that to our relationships we bring both old wounds and a longing to be met in deep intimacy with acceptance and love. A committed relationship is where we work all this out. The purpose of the difficulties we face in relationships is to help us grow. Relationship growth is like a birthing process where new awareness gestates slowly inside of us while we experience the wild ride of changing emotions, doubts, fears, hopes, and glimpses of new awareness. We alternately doubt our capability and feel confident that all will be well. But a relationship, like bringing in new life, is a mysterious journey. We do not know whom we are going to have the opportunity to love and care for or who we will become as a result of all the effort.

There will undoubtedly be times during the process when we want to give up, but like birth or any spiritual journey, a relationship presents us with tests and challenges along the way that ask us to become stronger and wiser. And if we stay the course, we forge a commitment to another that continues to grow and unfold. On the path of conscious loving, sex is a way we can release ourselves from our separate worlds and connect body and soul with our beloved. Lovemaking strengthens the bond between committed partners and creates an environment to explore the soul's longing to be one with another.

Our Marriage Culture: The Quest for Enduring Connection

Ours is a culture of marriage. In spite of the high rate of divorce, people seek to make their commitments permanent and recognized by family, community, and state. And when our marriages end, we usually do not give up on the institution, but instead create new marriages. The strong pull to marry goes beyond survival and procreation. Social and religious factors undoubtedly influence this. But marriage and marriage-like relationships reflect our need and desire to make our relationships lasting and committed. Commitment is a promise to be there for each other through whatever may come along. We want to know that we are not alone, even when we understand that being alone is the existential condition.

The Desire for Connection

The sexual connection bonds partners physically, emotionally, and spiritually. Lovers bask in the warm and glowing world they generate through their physical loving and that loving is a bridge to a vast love that is soulful and spiritual. Lovers find great comfort in the familiar bodies, tastes, smells, and sounds of each other. The generous and accepting arms of our beloved are a haven where we can embody our passionate love for another in breath-to-breath and flesh-to-bone contact. We are cleansed and released from our tensions and stresses in orgasmic waves, and lose our sense of being separate in the vast and mysterious ocean of loving.

In the beginning of a relationship, people are likely to have great sex because they find one another wonderful, new, and exciting. Desire and passion depose inhibitions and fears, at least to some degree. With the freshness of discovery, couples explore the wonders of each other tirelessly. While it isn't just sex that draws partners together in the first place, sex often occupies much of their time and interest in the early stages of their relationship. Inevitably, the newness and excitement give way to stages of the relationship that require partners to reflect and grow in order to continue to rediscover each other. Vatsyayana, Malyana Kalla, and other ancient writers recognized the role sexual loving could and should play in extending intimacy and closeness between partners. Through the Kama Sutra and the Ananga Ranga, they aimed to help lovers maintain over the long term the sense of ecstatic discovery and romance that marks the beginning of a relationship.

The Need to Preserve Your Sense of Self

Many people enter into relationships hoping to merge their lives with another in every way. People long for union, and have a drive to experience a feeling of oneness. When they go about this by spending all their time "mushed" together, they eventually deplete the erotic charge between them. The longing for peace and feeling as one are *our own* soul longings that we tend to project onto our relationships. When we think relationships can take care of all of our needs, hopes, and desires and guarantee us a permanent state of union, we are writing a recipe for a merged state that cannot sustain the passionate charge.

Merging with another we love and want to be close to is a highly pleasurable state. The sexual embrace is an ideal place for two adults to merge and become one. But many people think that they can extend the merged state indefinitely by spending all their time together and striving to enjoy all the same things. The price they may have to pay for becoming blurred together and undifferentiated is loss of self. Ultimately the effort to become totally agreeable extensions of each other has a negative effect on the erotic charge that thrives on the excitement and tension of polarities and newness. On the relationship path it is essential to experience yourself as an individual in a relationship, to bring yourself to your relationship whole and intact (though not necessarily perfect or complete).

> **Dr. Josie Suggests**
>
> Relying on someone else to be what you're not, to fill in the blanks and the gaps on your behalf, stunts your growth. Yes, couples need shared emotions and activities—sharing is the essence of relationships. But each partner needs his or her own identity, too.

How Attentiveness to Sexual Loving Can Strengthen a Committed Relationship

Sex is the language of love that unites a couple in body, mind, and spirit. Great sex elevates lovers to the peaks of ecstasy where they can glide indefinitely or zoom in a crescendo of orgasm that melds them in a shared quintessence. When partners meet feeling full and whole in themselves and present to each other, the intimacy of sexual loving envelops them in a bond of connectedness that can extend into all dimensions of their lives. Often when partners experience ecstatic bliss as a result of their willingness to be open and vulnerable during lovemaking, the intimacy they establish between them carries over into other aspects of communication. Their perceptions begin to shift, and they start to view openness and vulnerability as capable of generating intimacy and closeness beyond sex. There is risk, of course—risk is inherent in intimacy. But only by taking risks can partners build and strengthen the foundation of intimacy that supports and nurtures a relationship through time.

In some respects, relationships are like a bamboo grove. By themselves, a pair of bamboo stalks has little protection against the elements. But as the roots of each stalk grow deeper into the soil, they send out shoots that become more stalks. These stalks grow branches and leaves of the stalks that intertwine to form a dense, nearly impenetrable growth that keeps any other plants from growing in the same soil. Sexual loving can function the same way in a relationship. Over time, intimacy grows as shoots, stalks, branches, and leaves to support and bond the partners in such a way that it is difficult for potentially damaging thoughts, feelings, and actions to penetrate the relationship. Yet the relationship, like the bamboo grove, remains a living, dynamic, flexible entity. Neither partner loses individuality, yet both gain strength through their unity.

A relationship is a multi-faceted experience. While wonderful sex can strengthen a committed relationship that already has a solid foundation, it can't fix all problems (as much as we might wish that it could). Despite its potency, sex is only one form of communication that takes place between partners. It will be challenging for a couple who has trouble talking with each other in general to establish the level of intimacy that transcendent sexual union requires. But attentiveness to sexual loving—establishing lovemaking as an essential ritual in a relationship—can keep the bedroom from becoming a battleground. When you focus all of your attention on sharing pleasure with your beloved, on opening and being fully in the moment with your partner, it's difficult for worries, fears, and other thoughts to intrude. When you are fully present in your lovemaking, there is and can be nothing else.

> **CAUTION**
>
> **Out of Touch**
>
> Sex is at best a celebration that two whole people share without expectations. Though sexual loving can lead us to deeper bonding and higher states of sexual ecstasy, without other factors within the relationship—trust, love, honor, friendship—intimate communion does not grow deep roots.

Seeking Intimate Communion

Sex is one of the most powerful ways we know to feel connected to another. Unfortunately, many people use sex to get love, connection, or favors from another. When you give sex to get something, or use sex as a bargaining chip, you are traveling a path that leads in the opposite direction of sacred, intimate communion. You cannot find your self-esteem or sense of security through sex. Communion is what happens when we transcend our differences and sense of separation, and open to an open unbounded state. Meeting another in this expanded state is a soul-satisfying experience that we want desperately, but too often seek in the wrong places.

> **Sutra Sayings**
>
> Do not use this work, the Kama Sutra, solely to indulge and satisfy your desires. Attend to kama [sexual loving], but attend to dharma [ethics] and artha [possessions] with equal attention. In this way you do not become the slave of your passions, but rather obtain mastery over your senses.

In the West, people have become accustomed to using external things and substances as a way to avoid the pain of separation. We accumulate possessions. We use medications, alcohol, and drugs to alter our moods and emotions. We watch hours of television. We fall in love over and over and we use sex as a way to bolster ourselves, to feel more alive and connected, and to stave off the anxiety of our existential loneliness. The search to feel connected and whole through sex leads to a need for more and more stimulation to maintain the rush of adrenaline and excitement. Like a drug, sex used for filling the void in us postpones the emptiness for only a little while. Sex for the sake of sex can be physically and even emotionally thrilling, but it can't provide the lasting sense of connection that we long for. We must find this by befriending our fear and longing, and compassionately facing the emptiness we are trying to fill. We must ask ourselves what sort of holy hunger we are trying to satisfy and what we really want. Transforming the emptiness that drives us to be ever seeking more comes as we open and accept ourselves unconditionally.

The best sexual loving happens free of agendas. It is playful, joyful, and innocent. When you are open and natural in sex, the possibilities for pleasure, ecstasy, and sacredness unfold. There is a pure and simple beauty in this kind of loving. When people love each other consciously, they know that no matter how ecstatic their sexual meeting, it is a moment that will pass. But in that moment, they have the chance to become deeply aware and passionately connected with another and to the greater pulse of life through loving well.

Sacred Sexuality and the Kama Sutra

Sexuality is sacred when you honor and respect its role in your partnership and in your life. Like all things sacred, sexuality thrives on ritual. Ritual presents an experience as special, as worthy of reverence and awe. When you prepare the chamber of your lovemaking with objects that delight the senses, you establish this specialness.

Small, everyday rituals such as talking as friends, meditating together, sharing appreciations of each other, greeting each other with a warm, lingering hug when you return home, and spooning for a few minutes before falling off to sleep, are all ways to add a dimension of the sacred to your daily routine. Having a longer time on a regular basis for your special lovemaking ritual further enhances the element of sacredness in your relationship. Please enjoy the Kama Sutra together, and use its ancient wisdom to bring joy, both physical and spiritual, to the love you share with your beloved.

Use the Kama Sutra to create an intimate partnership based on sacred sexuality.

(Hrana Janto)

The Least You Need to Know

- ◆ A fulfilling relationship is one that embraces both intimacy and spirituality.

- ◆ Sex alone cannot provide either intimacy or spiritual connection. With intimacy and spiritual connection, however, sex can be the bridge that unites lovers in body, mind, and soul.

- ◆ Sex becomes sacred in a relationship when it becomes special and honored.

- ◆ Sexual loving has always been, and remains, an essential communication and bond between committed partners.

Glossary

abstinence   Voluntarily foregoing a pleasure, such as sex.

afterplay   Kissing, stroking, and caressing to extend intimacy and closeness after sexual union.

AIDS   An abbreviation for acquired immune deficiency syndrome. AIDS is spread through the exchange of body fluids such as takes place during sex. There is no cure for AIDS, which is ultimately fatal.

amphetamines   Chemicals that stimulate the nervous system.

Ananga Ranga   A Hindu love text, based on the Kama Sutra, that was written in the late fifteenth or early sixteenth century by Kalyana Malla.

anorexia   An eating disorder that results in self-induced starvation. Those who have this disorder have a distorted self-image and view themselves as fat, no matter how thin they really are.

anthropologist   A scientist who studies the origin, nature, relationships, societies, and living environment of human beings.

aphorism   A succinct statement of truth or principle.

aphrodisiac   A substance that increases or enhances sexual arousal.

archetype   A representation of a universal concept or behavior. The term is common in mythology.

aromatherapy   The use of essential oils in the form of fragrances to stimulate specific effects or results.

artha   Sanskrit term for material possessions or wealth.

Buddhism   An Eastern belief system that emphasizes self-enlightenment.

bulimia   An eating disorder also known as "binge and purge." Those who have this disorder eat normally or even overeat, then force themselves to vomit.

bull man   A man of sturdy build and hearty temperament, whose lingam measures eight finger-widths in length when erect.

caste   In Hindu society, a social level into which a person was born. Caste determined everything about how a person lived, from occupation to whom he or she could marry.

cervical cap   A form of contraception for women, it is a small latex cap that is placed over the cervix to prevent semen from entering.

cervical os   Means "mouth of the neck" and refers to the opening of the cervix.

cervix   The neck-like muscle between the vagina and the uterus.

chakra   A center, or wheel, of psychic energy within the human body.

circumcision   Surgical removal of the foreskin.

climax   Another term for orgasm.

clitoris   Highly sensitive erectile tissue at the upper junction of the labia.

concubine   In ancient India, a woman, other than his wife, with whom a man had an ongoing sexual relationship. Though the man might support the concubine in some way, he did not pay specifically for her sexual favors.

condom   A thin, protective sheath that covers the erect penis to contain the man's ejaculate. Condoms reduce the risk of pregnancy and sexually transmitted diseases. There is also a female condom, which fits inside the vagina.

cones   The cells on the retina that detect color.

contraception   The attempt to prevent pregnancy from occurring. Also called birth control.

courtesan   In ancient India, a woman whose sexual and social favors were available for a price to men of equal or superior status. Courtesans were typically wealthy, which gave them significant social standing.

Cowper's glands   A pair of glands within the man's body (below the prostate gland) that produce the fluid which appears at the tip of the penis during sexual arousal.

C-section   A surgical delivery in which the baby is delivered through an incision in the woman's belly. Also called Caesarian section.

cunnilingus   The technical term for oral sex performed on a woman.

deer woman   A woman of slight build and gentle temperament whose yoni is narrow and not very deep. Also called a doe woman.

dharma   Sanskrit term for ethics or virtue.

diaphragm   A form of birth control for women, it is a thin, dome-shaped shield made of latex that fits across the top of the vagina to keep sperm from entering the cervix.

duality   The view that mutually exclusive opposites, such as good and evil, govern existence. Also called dualism or dichotomy.

East/West psychology   An approach that blends the concepts of Eastern philosophy with the practices of Western psychology to view individuals in a holistic manner.

ectomorph   A body type characterized by a slender build, with small bones and slight musculature.

ego   In East/West psychology, the ego is the aspect of self that seeks to protect itself through control. In this context, the ego is also known as the false self or the personality.

ejaculation   A reflex action in which rhythmic muscle contractions propel semen through the urethra and out the opening of the penis.

ejaculation control   A learned process by which a man delays his ejaculation to experience multiple orgasms and extend his erection for prolonged lovemaking.

elephant woman   A tall, large-boned woman with a harmonious nature whose yoni is deep and cavernous.

endometrium   The soft, blood-rich layer of tissue that lines the interior of the uterus.

endomorph   A body type characterized by a large frame and rounded shape.

epididymis   The very long, tightly coiled tube that stores mature sperm within the testicle.

episiotomy   An incision made to widen the woman's vaginal opening during childbirth, to allow the baby to pass through without tearing these tissues.

erotica   Material, usually illustrations or writings, that is sexually arousing.

esoteric sexuality   The Tantric philosophy which recognizes that the powerful aspects of life, love, and sex can be vehicles to self-realization.

essence   In East/West psychology, the spiritual aspect of the self that knows absolute acceptance and unconditional love. The essence is also known as the soul or spirit.

essential oil   The oil that gives a plant its characteristic fragrance or flavor.

fellatio   The technical term for oral sex performed on a man.

fidelity   The state of being faithful to your partner.

foreplay   Kissing, embracing, caressing, and other stimulations to arouse desire before sexual union.

foreskin   A rounded hood of skin that covers the glans when the penis is relaxed. A circumcised man has had his foreskin surgically removed.

frenulum   The highly sensitive area on the penis just below the glans.

gay   A person whose sexual orientation is homosexual.

genitalia   The external sex organs.

glans   The highly sensitive "head" of the penis.

G-spot   The highly sensitive area on the inside front wall of the vagina.

hare man   A man of slight build and gentle ways, whose lingam measures six finger-widths (about three inches) in length when erect.

harmonized breathing   Breathing in conscious synchronization with your partner to establish a harmonic union between your energies.

heterosexual   A person who is sexually attracted to others of the opposite gender.

hierarchy of needs   A theory in psychology that says human needs exist at different levels. A person must meet his or her needs at one level to move onto the next level. The hierarchy of needs is drawn from the work of psychologist Abraham Maslow.

Hindu   Before 1800, a Hindu was a person who lived in India. This is the context of the term as used in this book. After 1800, the term came to define just those who practiced a particular belief system.

HIV   The abbreviation for human immunodeficiency virus, the virus that causes AIDS.

homosexual   A person who is sexually attracted to others of the same gender.

hormone replacement therapy (HRT)   The medical approach to replacing the body's natural estrogen supply following menopause with pills containing estrogen.

hormones   Chemical substances the body secretes that regulate various body functions.

humanistic psychology   An approach to understanding the human condition by looking for answers and explanations within the individual, rather than to external factors.

hymen   A ring of tissue just inside the vagina.

intimacy   The process of revealing yourself, with openness and vulnerability, to another.

kama   A Sanskrit term for love, usually interpreted to refer to sexual loving.

Kama Shastra Society   The secret organization established in the early 1880s by Richard Burton and others to publish and sell translations of the Kama Sutra and other ancient love texts.

Kama Sutra   Literally translated, Kama Sutra means "Love Aphorisms." We use the term today to refer to the document that originated in India during the fourth century C.E., though scholars believe it existed in oral form for centuries before that.

karma   The energy that an individual accumulates as the result of the actions and inactions of his or her life.

Kegel exercises   A series of "clench and release" exercises to strengthen the pubococcygeal muscle. Also called pubococcygeal or PC exercises.

labia   Liplike tissues surrounding the outer vagina. The labia majora are the larger outer tissues, and the labia minora are the smaller inner tissues.

lens   Clear element at the front of the eyeball that focuses light waves onto the retina.

lesbian   A woman who is homosexual.

limbic system   A ringlike area in the center of the brain that plays a role in feelings and the expression of emotion.

lingam   The Sanskrit term for the penis, usually referring to the male organ in its erect state.

love map   According to psychologist and sexologist John Money, the love map is the collection of ideals about what we find attractive in others. Each person begins forming his or her love map around age five, and refines it throughout life.

mare woman   A woman of sturdy build and vivacious personality, whose yoni is full and sensuous.

menopause   The period in a woman's life when menstruation ceases and she can no longer become pregnant.

mesomorph   A body type characterized by well-defined muscles and a sturdy build.

mixed message   In communication, a situation in which a person's words give one message but their actions or behaviors present a contradictory message.

monogamy   The condition of having one mate.

mons veneris   The soft pad of tissue over the pubic bone where the pubic hair starts growing.

mores   The sociological term for a culture's moral habits and customs.

mucus   A slippery, somewhat thick fluid that sensitive internal tissues secrete to keep themselves moist.

nadis   The invisible pathways or channels energy follows as it moves through the body.

nonduality   The view that existence is mutually harmonious.

olfactory   Pertains to the sense of smell.

orgasm   An intricate combination of physiological and emotional reactions that lead to an intensely pleasurable release of sexual tension.

ovary   One of two organs in the woman's body that produce eggs.

pap smear   The collection of cells scraped from the cervix that is examined under a microscope for signs of cancer.

passive-aggressive behavior   Behavior that indirectly expresses feelings, such as sarcasm, jokes, and jabs.

perineum   The sensitive tissue between the vagina and the anus in a woman or between the scrotum and the anus in a man.

penis   The tubular male sex organ through which either semen or urine pass from the man's body.

phallus   A term for the symbolic representation of the penis.

pheromones   Chemical substances people and animals produce that stimulate responses in others of the same species.

polygamy   The condition or practice of having more than one mate.

prana   Life energy or life force.

prostate gland   A gland within the man's body that produces the secretions that contribute to semen. It wraps around and connects to the urethra.

psychosomatic   Dealing with the mind and body in combination.

pubococcygeal muscle   A ring of muscle tissue at the base of the pelvis.

receptor cells   Specialized nerve cells in the skin that detect sensations such as pressure, temperature, and pain.

refractory period   The amount of time it takes for a man to be able to again develop an erection following ejaculation. This time varies among men and among sexual experiences.

retina   The light-sensitive membrane at the back of the eye.

ritual lovemaking The practice of setting aside a regular and specific time and place to honor and enjoy your partner through sexual loving.

rods The cells on the retina that detect light and dark.

sacred sexuality Sexual loving that honors the spiritual as well as the physical and the emotional.

safer sex Sexual habits and practices that aim to prevent the spread of sexually transmitted diseases, including AIDS.

scrotum The tissue pouch behind the man's penis that holds the testicles.

sentient A state of presence based on feelings and awareness.

serial monogamy A pattern of relationship in which the partners commit, one person at a time, to a number of other partners throughout their lifetimes.

semen The fluid of a man's ejaculation.

seminal vesicles A small pair of saclike glands above the prostate gland in a man's body that produce most of the fluid that becomes semen.

sexual morality The set of values and attitudes individuals and cultures hold and follow regarding sexual behavior.

sexually transmitted diseases (STD) Infectious diseases spread primarily through sexual contact. Among the most commonly known are HIV/AIDS, gonorrhea, syphilis, chlamydia, and genital herpes.

Shakti The yin force or energy of the feminine. In Hindu mythology, Shakti is the goddess of creation.

Shiva The yang force or the energy of the masculine. In Hindu mythology, Shiva is the god of all being.

soul mate Another person to whom you feel deeply connected at a spiritual level, as though you belong together and were meant to be with each other.

sperm The cells that carry one-half of the genetic material needed to create a new life.

stallion man A tall, firmly muscled man with an adventurous nature, whose lingam measures 12 finger-widths in length when erect.

sterilization A permanent form of contraception.

sutra A Sanskrit word that means "rules."

Tantra From the Sanskrit word meaning "weave" or "web," Tantra is a system of philosophy and psychology that seeks to embrace and unify life experiences beyond their apparent oppositions.

Tantric sex Within the context of Tantra, using sexual loving as both an act of pleasure and a vehicle of transformation and enlightenment.

tantrika A person, often a woman, who has mastered and embodies the Tantric teachings.

testicles The male sex organs. The pair of testicles hang outside the man's body within the scrotum. Also called testes, they produce testosterone, the male sex hormone, and sperm.

tubal ligation Surgery that cuts or ties off the fallopian tubes in the woman to prevent eggs from traveling from the ovaries to the uterus. A form of sterilization.

urethra In a man's body, the tubelike structure that carries either semen or urine out through the penis. In a woman's body, the urethra carries only urine.

uterus The muscular organ in a woman's body within which a baby grows.

vagina The muscular channel leading from the cervix to the outside of a woman's body. It serves both to receive the man's penis during sex and as the birth canal.

vasectomy Surgery that cuts or ties off the vas deferens in the man to prevent sperm from leaving the testes. A form of sterilization.

vas deferens The tubelike structure that carries sperm from the testicles into the man's body, where they mix with semen in preparation for ejaculation.

Vatsyayana Hindu scholar who lived in India during the fourth century C.E. and is credited with compiling the text we know as the Kama Sutra.

Viagra A common brand name for sildenafil, a prescription drug that can help a man with erectile dysfunction achieve firmer and more consistent erections.

Victorian period The years during the reign of England's Queen Victoria, from 1837 to 1901. The term Victorian has come to be synonymous with repression and restriction.

vulva The term for a woman's external genitalia, including the mons veneris, labia majora, labia minora, clitoris, and perineum.

withholding behavior Behavior that withholds thoughts, feelings, and physical contact when a person is angry or hurt.

yang The masculine essence or energy.

yin The feminine essence or energy.

yoni The Sanskrit term for the female genitalia.

Appendix B

Resources

You might want to know more about the Kama Sutra and other subjects we've discussed in this book. This section identifies a number of resources, including Web sites, translations, and other books, to help you broaden your knowledge.

Kama Sutra Translations

There are a number of translations of the Kama Sutra available. Richard Burton's work remains the classic, and appears in various titles under different editors. Three that are generally easy to find and are true to the original text are …

- *The Illustrated Kama Sutra, Ananga Ranga, and Perfumed Garden: The Classic Love Texts* (Rochester, Vermont: Park Street Press, 1991). Translated by Sir Richard Burton and F. F. Arbuthnot, edited by Charles Fowkes. This edition presents a significantly condensed version of the text highlighting the Kama Sutra's erotic teachings. The book contains many beautiful color illustrations featuring ancient works of art that give an intriguing context to the writing.

- *The Kama Sutra of Vatsyayana* (New York: Berkley Books, 1963), translated by Sir Richard Burton and F. F. Arbuthnot, edited by W. G. Archer. This text-only book is based on the translation Burton published in 1883, and includes Burton's footnotes and commentary.

◆ *The Complete Kama Sutra* (Rochester, Vermont: Park Street Press, 1994), translated by Alain Daniélou. A world-renowned artist, musician, and scholar, Daniélou presents the first comprehensive translation from the original Sanskrit manuscripts since Burton's work nearly two centuries ago. The text presents the sutras, along with interpretations from the twelfth-century Hindu scholar Yashodhara (excerpted from his commentary, the *Jayamangala*) and contemporary Hindu scholar Devadatta Shastri, whose interpretations incorporate material from other writings from the same time period as the Kama Sutra.

A text version of the Kama Sutra's original translation, *Vatsyayana: The Kama Sutra: The Classic Translation of 1883* by Sir Richard Burton, appears in electronic form at www.bibliomania.com/NonFiction/Vatsyayana/KamaSutra/.

Sacred Sexuality Resources

We refer to many of the following books in *The Complete Idiot's Guide to the Kama Sutra, Second Edition*. We've included some other titles here, too, as additional resources.

Amodeo, John, Ph.D. *Love and Betrayal: Broken Trust in Intimate Relationships.* New York: Ballantine Books, 1994.

Budilovsky, Joan and Eve Adamson. *The Complete Idiot's Guide to Meditation, Second Edition.* Indianapolis: Alpha Books, 2003.

Douglas, Nik and Penny Slinger. *Sexual Secrets: The Alchemy of Ecstasy.* Rochester, Vermont: Inner Traditions International, Ltd., 1999.

Feldman, Gail, Ph.D., and Katherine A. Gleason. *Releasing the Goddess Within.* Indianapolis: Alpha Books, 2003.

Fisher, Helen E., Ph.D. *Anatomy of Love: A Natural History of Marriage.* New York: W. W. Norton and Company, 1992.

Gottman, John, Ph.D. *Why Marriages Succeed or Fail and How to Make Yours Last.* New York: Fireside Books, 1995.

Hendricks, Kathlyn, Ph.D. and Gay Hendricks, Ph.D. *The Conscious Heart: Seven Soul-Choices That Inspire Creative Partnership.* New York: Bantam Doubleday Dell Publishers, 1999.

Hendricks, Harville, Ph.D. *Getting the Love You Want: A Guide for Couples.* New York: Owl Books, 2001.

Moran, Elizabeth and Val Biktashev. *The Complete Idiot's Guide to Feng Shui.* Indianapolis: Alpha Books, 1999.

Moore, Thomas. *Care of the Soul.* New York: HarperCollins, 1992.

———. *Soul Mates: Honoring the Mysteries of Love and Relationship.* New York: HarperCollins, 1994.

Odier, Daniel. *Tantric Quest: An Encounter with Absolute Love.* Rochester, Vermont: Inner Traditions International, Ltd., 1997.

———. *Desire: The Tantric Path to Awakening.* Rochester, Vermont: Inner Traditions International, Ltd., 2001.

Schnarch, David, Ph.D. *Passionate Marriage: Love, Sex, and Intimacy in Emotionally Committed Relationships.* New York: Henry Holt, 1998.

Trungpa, Chogyam. *Shambhala, Sacred Path of the Warrior.* Boston: Shambhala Publications, 1995.

Welwood, John. *Love and Awakening: Discovering the Sacred Path of Intimate Relationships.* New York: HarperCollins, 1997.

The following websites offer an array of accurate, useful information. Several also sell books, videotapes, and products that might be difficult to find elsewhere.

www.Tantra.com

This website is an excellent resource for accurate information. Through the e-sensuals catalog, the website sells books, videos, and quality products.

www.tantraworks.com

Posted and maintained by Nik Douglas (author of *Sexual Secrets: The Alchemy of Ecstasy*), this site provides information about the Kama Sutra, Tantric sex, and spiritual sexuality. The site also features numerous links to related sites.

General Sexuality Resources

American Association of Sex Educators, Counselors, and Therapists (AASECT)
Phone: 319-895-8407
Website: www.AASECT.org

This professional organization provides certification and continuing education programs for its members. It can direct you to certified professionals in your local area.

Planned Parenthood
Phone: 1-800-230-PLAN (1-800-230-7526)
Website: www.plannedparenthood.org

This nonprofit organization has clinics and offices in many locations throughout the United States Planned Parenthood provides information about sexual health, birth control, and pregnancy.

Sexuality Information and Education Council of the U.S. (SIECUS)
Phone: 212-819-9770
Website: www.SIECUS.org

SIECUS is a nonprofit organization providing educational materials and programs that promote sexuality as a healthy and natural dimension of life.

Sinclair Intimacy Institute
Website: www.bettersex.com

This website features in-depth and explicit information about all aspects of sexuality. The sexuality database is especially comprehensive. The Sinclair Intimacy Institute produces the best-selling *Better Sex Video Series*®.

Society for Human Sexuality
Website: www.sexuality.org

This website features articles and information about a wide range of sexual topics, including reviews of books, videos, and products. It also contains a calendar of sex-positive events taking place in several West Coast cities.

United States Association for Body Psychotherapy
7831 Woodmont Avenue
Bethesda, MD 20814
Phone: 202-466-1619
Website: www.usabp.org

This is a professional organization that provides continuing education for and listings of qualified professionals.

Index

F